The Second World War in the West

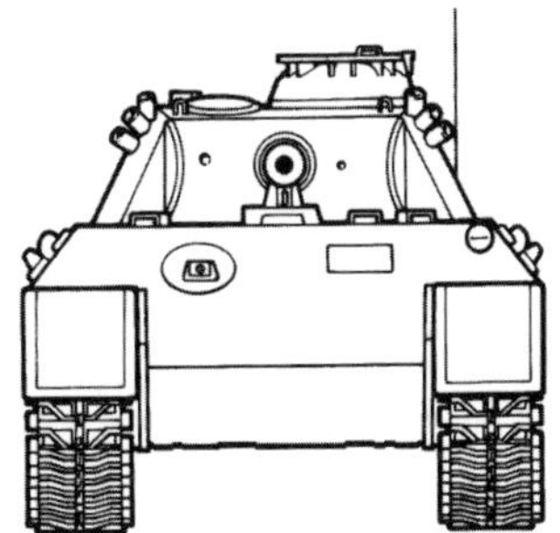

The Second World War in the West

Charles Messenger

General Editor: John Keegan

CASSELL&CO

'Total war is not a succession of mere episodes in a day or week. It is a long drawn out and intricately planned business, and the longer it continues the heavier are the demands on the character of the men engaged in it.'

GENERAL GEORGE C. MARSHALL, JUNE 1941

Cassell & Co
Wellington House, 125 Strand
London WC2R 0BB

First published 1999
Reprinted 2000

British Library Cataloguing-in-Publication Data
A catalogue record for this book is available from the British Library
ISBN 0-304-35224-1

Design, cartography and picture research: Arcadia Editions Ltd
Printed and bound in Italy by L.E.G.O. S.p.A.

Typeset in Monotype Sabon

ACKNOWLEDGEMENTS

I am deeply indebted to John Keegan for inviting me to write this volume in the History of Warfare series. I first met him when I was a cadet at the Royal Military Academy Sandhurst nearly forty years ago, when he helped to develop my deep interest in military history. His writings have proved an inspiration to me ever since.

I am also very grateful to Malcolm Swanston and his team at Arcadia for the devoted effort they put into creating the maps and diagrams and carrying out picture research.

Finally, my warmest thanks to Nick Chapman, Judith Flanders, Penny Gardiner and Caroline Knight at Weidenfeld. Their enthusiasm and encouragement have made working on this book a pleasure.

CHARLES MESSENGER

The rapidly expanding German army on parade, 1938.

Contents

KEY TO MAPS

Military units–types

infantry
armoured
motorized infantry
airborne
parachute
artillery

Military units–size

XXXXX army group
XXXX army
XXX corps
XX division
X brigade
III regiment
II battalion

Military unit colours

Allied
Germany
Poland
Finland

Military movements

attack
retreat
air attack

General military symbols

—XXXXX— army group boundary
—XXXX— army boundary
front line
defensive line
defensive line (3D maps)
field work
pocket or position
field gun
paratroop drop
sunken ship
airfield

Geographical symbols

urban area
road
railway
river
seasonal river
canal
border
bridge or pass
marsh
rocks

Map list

CHRONOLOGY

Key
w North-West Europe
e The Third Reich and the East
m The Mediterranean and the Balkans
a Africa and the Middle East

1939

e	1 Sep	German invasion of Poland
w	3 Sep	Britain and France declare war on Germany
w	7 Sep	French forces advance into Saarland but soon withdraw
w	9 Sep	British Expeditionary Force (BEF) begins to land in France
e	15 Sep	Warsaw surrounded
e	17 Sep	Soviet invasion of Poland
e	19 Sep	German and Soviet forces link up at Brest-Litovsk
e	27 Sep	Warsaw surrenders
e	6 Oct	Last Polish resistance ceases
w	9 Oct	Hitler issues orders for attack in the West
w	17 Nov	British and French decide on Plan D, a move into Belgium to defend against German attack
e	30 Nov	Soviet forces invade Finland
e	6 Dec	Russians begin fruitless frontal attacks on Mannheim Line

1940

e	7 Jan	Timoshenko takes command of Soviet forces in Finland
w	10 Jan	Mechlin incident, when German aircraft force lands in Belgium with plans for invasion of West. First prompt for rethink of plan
w	22 Jan	Hitler takes charge of planning for invasion of Norway
e	1 Feb	Timoshenko launches fresh offensive against Finns
e	11 Feb	Mannheim Line breached. Soviet–German economic agreement
w	1 Mar	US Secretary of State Sumner begins visit of warring countries to investigate prospects for peace
e	8 Mar	Russians capture port of Viipuri
e	12 Mar	Soviet–Finnish peace treaty
w	7 Apr	British air reconnaissance spots German invasion fleet en route to Norway
w	9 Apr	German invasion of Denmark and Norway
w	11 Apr	First British contingent sails for Norway
w	15 Apr	British landings near Narvik
w	16 Apr	Allied landings at Namsos
w	18 Apr	Allied landings at Andalesnes
w	26 Apr	Allied decision to evacuate southern Norway
w	10 May	German invasion of France and the Low Countries
w	13 May	Germans cross the Meuse
w	15 May	Dutch surrender
w	16 May	Allies begin to withdraw from Belgium
w	17 May	Germans enter Brussels
w	20 May	German armour reaches English Channel
w	25 May	Boulogne falls
w	26 May	Evacuation from Dunkirk begins
w	27 May	Calais falls
w	28 May	Allies finally capture Narvik. Belgium surrenders
w	3–8 Jun	Final Allied evacuation from Norway when troops and King Haakon of Norway leave Narvik
w	4 Jun	Evacuation from Dunkirk ends and Germans enter the port
w	5 Jun	German offensive across Rivers Somme and Aisne begins
w	11 Jun	Italy declares war on Britain and France
a	11 Jun	British patrols cross Egypt–Libya border
w	14 Jun	Germans enter Paris
a	14 Jun	British destroy guns in Libyan frontier forts
w	18 Jun	De Gaulle broadcasts to French people from London
w	20 Jun	Italian forces invade France
w	22 Jun	France signs armistice with Germany
w	24 Jun	France signs armistice with Italy and hostilities end the following day. First British Commando raid takes place that night on French coast
w	28 Jun	Britain recognizes de Gaulle as leader of the Free French
w	30 Jun	German forces occupy Channel Islands
a	4 Jul	Italians capture British frontier posts in Sudan
w	5 Jul	Vichy France breaks off diplomatic relations with Britain after bombardment of French North African ports
w	16 Jul	Hitler issues directive for invasion of Britain

w	19 Jul	Hitler makes final plea for peace with Britain
e	21 Jul	Estonia, Latvia, Lithuania become autonomous republics within USSR
e	31 Jul	Hitler informs his commanders of intention to attack USSR
w	1 Aug	Hitler makes it clear that invasion of Britain depends on success of Luftwaffe
e	1 Aug	USSR reaffirms neutrality
a	4 Aug	Italians invade British Somaliland, which they secure on 17 Aug
w	10 Sep	Luftwaffe's failure to gain air supremacy over southern England leads to invasion postponed until 24 Sept
a	13 Sep	Italian invasion of Egypt from Libya, which halts after three days
w	17 Sep	Hitler indefinitely postpones invasion of Britain
e	27 Sep	Germany, Italy and Japan sign Tripartite Pact
m	28 Oct	Italian troops invade Greece from Albania
m	4 Nov	Greeks mount counter-attack, driving Italians back into Albania
e	20 Nov	Hungary joins Tripartite Pact; 23 Romania joins; 24 Slovakia joins.
a	9 Dec	British Western Desert Force launches counter-offensive in Egypt
m	13 Dec	Hitler issues a directive for occupation of Balkans
e	18 Dec	Hitler issues formal directive for invasion of Russia

1941

a	5 Jan	Australians capture Bardia
a	17 Jan	Italians evacuate frontier forts they hold in Sudan
a	19 Jan	British forces enter Eritrea
a	20 Jan	Emperor Haile Selassie re-enters Abyssinia
a	22 Jan	Libyan port of Tobruk captured
a	24 Jan	British forces invade Italian Somaliland from Kenya
w	29 Jan	Opening of Anglo-Canadian-US ABC military staff talks
a	3 Feb	British forces begin to attack Keren, Eritrea
a	6 Feb	Australians enter Benghazi
a	6–7 Feb	Battle of Beda Fomm results in destruction of Italian Tenth Army in Libya
a	14 Feb	German forces begin to land at Tripoli, Libya
a	25 Feb	African forces occupy Indian Ocean port of Mogadishu
m	1 Mar	Bulgaria signs Tripartite Pact
w	4 Mar	Successful Commando raid on Lofoten Islands northern Norway
m	7 Mar	British ground troops land in Greece
w	8 Mar	LendLease becomes law in USA
a	19 Mar	British forces begin to liberate British Somaliland
a	24 Mar	Rommel attacks British in Libyan province of Cyrenaica
m	25 Mar	Yugoslavia signs Tripartite Pact
m	27 Mar	Coup in Yugoslavia results in Tripartite Pact being revoked
a	27 Mar	Keren falls
w	29 Mar	ABC talks conclude with agreement that priority would be given to defeat of Germany over Japan
a	1 Apr	Asmara, capital of Eritrea, surrenders. Pro-Axis revolt in Iraq
m	6 Apr	Axis forces invade Yugoslavia and Greece
a	6 Apr	African troops enter Addis Adaba, capital of Abyssinia
w	12 Apr	US forces establish bases in Greenland
e	13 Apr	Japan signs neutrality pact with Soviet Union
m	17 Apr	Yugoslavia surrenders
a	18 Apr	Indian troops start to land at Basra to begin quelling revolt in Iraq
a	25 Apr	Rommel had driven British forces in Cyrenaica back to Egyptian border, but Tobruk holds out
m	27 Apr	German forces enter Athens
a	9 May	British troops enter Iraq from Palestine
w	10 May	Hitler's deputy, Rudolf Hess, flies to Scotland
a	15 May	Failed British attack Brevity against Rommel
a	18 May	Amba Alagi, last main Italian fortress in northern Abyssinia, surrenders
m	20 May	German airborne assault on Crete
a	31 May	Iraq revolt ended
m	1 Jun	Germany secures Crete
a	8 Jun	Allied forces invade Vichy Lebanon and Syria from Palestine
a	15 Jun	Launch of Battleaxe, another abortive British attack against Axis forces on the Egypt–Libya border
e	22 Jun	German invasion of Russia
e	26 Jun	Finland declares war on Soviet Union
e	29 Jun	Finnish forces attack Karelian isthmus
e	1 Jul	Germans enter Riga, Latvia

e	3 Jul	Stalin broadcasts for first time since opening of German attack. Army Group Centre crushes the Bialystok pocket
m	4 Jul	Tito issues national call to arms in Yugoslavia
w	7 Jul	US Marines begin to relieve British garrison on Iceland
e	9 Jul	Vitebsk falls
e	12 Jul	Britain and USSR sign mutual assistance pact
a	15 Jul	Convention of Acre marks end of campaign against Vichy French in Lebanon and Syria
e	19 Jul	Hitler switches priority to Leningrad and Ukraine
e	20 Jul	Stalin makes himself People's Commissar for Defence
e	27 Jul	Germans enter Tallinn, Estonia
e	5 Aug	Army Group Centre produces huge Russian pocket at Smolensk
e	8 Aug	Army Group South reduces huge pocket around Uman
w	9–12 Aug	Roosevelt and Churchill meet off Newfoundland
a	25 Aug	British and Soviet forces invade Iran to prevent it joining the Axis
e	4 Sep	Leningrad put under siege
e	5 Sep	Hitler decides to advance on Moscow once more
a	17 Sep	British and Soviet forces occupy Tehran
e	19 Sep	Kiev falls
e	23 Sep	Army Group South enters Crimea
e	14 Oct	Army Group Centre reduces pocket at Bryansk
e	16 Oct	Non-essential government offices and foreign embassies begin to evacuate Moscow
e	18 Oct	Germans penetrate defence line eighty miles west of Moscow
e	24 Oct	Army Group South captures Kharkov
e	30 Oct	Army Group Centre halted by weather
e	15 Nov	Advance on Moscow resumes
a	18 Nov	Launch of British Crusader offensive into Libya
e	20 Nov	Army Group South captures Rostov-on-Don
a	27 Nov	Fall of Italian fortress of Gondar in northern Abyssinia marks end of campaign in East Africa
e	29 Nov	Soviet counter-attack on Rostov forces German withdrawal
e	5 Dec	German drive on Moscow halted and first of numerous Russian counter-attacks
a	7 Dec	British forces relieve Tobruk after an eight month siege
w	11 Dec	Germany and Italy declare war on USA
e	15 Dec	Organs of government ordered to return to Moscow
e	19 Dec	Hitler appoints himself C-in-C German Army
w	22 Dec	Opening of Anglo–US strategic conference in Washington, DC. Ended 13 January 1942
w	27 Dec	Successful Commando raid on Vaagso, south-west Norway
1942		
a	4 Jan	Axis forces complete withdrawal from Cyrenaica
a	21 Jan	Rommel launches fresh offensive into Cyrenaica
w	26 Jan	First US forces arrive in Britain
a	4 Feb	Rommel offensive halts in front of Gazala
e	8 Feb	Soviets create first significant pocket at Demyansk, south of Lake Ilmen
e	19 Mar	Soviet attempt to relieve Leningrad fails
e	5 Apr	Hitler issues directive for offensive into Caucasus
w	8 Apr	In midst of increasing Soviet agitation requesting it, US delegation arrives in Britain to discuss Second Front strategy
e	12 May	Soviet offensive launched south of Kharkov
a	27 May	Rommel launches assault on Gazala line
e	29 May	Soviet forces around Kharkov destroyed
a	21 Jun	Rommel captures Tobruk
e	30 Jun	German Sixth Army opens main summer offensive
a	30 Jun	British Eighth Army back on El Alamein Line in Egypt
a	1–27 Jul	Inconclusive first battle of El Alamein
e	3 Jul	Germans secure port of Sevastapol, Crimea, which had been under siege since October 1942
e	7 Jul	Germans enter Voronezh. Army Group A begins attacks into Donets Basin
w	24 Jul	Allied agreement reached to mount Torch landings in French North-West Africa
e	25 Jul	Army Group A breaks out across Lower Don
e	9 Aug	Maikop oilfields seized
e	10 Aug	German Sixth Army reaches outskirts of Stalingrad
w	19 Aug	Dieppe raid
e	24 Aug	Stalin orders Stalingrad to be held

a	30 Aug	Rommel assaults again at El Alamein, but is repulsed
a	23 Oct	Opening of Montgomery's assault at El Alamein
e	2 Nov	Army Group A advance into Caucasus comes to final halt
a	2 Nov	Final breakthrough battle begins at El Alamein
a	8 Nov	Torch landings in French North-West Africa
a	11 Nov	French in North-West Africa sign armistice with Allies. Axis begin to fly troops into Tunisia, and Allies make first advance here from Algeria
a	13 Nov	British re-enter Tobruk
e	19 Nov	Russian counter-offensive at Stalingrad opens
a	20 Nov	British re-enter Benghazi
e	23 Nov	German forces trapped at Stalingrad
a	24 Nov	Beginning of renewed, albeit fruitless, Allied efforts to reach Tunis
e	26 Nov	Hitler orders Paulus to stand fast at Stalingrad
e	30 Nov	Further Russian attacks on lower Chir
e	12 Dec	Von Manstein launches Stalingrad relief operation
e	16 Dec	Further Soviet attacks launched against Army Group B
e	28 Dec	Hitler sanctions further withdrawals, putting Stalingrad 125 miles east of main front

1943

e	3 Jan	Army Group A begins to withdraw from Caucasus
a	3 Jan	Axis forces begin a series of attacks in western Tunisia
e	8 Jan	Paulus rejects Soviet surrender demand
e	10 Jan	Final Soviet offensive against Stalingrad begins
e	12 Jan	Russians launch another Leningrad relief operation
e	13 Jan	Russian offensive across the Don
w	14–24 Jan	Casablanca Conference
a	23 Jan	British enter Tripoli
e	2 Feb	Final German surrender at Stalingrad
e	8 Feb	Russians regain Kursk
e	14 Feb	Rostov-on-Don liberated
e	16 Feb	Germans evacuate Kharkov
a	19 Feb	Rommel seizes Kasserine Pass, Tunisia, but is then rebuffed by the Allies
e	20 Feb	Germans launch counter-offensives in Ukraine
a	6 Mar	Montgomery throws back Rommel's assault against him at Medinine in eastern Tunisia
e	15 Mar	Kharkov recaptured
a	17 Mar	US forces under Patton capture Gafsa
a	20–27 Mar	Montgomery forces Axis troops out of the Mareth Line
a	7 Apr	Allied forces attack Fondouk Pass in western Tunisia
w	13 Apr	Gen Morgan appointed as COSSAC
e	13 Apr	Germans announce discovery of mass grave of Polish officers at Katyn
e	19 Apr	Jewish uprising within Warsaw ghetto. (Resistance ends on 16 May)
a	19–21 Apr	Montgomery rebuffed at Enfidaville
a	22 Apr	Opening of final Allied assault in western Tunisia
a	7 May	Fall of Tunis and Bizerta
a	11 May	Final Axis surrender in North Africa
w	12–25 May	Trident Conference Washington, DC confirms Italy to be knocked out of war before Second Front opened
e	4 Jul	German offensive against Kursk salient opens
m	10 Jul	Allied landings on Sicily
e	12 Jul	Soviet counter-attack at Kursk
w	15 Jul	COSSAC presents his Overlord plan to British Chiefs of Staff
m	23 Jul	US troops enter Palermo, Sicily
m	25 Jul	Mussolini arrested by Fascist Grand Council
e	5 Aug	Belgorod and Orel liberated
w	12–23 Aug	Quebec Conference approves Overlord plan
m	12 Aug	Axis forces begin to withdraw from Sicily
m	14 Aug	Italian government declares Rome an open city
m	17 Aug	American forces enter Messina, Sicily
e	23 Aug	Kharkov finally liberated
e	30 Aug	Taganrog liberated
m	1 Sep	Italian government accepts Allied armistice terms
m	3 Sep	British Eighth Army lands in toe of Italy
m	8 Sep	Eisenhower broadcasts Italian surrender
m	9 Sep	Allied landings at Salerno
m	10 Sep	German troops occupy Rome. British forces begin to land on Italian Dodecanese Is. in Aegean
m	12 Sep	Germans rescue Mussolini from house arrest

e	16 Sep	Germans evacuate Bryansk
e	22 Sep	Russians seize crossings over Dnieper
e	25 Sep	Smolensk liberated
m	26 Sep	British Eighth Army links up with Salerno beachhead
m	1 Oct	Allied forces enter Naples and Foggia
e	6 Oct	Soviet offensive launched towards Baltic states
m	13 Oct	US Fifth Army crosses River Volturno
e	6 Nov	Kiev liberated
m	6 Nov	Hitler appoints Kesselring C-in-C Italy
m	20 Nov	British Eighth Army crosses River Sangro
w	6 Dec	Eisenhower appointed Supreme Allied Commander for Overlord
m	8 Dec	US Fifth Army attacks force Germans to withdraw to Gustav Line
w	12 Dec	Rommel appointed to command Army Group B in defence of northern France and Low Countries
m	27 Dec	Canadian capture of Ortona marks end of Eighth Army advance

1944

e	14 Jan	Russians open further offensive to relieve Leningrad
m	17 Jan	Fifth Army opens attacks on Gustav Line
m	22 Jan	Allied landings at Anzio
e	26 Jan	Siege of Leningrad lifted
m	30 Jan	Beginning of four-month assault on Monte Cassino
e	1 Mar	Russians reach Estonian border
e	10 Mar	Uman liberated
e	19 Mar	German troops enter Hungary to help defend country
e	1 Apr	Finland approaches Moscow for an armistice
m	11 May	Alexander launches breakthrough of Gustav Line
e	12 May	Crimea cleared of German forces
w	15 May	Final presentation of plans for Overlord
m	17 May	Monte Cassino finally captured
m	23 May	Allied forces break out of Anzio beachhead
m	25 May	German glider *coup de main* on Tito's HQ forces him to flee Yugoslavia
m	5 Jun	US Fifth Army enters Rome
w	6 Jun	Normandy landings
e	10 Jun	Russian offensive against Finland launched
e	22 Jun	Russians launch Operation Bagration against Army Group Centre
w	27 Jun	Capture of Cherbourg
w	2 Jul	Von Rundstedt dismissed as C-in-C West and replaced by von Kluge
m	15 Jul	Allied advance north of Rome halted on River Arno
w	17 Jul	Rommel seriously wounded by marauding Allied fighter
w	18 Jul	Montgomery launches Operation Goodwood, an attack east of Caen
e	20 Jul	Attempt on Hitler's life at his HQ at Rastenburg in East Prussia
e	23 Jul	Russian forces enter Lublin
w	25 Jul	US First Army launches Operation Cobra to break through German defences
e	26 Jul	Russians reach the Vistula
e	31 Jul	Russians capture Kauna, capital of Lithuania
w	1 Aug	US Third Army begins break-out from Normandy
e	1 Aug	Polish Home Army rises against Germans in Warsaw
w	7 Aug	Eisenhower sets up forward HQ in Normandy
w	15 Aug	Allied forces land in South of France
e	20 Aug	Russians enter Rumania
w	21 Aug	Falaise pocket finally closed
e	23 Aug	Romania surrenders
w	25 Aug	Allied forces enter Paris
m	25 Aug	Allies renew offensive in Italy
w	28 Aug	Toulon and Marseilles liberated
w	3 Sep	Brussels liberated
w	4 Sep	Hitler recalls von Rundstedt to be C-in-C West
m	8 Sep	German forces begin to evacuate Greek islands
w	11 Sep	First Allied troops enter Germany
w	12 Sep	Port of Le Havre finally falls
w	12–16 Sep	Second Quebec Conference
w	17–26 Sep	Operation Market-Garden
e	17 Sep	Tallinn, Estonia falls to Russians
e	19 Sep	Finland signs armistice with Moscow
w	30 Sep	Calais liberated
w	1 Oct	First Canadian Army begins clearance of banks of River Scheldt
w	2 Oct	US First Army begins to attack West Wall between Aachen and Geilenkirchen
w	6 Oct	Opening of Battle of Huertgen Forest
e	7 Oct	Russians begin to drive Germans out of northern Finland

w	9 Oct	Hitler sees draft plan for Ardennes counter-offensive
e	11 Oct	Hungarian delegation signs armistice in Moscow. However, some Hungarian formations continue to fight on the side of the Germans
m	12 Oct	German forces evacuate Athens
m	20 Oct	Soviet forces and Tito's partisans liberate Belgrade
w	21 Oct	Americans secure Aachen
w	22 Oct	Hitler briefs von Rundstedt and Model on Ardennes attack
m	22 Oct	Fifth Army closes down its offensive against the Gothic Line
w	1 Nov	Amphibious assault on island of Walcheren
w	18 Nov	US Third Army enters Metz
m	3 Dec	Civil war breaks out in Greece. British troops are sent from Italy in order to quell it
w	16 Dec	Opening of Ardennes counter-offensive
w	22 Dec	Sixth Panzer Army comes to halt in Ardennes
w	26 Dec	Bastogne relieved
e	26 Dec	Budapest encircled
m	29 Dec	Eighth Army advance in Italy finally halted
w	31 Dec	Germans launch subsidiary offensive into Alsace

1945

e	1 Jan	Germans launch attack to relieve Budapest
e	12 Jan	Russians launch Vistula–Oder offensive
m	12 Jan	Truce brings hostilities in Greece to an end
e	20 Jan	Russians cross the German border
w	28 Jan	German salient created by Ardennes counter-offensive finally eliminated
e	4–11 Feb	Big Three conference at Yalta, Crimea
w	9 Feb	6th Army Group closed up to upper Rhine
e	13 Feb	Russians capture Budapest
e	15 Feb	German counter-attack from Pomerania into Russian flank
e	24 Feb	Russians attack into Pomerania
m	3 Mar	First German approach for an armistice in Italy
e	6 Mar	Germans launch offensive to secure Hungarian oilfield (halted 15 Mar)
w	7 Mar	US First Army seizes Rhine bridge at Remagen. (This collapsed on 18 March)
w	10 Mar	21st Army Group entirely closed up to Rhine
w	19 Mar	Hitler issues 'scorched earth' order
w	22 Mar	Patton achieves 'bounce' crossing of Rhine at Oppenheim
w	23 Mar	Montgomery begins to cross the Rhine at Wesel
w	26 Mar	US Seventh Army crosses Rhine near Worms
w	31 Mar	French First Army crosses Rhine near Germersheim
w	1 Apr	Army Group B trapped in the Ruhr pocket
w	4 Apr	British Second Army enters Osnabrueck and US Third Army captures Kassel
m	9 Apr	Final Allied offensive in Italy opens
w	11 Apr	US Ninth Army reaches River Elbe
w	12 Apr	Death of President Roosevelt
e	13 Apr	Russians secure Vienna
e	16 Apr	Russians open offensive across Oder to Berlin
w	17 Apr	Second British Army reaches Bremen
w	18 Apr	Ruhr pocket finally reduced
w	19 Apr	First US Army takes Leipzig
w	20 Apr	Seventh US Army captures Nuremberg
m	21 Apr	Bologna falls
w	25 Apr	Elements of First US Army and 1st Ukrainian Front link up at Torgau on River Elbe
e	25 Apr	Berlin encircled
m	27 Apr	Genoa falls
m	28 Apr	Mussolini killed by partisans
m	29 Apr	German forces in Italy surrender
e	30 Apr	Hitler commits suicide
w	2 May	21st Army Group enters Schleswig-Holstein
e	2 May	Berlin surrenders
m	2 May	British troops link up with Tito's forces near Trieste
w	4 May	Montgomery accepts surrender of German forces in north-west Germany, Denmark, Holland
w	7 May	German surrender ceremony in Reims
e	8 May	German surrender ceremony in Berlin
e	11 May	German forces in Czechoslovakia surrender

CHAPTER ONE

The Road to War (1919–39)

THE TRAPPINGS OF NAZI POWER. *Hitler leads a motorcade down from the Hofburgtheater towards the Town Hall in Vienna during the Anschluss of Austria. Ceremonial on a massive scale was designed to hypnotize both the German people and foreigners. Nowhere was this more evident than at the annual party rallies at Nuremberg. The overwhelming impression of disciplined mass restored the belief of the German people in both themselves and their country, throwing off the disillusion of the Weimar years, and binding them to Hitler. It also impressed other nations, helping to foster appeasement among the democracies and making Germany's neighbours more amenable to Hitler's demands. Both Mussolini and Stalin also encouraged these public shows of strength.*

The Road to War 1919–39

The first wave of air and mechanised attack will be followed up by motorised infantry divisions. They will be carried to the verge of the occupied territory and hold it, thereby freeing the mobile units for another blow. In the meantime, the attacker will be raising a mass army... He will do his best to launch the great blow so suddenly as to take the enemy by surprise, rapidly concentrating his mobile troops and hurling his air force at the enemy. The armoured divisions will no longer stop when the first objectives are reached; on the contrary, utilising their speed and radius of action they will do their utmost to complete the breakthrough into the enemy lines of communication.

HEINZ GUDERIAN'S *BLUEPRINT FOR BLITZKRIEG*, 1935

ALTHOUGH THE SLAUGHTER that had marked the Great War of 1914–18 had come to an end, 1919 was one of the most turbulent years that Europe had witnessed. In Russia civil war raged as the White forces, operating with the support of the western powers and Japan, tried to overturn the Bolshevik revolution. Three fronts had developed – Siberia, the Black Sea and the north. In the midst of this the Baltic states, Poland and Finland seized the opportunity to break away from the dominance that Russia had for so long exerted over them.

Austria–Hungary split apart, with left-wing extremist Bela Kun seizing power in Hungary. Turkey, too, seethed as a result of the loss of the Ottoman empire. Germany suffered the anguish of civil war as the Left tried to take control. The newly created democratic government was forced to leave Berlin for more peaceful Weimar, 150 miles to the south. In Bavaria, left-wing elements did establish a government and during their brief time in power even went so far as to declare war on Switzerland. The Weimar government, as it became known, was forced to call upon groups of soldiers who banded themselves into *Freikorps* and steadily crushed the militias of the Left.

In the meantime, the victorious Allies were drawing up the peace treaties which would formally bring the Great War to an end. They also desired to create a new world in which the slaughter of 1914–18 could not be repeated. The framework was to be President Woodrow Wilson's Fourteen Points of January 1918. Some, notably the French, whose main industrial region in the north of the country had been devastated by the war, wanted to extract the maximum revenge on Germany. To a large extent their desire was met, with Germany being forced to make heavy financial reparations for the damage she had caused. Her militarism was to be crushed for all time through stringent restrictions on the size of her armed forces. Conscription was banned, with the army being limited to 100,000 men, a tenth of its 1914 strength. Germany was to be allowed no air force, no tanks, and no guns above 150mm calibre. Her navy, much of which had been scuttled in Scapa Flow early in 1919, was restricted to a few elderly cruisers and smaller vessels. The need to give Poland access to the sea caused East Prussia to be isolated from the rest of Germany. Poland also received part of mineral-rich Silesia. Finally, the Rhineland was demilitarized and occupied by Allied troops and the coal-rich Saarland given to France to administer on behalf of the League of Nations. The same happened with Germany's former African colonies.

The Treaty of Versailles, bringing a formal end to the war with Germany, was signed on 28 June 1919. The Allies celebrated this with victory parades, but in Germany the swingeing terms caused resentment among certain sectors of the population. This was directed at the Weimar government, which had been forced to sign the treaty. The myth grew like a canker that the German armed forces had been betrayed at the end of the war by the politicians and others – the so-called 'stab in the back'.

Other peace treaties followed. That with Austria (Treaty of St Germain) recognized the disparate races that had made up the empire and the nationalism that this had engendered. A new state of Czechoslovakia was created, while the Austrian provinces in the Balkans were combined with Montenegro and Serbia to create Yugoslavia. Admiral Miklos Horthy, who had overthrown Bela Kun in March 1919 and established a right-wing dictatorship in Hungary, was forced through the Treaty of Trianon to cede large portions of territory to Czechoslovakia, Yugoslavia and Romania. This resulted in the population of Hungary being reduced from 16 to a mere 7 million. Bulgaria, which had also fought on the losing side, likewise had to cede territory.

A Freikorps *soldier engaging Spartacist snipers during the fighting in Berlin in early 1919. After the Treaty of Versailles the* Freikorps *went underground. Many joined the Nazis and became the backbone of the SA and SS.*

The last of the former belligerents to make peace was Turkey. The Treaty of Sèvres of August 1920 saw the dismemberment of the Ottoman empire, with France

EUROPE IN 1920

Versailles radically altered the map of central Europe. The granting of independence to the Baltic states and Poland displeased Russia, whose vassals they had formerly been. The isolation of East Prussia was to be a source of major German resentment. Polish rejection of demands for land links to it from the main part of Germany provided the spark that lit the fuse of the Second World War. The results of the creation of a Serb-dominated Yugoslavia would not, however, really be felt until after the death of Tito, over sixty years after Versailles.

being granted Syria, and Britain Palestine, Transjordan and Mesopotamia (soon to be renamed Iraq) as League of Nations' mandates. The Dardanelles were demilitarized, the Dodecanese ceded to Italy, and Greek troops allowed to occupy Turkish territory on both sides of the Bosphorus.

But the principal achievement of the peace conference was the creation of the League of Nations. This mirrored the concluding paragraph of Woodrow Wilson's Fourteen Points: 'A general association of nations must be formed under specific covenants for the purpose of affording mutual guarantees of political independence and territorial integrity to great and small states alike.' Contrary to French wishes, the League had no integral military element. Its purpose was merely to encourage, through disarmament agreements, mutual guarantees between nations, and international agreement not to resort to war until all other avenues had been thoroughly explored. For this the League would provide arbitration machinery. However, none of the vanquished nations was initially invited to join, and neither was Russia. Worse, as the League was setting up its headquarters at Geneva, the US Senate refused to ratify the Treaty of Versailles. Fears that the League would threaten the independence of American foreign policy, resentment that the British Empire had six votes to the United States's one, and traditional isolationism were the motivation for this. Woodrow Wilson's hopes that this would be reversed came to naught when he was decisively defeated in the 1920 presidential election by the Republican Warren Harding. Thus the League of Nations had to operate without one of the leading global powers.

As the League came into being, wars were still being fought. Taking advantage of the turmoil created by the civil war in Russia, the Poles invaded the Ukraine in summer 1919 and quickly closed to the River Beresina. The following year the Red Army, which had finally emerged victorious from the civil war, drove the Poles back literally to the gates of Warsaw. It seemed as though Poland would once more become a Russian satrap, but an eleventh-hour counter-offensive turned the tables on the now over-extended Red Army. Through the subsequent 1921 Treaty of Riga, Poland was allowed to keep most of her territorial gains.

That same year Polish irregulars tried to annexe the rest of Silesia. Forbidden by the Allies to employ the Reichswehr, the Weimar government was forced to use the *Freikorps*, which had been officially banned, to repel the invaders. Thus Poland found herself with two resentful neighbours. Indeed, the Polish problem was one reason why Germany and Russia, now Europe's outcasts, had signed the Treaty of Rapallo in April 1922. This was a declaration of mutual friendship seemingly in accord with the League of Nations, but secret clauses enabled the Germans to set up covert arms factories in Russia, and later to send selected officers to train in armoured and air warfare in exchange for technical advice.

The peace terms also led to discontent in Turkey. Early in 1921, the sultanate was overthrown by Kemal Ataturk. He turned on the Greek forces occupying parts of mainland Turkey and drove them out. This posed a threat to British and French forces policing the demilitarized zone and for a time war seemed imminent.

Europe in 1920
(post peace treaties)
Arctic Circle
Iceland
(Danish)
Norwegian Sea
(Danish)
NORWAY
SWEDEN
FINLAND
Leningrad
Helsinki
Tallinn
Stockholm
ESTONIA
Oslo
Riga
LATVIA
LITHUANIA
Kaunas
USSR
Baltic Sea
North Sea
DENMARK
Copenhagen
Danzig
(free city under League of Nations)
Königsberg
East Prussia
Glasgow
Edinburgh
UNITED KINGDOM
IRELAND
Dublin
Liverpool
Hamburg
Amsterdam
NETHER.
Berlin
Warsaw
Brest Litovsk
Birmingham
Bristol
London
POLAND
GERMANY
Calais
Brussels
BELGIUM
LUX.
Rhine
Frankfurt
SAAR
(autonomous under League of Nations)
Prague
CZECHOSLOVAKIA
Cracow
Lvov
Paris
Vienna
Budapest
Orléans
ATLANTIC OCEAN
AUSTRIA
HUNGARY
ROMANIA
Bern
SWITZ.
FRANCE
Lyon
Bordeaux
Milan
Trieste
Venice
Genoa
Belgrade
Bucharest
Danube
Black Sea
YUGOSLAVIA
BULGARIA
Sofia
Marseille
ANDORRA
ITALY
Adriatic Sea
ALBANIA
PORTUGAL
Rome
Barcelona
Madrid
SPAIN
Naples
TURKEY
Aegean Sea
GREECE
Balearic Is.
Smyrna
Athens
Alicante
Cádiz
Gibraltar
(British)
Almeria
Mediterranean Sea
(Italian occupied)
Tangier
(international zone)
Algeria
(French)
Tunisia
(French)
Morocco
(French)
Libya
(Italian)

Colonel (later Major General) J. F. C. Fuller. His writings drew from both his experience with tanks during 1916–18 and his knowledge of military history. Both the Red Army and Germany took much note of them. At home his outspoken frustration at the failure of the British Army wholly to embrace his ideas eventually terminated his career as a soldier, causing him for a time to embrace Fascism.

Eventually, in July 1923, the Allies agreed to drop all claims to mainland Turkey. This marked the first significant revision of the peace treaties.

The truth was that Britain and France could not afford to act as the world's military policemen; 1914–18 had drained them physically and financially. They had dismantled their vast war machines as quickly as they could and were now bent on reconstruction of their exhausted economies. French defence policy was based on the need to secure her eastern borders so that Germany would not contemplate another invasion like those of 1870 and 1914. Because the main industrial regions lay close to her most vulnerable borders, the conclusion was that any future war must be fought beyond them. Yet, at the same time, French military thinking in the 1920s was dominated by the belief that the *poilu* was at his most effective in defence, as shown by his action during the long bloodbath of Verdun in 1916. This was in stark contrast to the 1914 theory that the strength of the French soldier lay in that quality of *élan* which made him unstoppable in the attack. Static defence thus became the cornerstone of French policy as was finally realized at the end of the 1920s with the construction of the Maginot Line, named after the then defence minister who had himself been badly wounded at Verdun.

In Britain the military conservatives regarded the trench warfare of 1914–18 as an aberration and were relieved by the prospect of getting back to 'real soldiering'. This meant reverting to the traditional priority of defence of empire. But the need to police the mandates in the Middle East quickly placed an intolerable strain on the British Army, slowing down demobilization. It was now that the Chief of the Air Staff, Hugh Trenchard, stepped in, proposing that the newly independent Royal Air Force take over responsibility for the Middle East at a fraction of the existing costs. The government gratefully accepted this plan, and the policy of air control was born.

Yet, in spite of seeming military stagnation, there were some who sought to draw valid lessons from 1914–18 for the future. They began with the premise that the internal combustion engine had altered the nature of war. One school of thought concerned itself with air power. Initially led by the Italian General Guilio Douhet, it argued that the aircraft, by virtue of its ability to overfly seas and armies, could strike at the very heart of the enemy – his government, industry, and, above all, the morale of the population.

The other major school of military theory concerned itself with a weapon which had been created during the war to overcome the deadlock on the Western Front.

It was Colonel J. F. C. Fuller, lately chief of staff at the headquarters of the British Tank Corps in France, who led the way in arguing that the tank would revolutionize war on land, and, by increasing the pace of operations, would make static warfare a thing of the past. He was joined by a wartime soldier turned journalist, Captain Basil Liddell Hart. They likened the old style of warfare to the brute force of a cudgel directed at the enemy's mass. In contrast, armoured warfare was as the thrust of a rapier aimed at the heart of the opposing army – its command, control and communications. With these disrupted, the enemy would be unable to react in time and his defeat would be inevitable.

The British took sufficient note of these theories to establish, temporarily, a brigade-sized all-arms mechanized force in 1925. Little came out of the trials, however. The financial resources were not available to create the mechanized army that Fuller and Liddell Hart envisaged. Furthermore, the artillery and infantry feared that their individual identities would be lost. Finally, armoured forces were viewed as offensive in nature and to create them in any strength would be to run counter to the climate of international disarmament which existed at the time. In any event, there were many who believed that the tank should be retained in just its original role, that of infantry support. Indeed, the Americans went so far as to enshrine this in an Act of Congress, making tanks part of the infantry.

It was the United States, however, which had taken the lead in disarmament, compensating in some measure for its failure to join the League of Nations. During the winter of 1921–2 a naval disarmament conference was held in Washington, DC. The result of this was that limits were placed on the size of future capital ships, and the navies of Britain, France, Italy, Japan and the United States were to maintain

THE MAGINOT LINE

A cross-section of the Maginot Line. Apart from covering the Franco-German border, another section was constructed in the French Alps to defend against a possible attack by Italy. The Line was first manned in 1936. It was armed with 131mm howitzers, 75mm guns, mortars, anti-tank guns, machine-guns and grenade throwers.

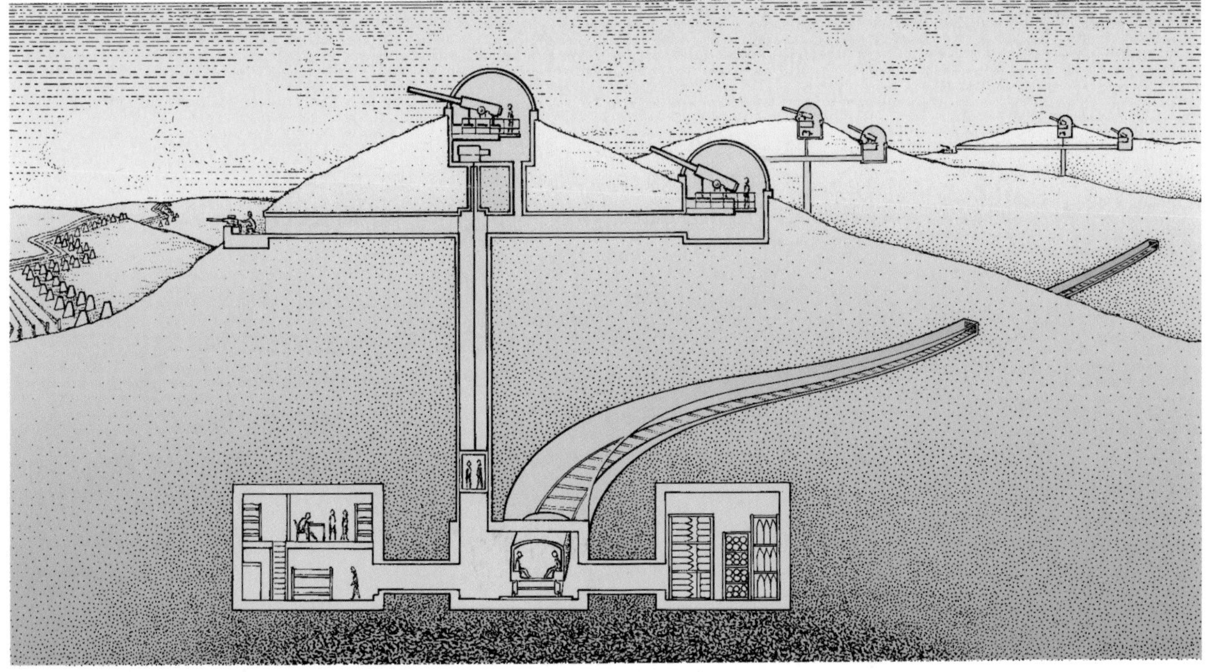

their existing proportions of major warships. But, at a further conference held at Geneva in the summer of 1927, the Americans failed to get agreement from Britain and Japan for the same proportionality to apply to all classes of warship. They had more success three years later when, under the London Naval Treaty, these two countries did agree to this proposal and to a five year moratorium on capital shipbuilding. This time, however, France and Italy stayed outside the treaty because they were unable to agree the proportions *vis-à-vis* each other's navies. The international jurists meeting at the Hague during 1925 were similarly frustrated. They succeeded in drawing up draft rules on the conduct of air warfare, with emphasis on avoiding attacks on civilian targets, but not a single nation was prepared to ratify them.

During the 1920s a new force began to emerge in Europe. Italy, although one of the victors of the late war, suffered in its immediate aftermath from a series of weak governments. Civil unrest, especially strikes, grew. To counter this, a right-wing movement called the *Fascisti* developed in northern Italy, with journalist Benito Mussolini quickly rising to lead it. Initially they had little popular support, but in autumn 1921 began a campaign of moving into one city after another, gaining control by taking over the public utilities. Then, in August 1922, the Socialist opposition declared a general strike. Frustrated by the central government's inability to deal with it, Mussolini and his followers took over the national transport system. Two months later the Fascists made their celebrated march on Rome and took over the reins of government, vowing to modernize the country.

The path which brought Adolf Hitler and his Nazi Party to power in Germany was, however, to be a much longer one than Mussolini's. Its start point was the German Workers Party formed in 1919. Its manifesto called for the restoration of Greater Germany, the abrogation of the peace treaties, and the denial of German citizenship to Jews. It was renamed the Nationalsozialistische Deutsche Arbeiterpartei (NSDAP) in 1921, with Hitler taking control. By early 1923 Germany was falling badly behind in reparations payments to the Allies. French troops therefore occupied the industrial Ruhr. Not only did this result in galloping inflation, but it also provided right-wing parties, like the NSDAP, with a rallying cry. Chancellor Gustav Stresemann, fearful that the country was on the verge of total collapse, declared a state of emergency and agreed to resume reparations payments. Consequently, the French withdrew from the Ruhr.

The Right saw Stresemann's action as a climbdown. In Bavaria, where feeling against him was strongest, Hitler formed an alliance dedicated to toppling the Weimar republic. Among his supporters was the now venerable Field Marshal Erich von Ludendorff. On 9 November 1923 Hitler and his followers attempted a putsch in Munich, but it was put down by the police and the army. Hitler was imprisoned for a short time and the NSDAP banned in Bavaria.

Matters began to ease for Germany with the introduction of the Dawes Plan in April 1924. This modified the rate of reparations payments, although they remained high, and the economy began to pick up. The situation improved still more in August 1929, when, under the Young Plan, the reparations payments were stretched even further and the Allies agreed to withdraw their garrisons on the west bank of the Rhine. In 1926 Germany was admitted to the League of Nations, and at the beginning of the following year the Inter-Allied Control Commission, responsible for monitoring German armaments, was withdrawn. All this served to weaken support for the Right.

The prospects for future peace were strengthened by the December 1925 Locarno Treaties, through which Britain and Italy agreed to act as guarantors of the national borders within western Europe. Three years later, more than sixty nations pledged to outlaw war by signing the Kellogg–Briand Pact. The League of Nations, too, successfully mediated in a number of territorial disputes.

In October 1929, however, came the Wall Street Crash. Its reverberations were felt all over the world, nowhere more so than in Germany, whose fragile economy took a severe battering. Unemployment rose sharply and with it came increased

Vickers Mediums of Britain's 1st Tank Brigade exercising on Salisbury Plain, 1931. Much time was spent in manoeuvring the tanks like fleets at sea, using hand signals and radio. Not for another eight years would the British Army begin to create armoured divisions.

political polarization to the extreme Left and extreme Right. The elections of the following year witnessed much street violence between Communist and Nazi thugs. They also saw Hitler win over a hundred seats in the Reichstag, making his party the second largest. The government's deflationary policies caused unemployment to rise even further, thus increasing the political polarization. This enabled Hitler to challenge Field Marshal Erich von Hindenburg for the presidency in 1932. He lost, but gained over a third of the total vote, with the Communist leader Ernst Thälmann coming a poor third. That same year the Allies agreed to waive the remainder of Germany's reparations payments, but this did not prevent the NSDAP from becoming the largest party in Germany as a result of elections held that July.

Hitler, however, refused to join other parties in a governing coalition and fresh elections had to be held. The Nazi vote fell slightly and von Hindenburg appointed General Kurt von Schleicher as chancellor. Unable to form a government, he was forced to rule by decree. Hitler isolated von Schleicher even further by forming an alliance with Franz von Papen, a previous chancellor. Accordingly, von Hindenburg now appointed Hitler as chancellor in von Schleicher's place, with von Papen as his deputy.

One of Hitler's first steps was to call for fresh elections, but a week before they took place there was a fire at the Reichstag. Hitler blamed the Communists, but it is almost certain that the fire had been started by the Nazis. The elections saw the Nazis win sufficient seats to gain total power and Hitler wasted little time in getting legislation passed which virtually prohibited all political parties other than the NSDAP. Thus by the spring of 1933 he was in almost total control of Germany. Just over a year later, on 2 August 1934, Hitler's power became absolute on the death of von Hindenburg. By this time global peace was beginning to come under threat.

In 1931 the Japanese Kwantung Army seized Mukden and then overran the remainder of Manchuria. They then established the puppet state of Manchukuo. Not until early 1933 did the League of Nations make a protest; the Japanese reaction was to revoke its membership. During this time an international disarmament conference, which had been convened in February 1932, was taking place in Geneva. The aim was for all the nations of Europe to reduce their armed forces to the same size as those of Germany. The main obstacle proved to be France, who considered the proposal to be too great a threat to her security. The Germans, on the other hand, demanded the right to rearm if agreement was not reached. They became even more strident after Hitler came to power, and in October 1933 he also took his country out of the League of Nations when the other nations refused to allow German rearmament. Thus the Geneva conference was left in tatters. It marked the end of attempts to pursue international disarmament.

In fact, German plans for rearmament had been in place for some years. General Hans von Seeckt, commander-in-chief of the Reichswehr until 1926, realized only too well that his 100,000-man army was not strong enough to defend Germany's western and eastern borders simultaneously. He therefore structured it as a cadre to provide the framework for a massive expansion in time of war. One of its key features was the *Führerarmee* concept, which laid stress on training soldiers to fill posts at command levels higher than those they were in. This was to serve the army well during 1939–45. Von Seeckt also acknowledged that future war was likely to be very much more mobile than in 1914–18 and it was he who was instrumental in inserting the secret clauses concerning sending selected officers to train in Russia under the Treaty of Rapallo. Furthermore, although Versailles prohibited Germany from having an air force, von Seeckt set up a covert air office within the war ministry.

Once the Allied Control Commission had left Germany, it became possible to begin clandestine development of modern weapons within the country. Indeed, Alfred Krupp, the German armaments tycoon, later stated that most of Germany's significant artillery weapons of 1939–45 had been developed before Hitler came to power. The Germans also took note of the writing of foreign military theorists, especially J. F. C. Fuller. It was these, combined with the infiltration tactics used by the *Sturmtruppe* during 1917–18, which led to the blitzkrieg concept.

But while the British continued their experiments with armoured warfare, it was the Russians who made the most spectacular advances. During the early 1920s there had been an intense debate as to what shape the Red Army should take. One school of thought was led by former officers of the Imperial Army who had thrown in their lot with the Bolsheviks. They wanted to create a regular army, with emphasis on defence. Some who had risen to prominence during the civil war – men like M. V. Frunze and Mikhail Tuchachevski – also wished for a regular army. Drawing on the mobile warfare which largely characterized the civil war, they wanted a highly mobile army, which, in Frunze's words, would be 'impregnated in the spirit of bold and energetically conducted offensive operations' and be the tool for exporting Communism abroad. Finally, there was Leon Trotsky, the Commissar for War during

Turretless German PzKw I tanks being used for training, mid 1930s. Normally armed with machine-guns, these tanks made up the first Panzer battalion, which was formed in 1934. By 1937 the force had grown into a Panzergruppe *of three divisions.*

the civil war. He, too, wanted to see Communism exported, but argued that a regular army ran counter to the Marxist principle of drawing on the mass of the people. Consequently, the army should be a militia, as it had been during the civil war.

Once Josef Stalin had assumed power on the death of Lenin in 1924, Trotsky fell from favour and was forced to flee abroad. In a similar manner, the ex-Imperial Army school was also discredited. Thus Frunze, who succeeded Trotsky as Commissar for War, and his school won out. He, too, took note of Fuller's writings, as well as German military literature, but realized that the Red Army could not be modernized until Soviet industry had been overhauled and brought up to date. Frunze's deputy, Tuchachevski, who succeeded him on his death in autumn 1925, pursued the same policy. Hence, when Stalin launched his first Five Year

Plan in 1928, the primary driving force behind it was the creation of an effective munitions industry.

The Red Army's 1929 Field Service Regulations spelt out how it would operate once modernized. The ideal, they stated, was the encirclement of the enemy through attacks by armour and cavalry. If the enemy's flanks proved too strong, then breakthrough operations would be needed. These would require strong artillery support and the co-operation of all arms. The Red Air Force would play its full part in providing direct support to the ground forces. At base, though, the Red Army still regarded the infantryman as its prime tool, and Tuchachevski found it an uphill struggle to marry his high-speed-manoeuvre-warfare concepts to the underlying Marxist–Leninist doctrine that strength lay in mass.

Even so, by the mid 1930s the Red Army had a formidable armoured force. Tuchachevski had also introduced paratroops and was conducting ambitious manoeuvres with combined arms. Foreign observers were impressed, although the more astute of them were aware that, as a whole, the Red Army was still an unwieldy mass – 'a bludgeon, quite incapable of rapier work', as one of them wrote.

March 1935 was a momentous month for Germany. First, German troops reoccupied the Saarland, whose inhabitants had overwhelmingly voted to be restored

Soviet T26 tanks on manoeuvres, 1935. While they appeared impressive on parade, the Red Army's armoured formations lacked the flexibility of the German model because few of the tanks were equipped with radio. Paucity of communications would remain throughout 1941–5.

to Germany in a League of Nations plebiscite held a few weeks earlier. Then, on the 9th, Hitler announced to the world that Germany had an air force. Suspicions that he was creating one had grown during the previous twelve months, but now it was a *fait accompli*. A week later, Hitler announced a massive expansion of the army. Versailles was well and truly dead.

Hitler saw the Luftwaffe as essentially a political weapon which he could use to further his aim of recreating a Greater Germany. To this end it had to be superior to or at least match other European air forces in numbers of aircraft. Consequently, in

1934 a plan was drawn up calling for 4,000 aircraft by the end of the following year. Two thousand of these aircraft had already been produced by the end of 1934. As for the army, the original plan, drawn up at the end of 1933, entailed expanding it to twenty-one divisions by 1937. The additional manpower was to be found from one-year volunteers. By March 1935 Hitler was demanding a further increase, to thirty-six divisions. This could only be met by conscription. This meant drawing on those born during the so-called 'white years' of 1914–18, when the birth rate fell dramatically. Furthermore, industry found it hard to increase weapons production to match the accelerated expansion. One significant example of this was that, while three Panzer divisions had been formed by October 1935, the remainder of the army had to rely largely on horse-drawn transport, and would continue to do so.

When it came to strengthening the Germany navy, Hitler had no wish for a repeat of the pre-1914 Dreadnought race, which would merely serve to antagonize Britain. Consequently, through the Anglo-German Naval Agreement of June 1935, Germany agreed to restrict her surface fleet to just over a third of that of the Royal Navy, but would be allowed parity in submarines. This concession reflected a British belief that the submarine no longer posed the threat that it had during 1914–18, an attitude which they would have cause to regret.

Yet Britain and France were still uneasy and began slowly to rearm in that same year of 1935. At the time governments perceived that the main threat was the bomber. Consequently, rearmament was initially directed at increasing the size of the British and French air forces so as to provide a deterrent to the Luftwaffe.

That 1935 marked a turning-point in European affairs during the interwar years was further reinforced in October. Mussolini had been disappointed that, unlike France and Britain, Italy had been awarded none of Germany's former African colonies. True, Italy already possessed Libya, Eritrea, and Italian Somaliland, but Mussolini wanted more and cast his eyes on Abyssinia (which the Italians had tried without success to seize in the 1890s). After peaceful overtures had failed, Italian troops invaded the country in October. The League of Nations protested, but the only positive action it took was to impose limited economic sanctions on Italy. Since these did not include coal or oil, and neither the USA nor Germany, not being League members, was bound by them, the sanctions had little effect, with Abyssinia being totally overrun by May 1936. Indeed, sanctions merely served to drive Mussolini into Hitler's arms, and on 1 November 1936 they signed the Berlin–Rome Axis. This made war in Europe possible, and from now on Britain and France would strive to prevent it breaking out.

Taking advantage of British and French concern over Abyssinia, Hitler sent his troops into the still-demilitarized Rhineland in March 1936. It was a calculated gamble, since the German army, still in the throes of expansion, was hardly ready for war. It worked, and served to boost Hitler's confidence still further. True, as a result of the German move, the French and British held military staff talks, but they reached no firm conclusions on how further German expansion might be countered.

London and Paris were further distracted in the late summer of 1936 by the

Spanish Civil War. Increasing rivalry between the Left and Right in the country resulted in land seizures, strikes and street violence. This culminated in a revolt by army garrisons in Spanish Morocco led by General Francisco Franco in July 1936, a revolt which quickly spread to the mainland. While Comintern, Moscow's instrument for the export of Communism, agreed to support the left-wing Republican government with volunteers and money, German and Italian aircraft arrived in Spanish Morocco, at Franco's request, and airlifted his troops across the straits to Spain.

The British and French, alarmed that the conflict might widen, declared their non-intervention and tried to persuade other nations to do the same. Hitler, Mussolini, and Stalin, while agreeing in principle to do so, in practice ignored the plea. Soon each was sending ground and air contingents to Spain. There were, too, the International Brigades, largely formed of idealist volunteers from the democracies, who fought on the Republican side, while a smaller number joined

Italian forces on the march during the invasion of Abyssinia, 1936. The Italians used large numbers of indigenous troops, recruited from their African possessions. It was, however, the use of modern weapons, which included poison gas, that proved too much for the Abyssinians.

Franco's Nationalists. For the dictatorships, Spain quickly became a weapons-testing laboratory. In the air, German Messerschmitt Me109s duelled with Russian Poliakarpov I-15s and I-16s, while on the ground German, Italian and Russian tanks met each other in battle for the first time.

It soon became clear that the Nationalists, with their German and Italian backing, were gaining the upper hand. Yet the war was to drag on for almost three years before the last Republican resistance ceased. The military lessons that came out of it were, it was to be later shown, somewhat misleading. Attempts to use tanks *en masse*, without co-operating with other arms, largely failed and the general conclusion drawn in many quarters was that their only true role was the traditional one of infantry support. There was also the belief that the war had shown that the anti-tank gun had outstripped the tank, thus implying that defence was superior to offence. For the world at large, however, the event which had the most impact took place on 26 April 1937, when aircraft of the German Condor Legion bombed the Basque town of Guernica. This seemed to provide confirmation that future conflict would be dominated by the bomber, with its power to make war total.

Unlike others, the Germans were careful not to draw too many tactical lessons from Spain. They did, however, begin to perfect the art of close air support of the ground forces, with the Junkers Ju87 Stuka dive-bomber making its operational debut. In Russia, however, the Spanish Civil War took place at a time of upheaval. This was caused by Stalin's purges, which had been ostensibly triggered by the murder of Sergei Kirov, Secretary of the Leningrad Regional Communist Party, on 1 December 1934. This started a wave of arrests, which spread ever wider and soon engulfed every walk of life. Eventually it reached the Soviet armed forces. The results were devastating. Three out of the five marshals, including Tuchachevski, perished, as did fourteen out of sixteen army commanders. All eight of the leading admirals of the Soviet navy lost their lives. But the purges spread downwards as well, even to junior officer level. Indeed, some estimates state that almost half of the officer corps

Republican volunteers leave for the front early in the Spanish Civil War. Increasing political factionalism weakened the effectiveness of the government forces. The support given by Moscow did not match that given by the Germans and Italians to Franco and his Nationalists, who also enjoyed the advantage of forces based largely on a combat-experienced army from North Africa.

was shot or imprisoned. It was the Red Army which suffered worst, with all Tuchachevski's hard work being undone on the pretext that Spain had shown that his theories were worthless. Apart from inexperienced and often low-calibre officers being appointed in place of those purged, the Red Army reverted to its traditional reliance on mass with armoured formations broken up, their tanks being largely restricted to infantry support.

The worsening situation in Europe and elsewhere caused Britain and France to speed up their rearmament. In Britain a bewildering series of RAF expansion plans followed one another in rapid succession, with Scheme F calling for a strength of 8,000 aircraft. In spite of efforts to expand the aviation industry, only 4,500 had been achieved by spring 1938 and many of these were obsolescent types, ordered under previous schemes. The French aviation industry was in a very much worse state and could only produce a fraction of the aircraft required. In 1936 it was nationalized, but it was to take time for the beneficial effects of this to be felt. By 1939, it was still producing only 600 aircraft a year, while the Germans were building 3,000.

German infantry 'goose-step' past the saluting base. Hitler's army did not, however, otherwise readopt the traditions of the old Imperial Army. Instead, so as to maintain primacy over Hitler's political troops – SA and SS – in the defence of Germany, every soldier had to swear a personal oath of loyalty to the Führer.

As in 1914 the French agreed that the British should take the lead when it came to naval operations, with the French navy concentrating most of its effort in the Mediterranean. The Royal Navy's posture during the 1920s and early 1930s had been based on the premise that the main naval threat was from Japan, and that only relatively small forces would be needed in the Mediterranean and home waters. Abyssinia and the realization that the 1930 London Naval Treaty would expire in 1936 caused a rethink. Thus, in 1935 a plan was drawn up which called for a significant increase in aircraft-carriers, cruisers and destroyers so as to ensure that the German navy did not gain control of home waters while the Far East was being reinforced.

The British Army came a poor third when it came to rearmament. The original plan envisaged five divisions being sent to the Continent, to be reinforced by Territorial Army (TA) formations once they were ready. It soon became clear, however, that the money being poured into expanding the RAF left little for the ground forces. Hence, at the end of 1936 there was a review of the army's role in general war. This concluded that coalition interests were best served by the Royal Navy and the RAF. Only two divisions were now earmarked for a token expeditionary force. This also had the advantage of avoiding the possibility of another very costly casualty bill and became known as the Doctrine of Limited Liability. Indeed, the continental commitment was now in last place in the army's priorities, with the top being home defence, followed by imperial defence, especially of Egypt in view of the growing Italian threat. The primary element of home defence was seen as against air attack. To this end the TA was given a new priority – the manning of anti-aircraft guns and searchlights. Fear of the bomber had also prompted the government to set up an Air Raid Precautions (ARP) organization in 1935. This was initially on a voluntary basis, but in 1937 it was made compulsory for local government to organize.

The French army was still firmly wedded to the Maginot Line. Yet one officer had dared to question reliance on this to the exclusion of all else in defence policy. This was Charles de Gaulle, who expounded his ideas in a book, *The Army of the Future*, published in 1933. He argued that France's falling birth rate meant that it could no longer sustain its traditional mass conscript army. Instead, the core of the army should be a 100,000-man professional armoured force. This was dismissed by most politicians, who argued that there was little point in having an offensive-based army when so much money had been spent on the Maginot Line. In any event, political suspicion of a regular army lay deep in France.

Yet Hitler's reoccupation of the Rhineland did jolt some into realizing that the French army had serious defects compared to the new German army. It was recognized that something was needed to counter the Panzer force, but the conservative view that the primary role of the tank was infantry support still dominated. The politicians, too, were concerned not do anything to disturb the sense of security engendered in the French people by the Maginot Line. Furthermore, there was the false lesson from Spain that the defence was still dominant.

In Germany it was different. The *Wehrmacht* (armed forces) continued to expand, with the army rising to thirty-nine divisions by the autumn of 1937. Hitler was now devoting his attention to creating the Greater Germany he had dreamt of for so long. His first target was Austria. Bound to Germany by a common language, there was already a strong Nazi following within the country that for some time had been at work paving the way for a German takeover. Early in 1938 matters reached such a pitch that the Austrian chancellor, Kurt von Schuschnigg, complained to Hitler, but was rebuffed. He therefore decided to hold a plebiscite on whether the Austrian people wished to retain their independence. Fearful that it might produce the wrong result, Hitler ordered his troops across the border on 12 March, the very eve of the vote. It was a bloodless invasion, with *Anschluss* (union) being achieved in less than twenty-four hours. The only flaw was the performance of the Panzer arm, which spearheaded the invasion. Lack of organization and inexperience caused a sizeable proportion of its vehicles to break down or run out of fuel.

Hitler now turned on Czechoslovakia, especially the westernmost province of Sudetenland, which contained a significant ethnic German minority. This, as the Austrian Nazis had done, began to agitate for total autonomy at Hitler's prompting, and he made it clear that he was prepared to use force if necessary. The Czechs refused to be cowed, and mobilized. Recognizing the not insignificant Czech military

HITLER'S ANNEXATIONS 1936–9

Apart from remilitarizing the Rhineland, Hitler's annexations had the effect of isolating Poland.

BELOW: *Ethnic Germans welcome the army's entry into Sudetenland, 1 October 1938. In contrast, when German forces entered Prague the following March, they were greeted by sullen silence.*

strength, Hitler did not take immediate military action, even though it was clear that neither Britain nor France was prepared to go to war over Czechoslovakia. But, as the summer of 1938 wore on, the tension grew. London and Paris became increasingly concerned that this might result in general war.

In early September the British prime minister Neville Chamberlain flew to Germany and obtained Hitler's assurance that Sudetenland was his final territorial ambition. But the policy of allowing him a free hand had to be sold to the French and the hapless Czechs. In the meantime, both Britain and France carried out a partial mobilization, which included erecting anti-aircraft defences in their respective capitals. The French accepted the proposal and told the Czechs that they would withdraw all support from them if they did not allow Germany to annexe the German-speaking region of Sudetenland. At the end of September, at Munich, at a

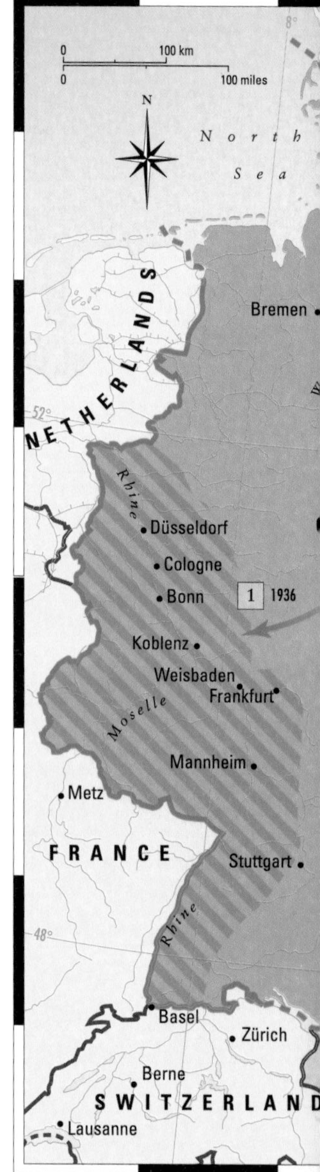

meeting of Hitler, Mussolini, Chamberlain, and the French prime minister Daladier, the whole of Sudetenland was signed away and German troops entered the province in triumph on 1 October.

The relief in Britain and France that war had been averted was intense, with the British acclaiming Chamberlain a hero after he declared, on his return from Munich, that he had brought 'peace in our time'. Yet, just four weeks after he had occupied Sudetenland, Hitler turned his eyes on Poland. He demanded that the Poles hand over the port of Danzig and that Germany be allowed to establish road and rail links with East Prussia across the Polish Corridor. The Poles, not unnaturally, refused. Hitler, however, was prepared to bide his time, especially since there was growing unrest in two other Czech provinces – Slovakia and Ruthenia – which wanted greater autonomy. Eventually President Hacha was forced to sack

Mussolini and Hitler meet in Munich, September 1938, before the signing of the pact which sealed Czechoslovakia's fate. Mussolini's delusions of grandeur were eventually to make him a mere puppet of Hitler.

the two premiers. That of Slovakia complained to Hitler, who now demanded Slovakian independence. Hacha went to Berlin to object to this interference in internal Czech affairs, but was subjected to such a browbeating that he agreed to place his country under German protection. Once more German troops crossed the border into a neighbouring state and in mid March 1939 Czechoslovakia found itself dismembered between Germany and a Hungary still under the Horthy regime.

Thus Hitler tore up the Munich Agreement. The reaction of the western democracies was, however, merely one of mild protest. Encouraged by this, Hitler now reiterated his Polish demands, which were again turned down. Two days later, on 23 March 1939, his troops marched into the port of Memel on the Polish–Lithuanian border. The Poles immediately warned Hitler that any similar occupation of Danzig would mean war.

It was now that Britain and France finally woke up to the fact that the only way in which Hitler could be stopped was to stand up to him. Accordingly, they declared at the end of March that they would stand by Poland in the event of German aggression. During the previous winter they had, however, been reviewing their joint military plans. The French had been unimpressed by the offer of a token British Expeditionary Force (BEF) and in consequence it was increased to four infantry and one armoured divisions, with a further four TA divisions earmarked as reinforcements. Now, as a result of the stand over Poland, the British government announced a doubling in size of the TA. The manpower for this was to be found through limited conscription, which came into force in spring 1939. Unfortunately, given that air and naval expansion continued to enjoy priority, the industrial resources required to equip this larger army were not initially available.

As these new measures were being introduced, there was another development on the continent of Europe, this time in the south-east. Mussolini, jealous of Hitler's successes, decided to copy him and sent troops across the Adriatic to Albania, which had been under Italian influence for the past fifteen years. This continuing land-grabbing now caused US president, Franklin Roosevelt, to become concerned. In mid April 1939 he sought assurances from Hitler and Mussolini that they would not attack other European nations. Unfortunately, Roosevelt was on weak ground, since during the period 1935–7 Congress had passed a series of Neutrality Acts which forbade the United States from entering a war that was already raging. The two dictators were well aware of this and ignored Roosevelt's request.

The war clouds now began to loom ever larger over Europe. At the end of April Hitler reiterated his Polish demands, this time renouncing a non-aggression pact which he had made with Poland in 1934 to safeguard his eastern border while he carried out his expansionist policies elsewhere in Europe. Hitler then ordered plans to be drawn up for the invasion of Poland. This was done in great secrecy by a small team led by the recently retired General Gerd von Rundstedt. Another ominous sign of approaching doom came in May, when Italy and Germany signed the Pact of Steel through which they guaranteed support for each other in any future war.

1 September 1939 – German troops remove a frontier barrier prior to entering Polish territory. The invasion did not take Warsaw by surprise, but with a traditionally hostile Soviet Union on her eastern border, and a German-occupied Czechoslovakia to the south, an effective defence was virtually impossible.

The western democracies did, however, have one ray of hope. In April 1939 the Soviet Union proposed a ten-year alliance with Britain and France. London and Paris welcomed this, seeing it not only as a more effective means of protecting Poland, but also as a way to present Hitler with the threat of simultaneous war on both fronts, which Germany had traditionally tried to avoid. Negotiations continued throughout much of the summer, but it was Poland itself which was the sticking-point. Anathema towards their eastern neighbour meant that the Poles would never allow Russian forces on to their territory.

Hitler, realizing what was in the wind, also began to make secret overtures to Moscow. On 23 August Germany and the Soviet Union signed a non-aggression pact, taking Britain and France, as well as much of the rest of the world, by surprise. What had caused this volte-face was that Hitler was prepared to give Stalin the eastern part of Poland after the country had been overrun and would also allow him a free hand in the Baltic states.

Throughout August the German armies had been steadily deploying close to the Polish border under the pretext of manoeuvres. Hitler gave orders that the invasion was to begin in the early hours of 26 August. That afternoon the troops began to move forward to their jump-off positions. They were to be preceded by special squads who were to secure Polish bridges close to the border. Suddenly, at 8 p.m. on the 25th a postponement order was sent out.

On that same day Britain and France had made a formal alliance with Poland, something Hitler had not expected. Furthermore, Mussolini declared that his country was not yet ready for war and offered to mediate between Berlin and Poland. The western allies tried to persuade the Poles to negotiate, but they were adamant. While this was going on, the German forces remained in their assembly areas, many helping out with the local harvest in order to pass the time.

At 4 p.m. on 31 August the German army higher command sent out another order. The attack would begin at 4.45 the following morning. This time there would be no cancellation.

CHAPTER TWO

The Triumph of Blitzkrieg (1939–40)

German PzKw III with short-barrelled 50mm gun. The Panzer troops wore a black uniform, which served to hide oil stains. The black beret, copied from the British Royal Tank Corps, was discarded after the earlier campaigns for a black side hat. The campaigns in Poland and the West demonstrated the increased pace of operations generated by armoured fighting vehicles with efficient radio communications handled by quick-thinking commanders who led from the front. They enabled the Germans to maintain the initiative and prevent timely reaction by their enemies. Yet, many senior German commanders still thought on traditional lines and took time to adjust to Blitzkrieg. Their dilemma was largely brought about by the infantry main body still being reliant on its feet.

THE TRIUMPH OF BLITZKRIEG 1939–40

THE POLISH CAMPAIGN

Forced to adopt a linear defence and lacking the necessary mobility, the Poles were unable to deploy reserves in time to counter the German Blitzkrieg. The Soviet invasion sealed Poland's fate.

At the switchboard, which was receiving bad news at monotonous one-minute intervals, there was no longer any reaction; one officer would acknowledge messages in a quiet, soft voice, another with an almost hysterical giggle – 'Ah yes, your left has been driven in; oh, I see, they're behind you. I'll make a note of it!' Everyone else in the room, prostrate and silent, was sitting about in armchairs.

ANDRÉ BEAUFRÉ, A JUNIOR STAFF OFFICER AT THE FRENCH HQ
NORTH-EAST THEATRE, MAY 1940

THE GERMAN GROUND FORCES that invaded Poland at dawn on 1 September were organized in two army groups and totalled forty infantry, six Panzer, two light (each comprising motorized infantry and a light tank battalion), and four motorized divisions. A further army group was also deployed to Germany's western borders, part of it occupying the Siegfried Line, which had been constructed to counter the French Maginot defences. To support the forces attacking Poland, the Luftwaffe fielded some 1,700 aircraft. It had two principal roles: the first, to destroy the Polish air force, if possible on the ground; the second, to provide support for the ground forces. This was not so much direct support on the battlefield, but more on interdiction targets so as to disrupt Polish communications and prevent the deployment of reserves and supplies. A subsidiary target was to be the Polish war industry, but attacks on purely civilian targets were strictly prohibited.

BELOW: *German infantrymen watch the bombardment of Warsaw. Having surrounded it, they were content for bombs and shells to force its surrender, rather than be committed to costly fighting in the streets of the Polish capital.*

Campaign in Poland
1–28 September 1939
German advance
Russian advance
Polish retreat
German field work
Polish defensive lines
Polish positions
German-Russian demarcation line
1 Polish positions 5 September 1939
2 Polish positions 6–14 September 1939
3 Polish positions 15–28 September 1939
Baltic Sea
LITHUANIA
East Prussia
POLAND
GERMANY
USSR
Protectorate of Bohemia-moravia
Slovakia
Ruthenia
AUSTRIA
HUNGARY
ARMY GROUP NORTH BOCK
KUECHLER
GUDERIAN
POZMORZE
KLUGE
WODRIG
MODLIN
NAREW (elts)
MODLIN and NAREW (elts)
BELORUSSIAN FRONT
PORMORZE
POZNAN
LODZ
CRACOW
UKRANIAN FRONT
CARPATHIAN
BLASKOWITZ
HOEPPNER
REICHENAU
KRAKOW
ARMY GROUP SOUTH RUNDSTEDT
LIST
Königsberg
Lablau
Insterburg
Kaunas
Wilno
Kalvarya
Suwalk
Grodno
Gdynia
Danzig
Elbing
Lauenburg
Stulp
Kolberg
Koslin
Stettin
Allenstein
Lomza
Bialystock
Baranowicze
Bydgoszcz
Scneidemühl
Landsberg
Inowroclaw
Wloclawek
Plock
Roznan
Poznan
Warsaw
Siedlce
Brest-Litovsk
Guben
Kock
Lodz
Kalisz
Leszno
Glogou
Tomaszon
Radom
Lublin
Breslau
Kielce
Czestochwa
Oppeln
Katowice
Cracow
Tarnow
Rzeszow
Lvov
Przemysl
Sambor
Prague
Kutna Mora
Olamouc
Nowy Sacz
Nowy Targ
Brno
Stanislowow
Presov
Znojmo
Trengin
Zvolen
Uzingorod
Trnava
Bratislava
Vienna
Miskolc
Debrecen
Budapest
Vistula
Warta
Oder
Bug
Dneister
Danube
Tisza
6000
3000
1500
600
300
0 ft
0 100 km
0 100 miles

The pride of the Polish army was its cavalry, which had a long tradition, including its famous Lancers who had fought for Napoleon. On more than one occasion Polish cavalry charged German tanks, with an inevitable result. It confirmed that shock action on the battlefield was now the tank and not the horse.

The Polish army could match the invading forces numerically, but it laboured under a number of disadvantages. Most critical was that the German annexation of Czechoslovakia had significantly increased the length of Poland's western borders. This gave the Poles little option but to adopt a linear defence. Furthermore, their army's weapons and equipment did not match those of the Germans. While the thirty infantry divisions were on a par with their opponents, both being largely reliant on their feet, the Poles had only one tank and two motorized brigades, the former being equipped with obsolete tanks. Indeed, the cream of the army was the eleven cavalry brigades. The Polish air force was in an even worse condition, numbering a mere 450 aircraft, almost all obsolete types.

Even though the Poles deployed many of their aircraft to satellite airfields, the Luftwaffe had little difficulty in achieving air supremacy. On the ground the attacks were spearheaded by the Panzer divisions, supported by the motorized infantry and light divisions. These achieved penetrations which were widened by the conventional divisions, who covered up to twenty-five miles per day on their feet. The Poles fought with sometimes fanatical bravery, but the sheer pace of the German advance, combined with the Luftwaffe's interdiction attacks, proved too much, and many found themselves trapped. Yet not all went to plan for the Germans. Hesitancy and poor co-ordination were frequent during the early days.

Indeed, the Panzer commanders, especially General Heinz Guderian, one of the chief architects of Germany's armoured forces, soon realized that they needed to lead from the front so as to imbue their troops with the necessary urgency. They also found themselves frustrated by higher commanders fearful of allowing the tanks to get too far ahead of the main body. Consequently, the Panzer divisions were often reined back.

The Poles' main hope was that if they kept fighting, their western allies would launch an attack to relieve the pressure. France and Britain had declared war on Germany on 3 September, after their ultimatum to Hitler to withdraw his troops from Poland had been rejected. While both Japan and the United States were quick to declare their neutrality, the British dominions followed the mother country with declarations of war. This was, however, only after the matter had been debated by their respective parliaments – an indication of their increased autonomy over the situation of twenty-five years earlier.

Not until 8 September did the French take offensive action, but hardly on the scale hoped for by the Poles. Nine divisions made a hesitant advance into the Saarland, but they halted before they got out of range of the guns in the Maginot Line. It caused the Germans hardly a ruffle and the remorseless advance ever deeper into Poland continued. On 15 September the Germans surrounded Warsaw, but the Poles rejected demands to surrender their capital. It was therefore subjected to

PzKw IIIs, armed with a 37mm gun, await the order to advance. These provided the backbone of the Panzer divisions during the first phase of the war. The lighter PzKw Is and IIs were used mainly for reconnaissance, while the larger PzKw IV, with its short barrelled 75mm, was used for fire support. Later the IV was equipped with a long barrelled 75mm and largely superceded the III.

STUKA TACTICS

How Junkers Ju87 Stuka dive-bombers operated with the Panzer divisions. The secret was good air–ground communications, with a Luftwaffe officer with radio accompanying the Panzer formation commander. The almost vertical dive enabled a high degree of accuracy in delivering its bombs, but some Stuka crews perished because the pilot did not pull out of his dive in time.

massive artillery and air bombardment. Two days later the Red Army invaded Poland from the east, declaring that it no longer existed as an independent state.

The Poles continued to fight on. Warsaw held out until the 27th and only surrendered because the public utilities, including the water supplies, had been destroyed. Next day, ten Polish divisions which had been trapped in the Modlin area since 10 September, also surrendered. This marked the virtual end of the fighting, although resistance on the Baltic coast did not finally cease until 1 October, at which point the French withdrew their forces from the Saarland.

A dark shadow now fell over dismembered Poland. In the western half of the country the Germans were soon persecuting the large Jewish population, confining many of them to ghettoes in the cities. In the east the Russians, determined that Poland would never again enjoy independence, purged the intelligentsia. Meanwhile, in Paris General Wladyslaw Sikorski had established a government-in-exile, the first of many, and Poles, many of them reaching France after incredible adventures, rallied to his flag.

Hitler, having removed the Polish problem, was keen to turn on Britain and France as soon as possible, and no sooner had the fighting ended than the troop trains began to roll westwards. He did, however, on 6 October propose peace if the western democracies would recognize the status quo in eastern Europe. Not surprisingly, London and Paris immediately rejected this, and three days later Hitler issued orders for an invasion. His main object was to secure the North Sea and Channel coasts. These would become 'a basis for successful air and sea operations against Britain' and provide 'a broad protective zone for the Ruhr'. As in 1914, the attack would take in the neutral Low Countries, but this time also encompassed Holland. During its course Hitler expected to destroy the bulk of the Allied armies. As for the Maginot Line, he intended merely to tie down the French forces holding it without attempting to attack.

Hitler ordered the attack to be mounted in mid November, but his generals were unwilling. For a start, they needed time to assimilate the lessons of the Polish campaign. They also recognized that the enemy in the West was far more formidable than Poland had been. As a result there was a series of postponements.

Across the Franco-German border the British and French were assembling their forces. The BEF duly crossed the Channel and took up position in northern France. It was accompanied by an RAF contingent. But the BEF was lacking its armoured division, which, because of the problems in equipping it, would not be ready before spring 1940. In the meantime, the French had become conscious of the fact that the Maginot Line extended only as far as the border with Luxembourg. Consequently, work began to extend it northwards. The Allies were also convinced that the most likely German invasion route was north of the heavily wooded Ardennes. But in the extreme north of France there were no suitable natural features on which to base a defence. It was also one of the country's key industrial areas. The result was Plan D. As soon as the Germans attacked the northern French armies, the BEF would move into Belgium and take up positions along the Albert Canal and Rivers

Dyle and Meuse. The problem was that the Belgians, keen to preserve their neutrality above all else, refused to allow even reconnaissance parties across their border. All detailed planning had therefore to be from the map.

Thus, apart from the odd patrol clash in front of the Maginot Line, the Western Front remained quiet. In the air both sides carried out reconnaissance flights and occasionally bombed each other's ships. RAF bombers also dropped leaflets over Germany. The pre-war belief that, on the outbreak of war, cities would be attacked indiscriminately with gas bombs as well as conventional ones, had not materialized, both sides fearing retaliation in kind. Thus, many of the children evacuated to the rural areas from Britain's cities at the outbreak of war began to drift back to their homes. It did, indeed, appear to be a 'phoney war', as one US commentator expressed it.

Only at sea was there any action. The Royal Navy instituted a blockade of German ports at the outbreak of war, as well as organizing its merchant vessels in home waters and the north Atlantic into convoys, although little could be

THE RUSSO-FINNISH WAR
Although the Soviet attacks took place on a wide front, the critical sector was in the Lake Ladoga region in the south where the Finns had constructed the Mannerheim Line.

spared to escort them. While Hitler had torn up the Anglo-German Naval Agreement and ordered an expansion of his U-boat fleet, there were only fifty-seven U-boats in commission at the outbreak of war, too few to make a significant impact, although one sank a British aircraft-carrier and another penetrated the Home Fleet's anchorage at Scapa Flow and sank a battleship. But Hitler had also deployed pocket battleships to waiting areas before the outbreak of war. One of these, *Graf Spee,* created havoc in the shipping lanes in the Indian Ocean and south Atlantic before eventually being trapped by British cruisers in the Uruguayan port of Montevideo in December, where her crew scuttled her. This marked the only Allied success in the opening months of the war.

In November 1939, however, the focus began to switch in part to Scandinavia. After the overrunning of Poland, the Soviet Union had quickly brought Latvia, Lithuania and Estonia under her control through a series of 'mutual assistance' pacts. The Russians now turned to their northern neighbour, Finland. To secure the Gulf of Finland and the Barents Sea, they demanded of the Finns the lease of Finnish ports, especially Viipuri and Petsamo, as well as territory on the shores of Lake Ladoga and the Gulf of Finland. In return Finland would receive parts of desolate Karelia. The Finns, seeing what was happening in the Baltic States, refused. Stalin therefore lost patience and on 20 November launched a multi-pronged invasion, which included the air bombing of Finnish towns.

The Finnish armed forces were only a fraction of the size of those ranged against them. Yet, to the surprise of the world, they easily repulsed the initial

BELOW: *Finnish ski patrol and frozen Russian corpses, December 1939. These patrols were very effective in penetrating the Soviet lines and mounting 'hit and run' raids, which did little for the morale of the Red Army troops.*

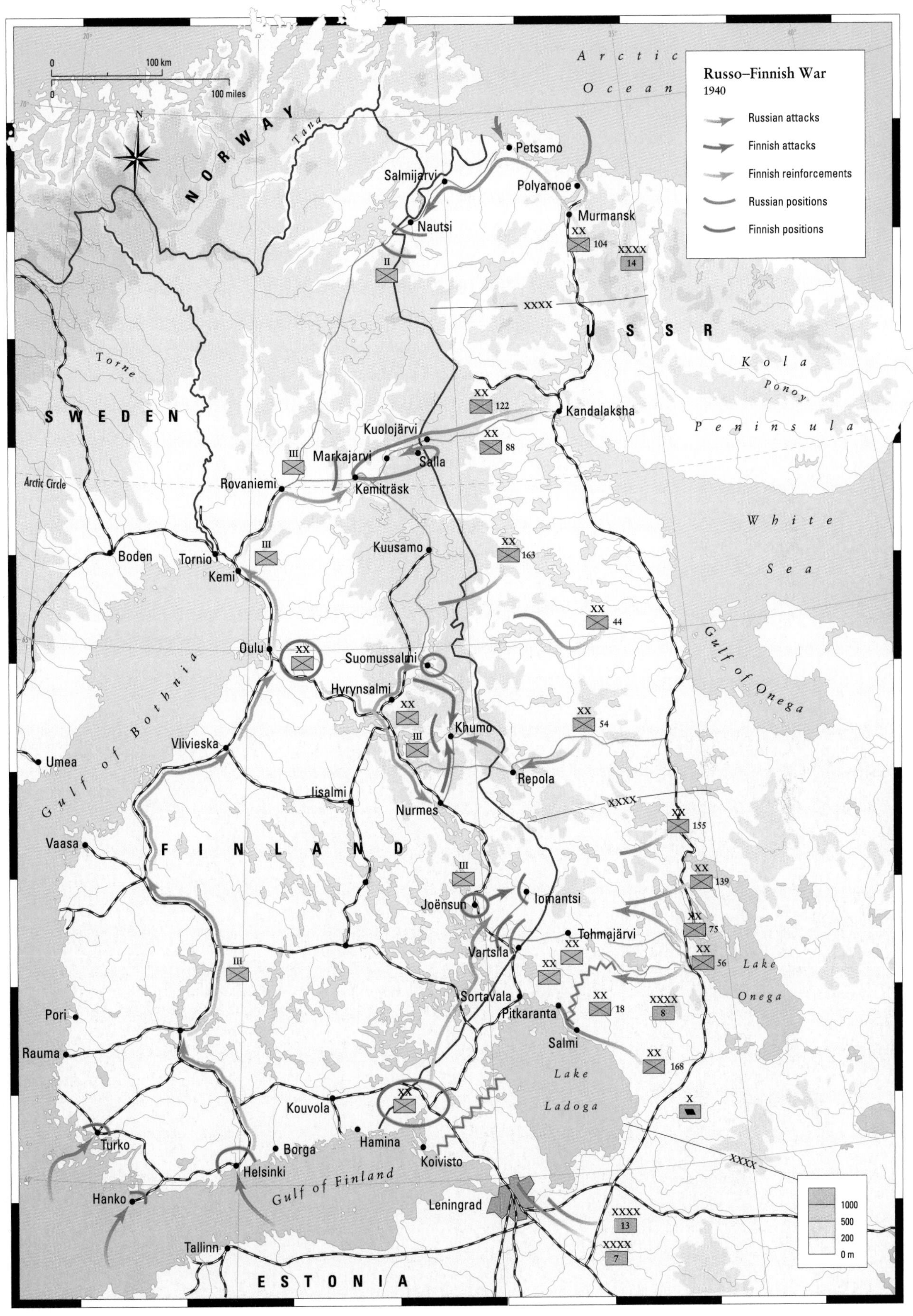
Russo–Finnish War
1940
Russian attacks
Finnish attacks
Finnish reinforcements
Russian positions
Finnish positions
100 km
100 miles
Arctic Ocean
NORWAY
SWEDEN
FINLAND
USSR
ESTONIA
Kola Peninsula
White Sea
Gulf of Onega
Gulf of Bothnia
Gulf of Finland
Lake Onega
Lake Ladoga
Arctic Circle
Petsamo
Polyarnoe
Murmansk
Salmijärvi
Nautsi
Kandalaksha
Kuolojärvi
Markajarvi
Salla
Kemiträsk
Rovaniemi
Kuusamo
Boden
Tornio
Kemi
Oulu
Suomussalmi
Hyrynsalmi
Khumo
Repola
Vlivieska
Umea
Iisalmi
Nurmes
Vaasa
Joënsuu
Iomantsi
Tohmajärvi
Vartsila
Sortavala
Pitkaranta
Salmi
Pori
Rauma
Kouvola
Hamina
Koivisto
Turko
Borga
Helsinki
Hanko
Leningrad
Tallinn
1000
500
200
0 m

OPPOSING PLANS IN THE WEST

The Allied Plan D unwittingly played into German hands.

Russian attacks. As the weeks wore on, the Red Army continued its attacks, but suffered sharply rising casualties and could make little headway – Stalin's purges of the military had come home to roost. Britain and France began to take note and decided to send arms to the Finns, but with the other Scandinavian countries being neutral, delivering them was a problem.

Early in January 1940 Stalin ordered one of the few senior commanders who had survived the purges to take charge of the operations against Finland. Semyon Timoshenko reorganized his forces and launched another series of attacks at the beginning of February. At the same time, the British and French finally decided to send troops to help the Finns, planning to pass them through northern Norway. It was, however, too late. The Finns began to wilt under the Russian pressure, and, in early March, sent a deputation to Moscow. In order to preserve their independence, they were forced to concede much more than the original Soviet demands. This left them embittered. As for the Russians, the military difficulties that they had experienced resulted in a massive overhaul of their armed forces.

In western Europe the winter of 1939–40 was a cold one, which gave the German commanders another reason for not launching the offensive. But some were beginning to question Hitler's concept of operations. The most vociferous of these was Erich von Manstein, chief of staff to Army Group A. He believed that Hitler's objective of the North Sea and Channel coasts was too limited and would

The French Char B tank appeared formidable. With armour twice the thickness of any German tank it was armed with a turret-mounted 47mm gun and a hull-mounted 75mm. But the small size of the turret meant that the commander had both to fire and load the 47mm in addition to his other duties. The effectiveness of the 75mm was much diminished because it had no traverse and could only be aimed by moving the tank itself.

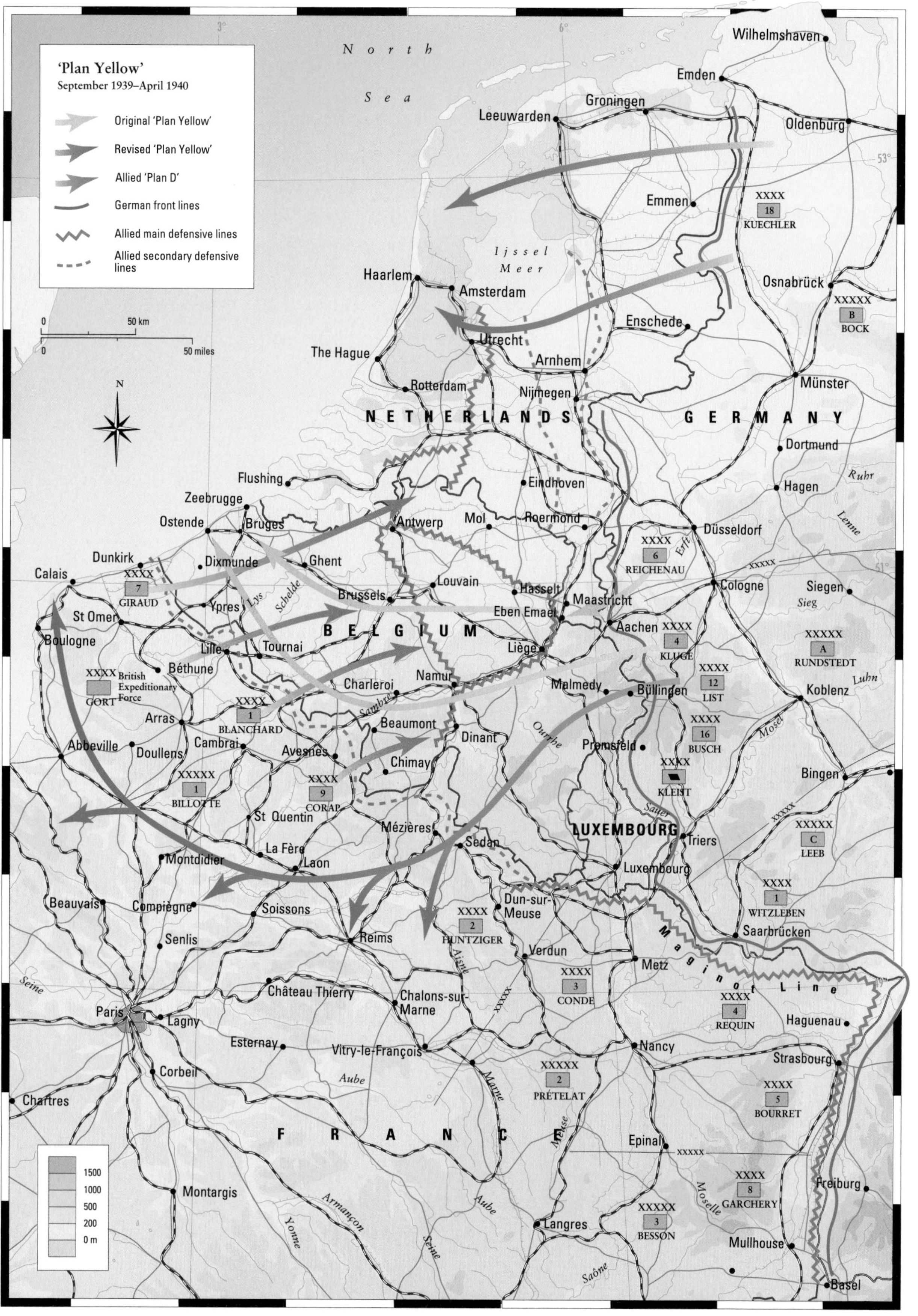

'Plan Yellow'
September 1939–April 1940
Original 'Plan Yellow'
Revised 'Plan Yellow'
Allied 'Plan D'
German front lines
Allied main defensive lines
Allied secondary defensive lines
0 50 km
0 50 miles
N
North Sea
Ijssel Meer
NETHERLANDS
GERMANY
BELGIUM
LUXEMBOURG
FRANCE
Maginot Line
Wilhelmshaven
Emden
Groningen
Leeuwarden
Oldenburg
Emmen
XXXX 18 KUECHLER
Haarlem
Amsterdam
Osnabrück
XXXXX B BOCK
Enschede
Utrecht
The Hague
Arnhem
Rotterdam
Nijmegen
Münster
Dortmund
Flushing
Eindhoven
Hagen
Ruhr
Zeebrugge
Ostende
Bruges
Antwerp
Mol
Roermond
Düsseldorf
Lenne
XXXX 6 REICHENAU
Erft
Dunkirk
Calais
XXXX 7 GIRAUD
Dixmunde
Ghent
Louvain
Hasselt
Maastricht
Cologne
Siegen
Sieg
Brussels
Eben Emael
St Omer
Ypres
Lys
Schelde
Aachen
XXXX 4 KLUGE
XXXXX A RUNDSTEDT
Boulogne
Lille
Tournai
Liège
Béthune
Namur
Malmedy
Büllingen
XXXX 12 LIST
Luhn
XXXX British Expeditionary Force GORT
Charleroi
Sambre
Koblenz
XXXX 1 BLANCHARD
Arras
Beaumont
Dinant
Ourthe
Prümsfeld
XXXX 16 BUSCH
Mosel
Abbeville
Doullens
Cambrai
Avesnes
Chimay
XXXX KLEIST
Bingen
XXXXX 1 BILLOTTE
XXXX 9 CORAP
St Quentin
Sauer
Mézières
LUXEMBOURG
Triers
XXXXX C LEEB
La Fère
Sedan
Montdidier
Laon
Luxembourg
XXXX 1 WITZLEBEN
Beauvais
Compiègne
Soissons
Dun-sur-Meuse
XXXX 2 HUNTZIGER
Saarbrücken
Senlis
Reims
Aisne
Verdun
Metz
Seine
XXXX 3 CONDE
Château Thierry
Chalons-sur-Marne
XXXX 4 REQUIN
Paris
Lagny
Haguenau
Esternay
Vitry-le-François
Nancy
Strasbourg
Corbeil
Aube
Marne
XXXXX 2 PRÉTELAT
XXXX 5 BOURRET
Chartres
Meuse
Epinal
1500
1000
500
200
0 m
Montargis
Armançon
Moselle
XXXX 8 GARCHERY
Freiburg
Yonne
Aube
Seine
Langres
XXXXX 3 BESSON
Mullhouse
Saône
Basel

DENMARK AND NORWAY

Simultaneous landings along the Norwegian coast facilitated the German advance northwards. Only at Narvik did the Allies enjoy any degree of success, but it was shortlived.

still leave sizeable French forces intact. Furthermore, thrusting through the Low Countries was too obvious, echoing, in some ways, the 1914 von Schlieffen plan. Instead, he argued, the main thrust should be conducted by Army Group A, with the bulk of the armour, through the heavily wooded Ardennes in southern Belgium. This would make a much deeper hook to the English Channel, with Army Group B, once it had overrun Holland and Belgium, turning south to act like a hammer on the anvil created by Army Group A. Von Rundstedt, von Manstein's superior, supported him, but at first his proposals met with little enthusiasm.

On 10 January 1940 a Luftwaffe communications aircraft force-landed in Belgium. On board was a liaison officer with details of the attack plans, which he was able only partially to destroy. The Belgians said nothing, but the odds that the plan had been compromised were high. Therefore, six days later, Hitler decreed a postponement until the spring. This gave von Manstein another opportunity to push for his alternative plan. After it had been demonstrated during war games conducted on maps, Hitler eventually agreed. *Fall Sichelschnitt* (Plan Sickle) was officially adopted on 6 March. His next move was to pressure Mussolini into honouring the Pact of Steel. The two dictators met in the Brenner Pass, close to the Italo-Austrian border, and Mussolini assured his ally that he would join in the attack when it took place.

ABOVE: *French* Chasseurs Alpins *in Norway, April 1940. The French contingent also included a brigade of Polish troops. After the fall of Poland, the country's forces were reorganized in France, from where they later moved to Britain.*

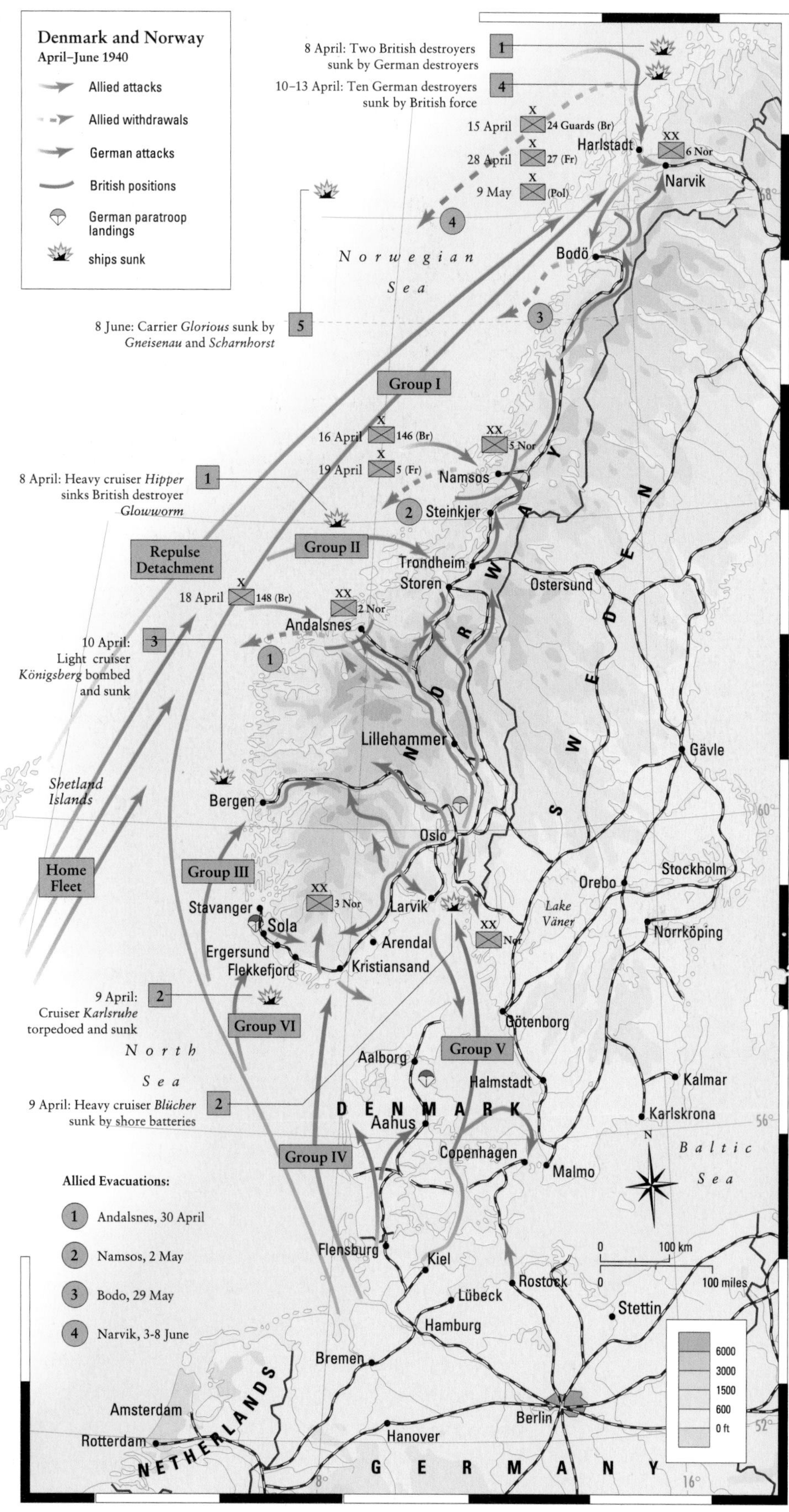

Denmark and Norway
April–June 1940
Allied attacks
Allied withdrawals
German attacks
British positions
German paratroop landings
ships sunk
8 April: Two British destroyers sunk by German destroyers
10–13 April: Ten German destroyers sunk by British force
8 June: Carrier Glorious sunk by Gneisenau and Scharnhorst
8 April: Heavy cruiser Hipper sinks British destroyer Glowworm
10 April: Light cruiser Königsberg bombed and sunk
9 April: Cruiser Karlsruhe torpedoed and sunk
9 April: Heavy cruiser Blücher sunk by shore batteries
Allied Evacuations:
1 Andalsnes, 30 April
2 Namsos, 2 May
3 Bodo, 29 May
4 Narvik, 3-8 June
15 April 24 Guards (Br)
28 April 27 (Fr)
9 May (Pol)
6 Nor
16 April 146 (Br)
19 April 5 (Fr)
5 Nor
18 April 148 (Br)
2 Nor
3 Nor
Group I
Group II
Group III
Group IV
Group V
Group VI
Repulse Detachment
Home Fleet
Norwegian Sea
North Sea
Baltic Sea
Shetland Islands
Harlstadt
Narvik
Bodö
Namsos
Steinkjer
Trondheim
Storen
Andalsnes
Ostersund
Lillehammer
Gävle
Bergen
Oslo
Stockholm
Orebo
Lake Väner
Norrköping
Stavanger
Sola
Larvik
Arendal
Ergersund
Flekkefjord
Kristiansand
Götenborg
Aalborg
Halmstadt
Kalmar
Karlskrona
Aahus
Copenhagen
Malmo
Flensburg
Kiel
Rostock
Lübeck
Hamburg
Stettin
Bremen
Berlin
Amsterdam
Rotterdam
Hanover
NORWAY
SWEDEN
DENMARK
NETHERLANDS
GERMANY
0 100 km
0 100 miles
6000
3000
1500
600
0 ft

German troops advance through a Norwegian village which has been set on fire by the Luftwaffe. Apart from an ill-coordinated command and control structure, the French and British forces in Norway were seriously disadvantaged by the almost total German air supremacy.

In the Allied camp there were also changes. While Chamberlain was still Britain's prime minister, his fellow appeaser Edouard Daladier was replaced in late March by a new government led by Paul Reynaud, one of the few politicians who had supported de Gaulle's concept of a professional armoured core to the French army. One of Reynaud's first actions was to agree with Chamberlain that neither Britain nor France would make a separate peace with Germany.

As March turned to April, there was still no German move. A relieved Chamberlain therefore told the British people 'Hitler has missed the bus.' Within little more than a month he would have cause to eat his words.

During the early months of 1940 both sides had turned increasing attention to Norway. The British and French not only wanted to use it to pass troops and supplies through to Finland, but were also concerned over supplies of Swedish iron ore to Germany which, in the winter months, were sent through the northern Norwegian port of Narvik. The German navy, too, was attracted by Norway as an ideal northern base from which to harry British trade routes in the north Atlantic. Hitler therefore ordered plans for an invasion to be drawn up. Similar British and French plans were, however, thwarted when Finland's surrender removed their pretext for action. At the end of March, they decided to mine Norwegian territorial waters instead, but also to have troops ready to send if the Germans should invade.

On 5 April, after warning the Norwegian and Swedish governments, the minelaying forces sailed. But Hitler had already given invasion orders. While one force overran Jutland and the Danish islands, the Norwegian expedition would sail in six groups which would land at various points on the country's long coastline. RAF aircraft spotted those bound for Trondheim and Narvik on the 7th, but a gale prevented the Royal Navy from intercepting them. The German attack itself took place on the 9th. Denmark was overrun within less than twenty-four hours. Paratroops were used to seize key Norwegian airfields, enabling the Luftwaffe to use them as bases. Oslo, the capital, was quickly taken and the only Norwegian success on that day was the sinking of the cruiser *Bluecher* by a coastal battery in Oslo Fjord.

The first British contingent sailed on the 11th, but amid much confusion, with troops being embarked and then disembarked, becoming separated from much of their heavy equipment in the process. Indeed, muddle was to dominate the campaign and was largely caused by lack of clear-cut command and control at the higher levels. The Allied plan was to land contingents on the Norwegian coast. These would then co-operate with local Norwegian forces to halt the German thrust northwards, as well as reducing those forces which had landed at Trondheim and Narvik. Unfortunately, the Germans enjoyed almost total air supremacy and were also able to bypass the Allied forces. Hence, one after another, they had to be evacuated. Only at Narvik did the Allies enjoy any success, isolating the German forces there and eventually capturing the port at the end of May, with the German garrison slipping across the border into Sweden. By this time the Allies were facing catastrophe many hundreds of miles to the south, and in early June the Narvik force, now out on a very long limb, was withdrawn, leaving Norway under total German control.

On 10 May 1940 the long-awaited German invasion of the West began. On that same day Neville Chamberlain was succeeded by Winston Churchill as prime minister of Britain. On paper the Allies appeared formidable. The Dutch could field ten divisions and their numerous waterways provided good natural obstacles. The Belgian army had a strength of twenty-two divisions and had constructed modern defences to replace the old Liège forts of 1914. France had mobilized no fewer than 104 divisions, while by May 1940 the BEF had grown to ten divisions. Facing them, the Germans had mustered some 135 divisions. Beneath these bald figures the situation was rather different.

The Dutch army was ill equipped and riddled with pacifism, the result of over a hundred years of strict neutrality. The Belgians, too, lacked modern weapons, especially anti-aircraft artillery. The BEF looked modern, especially since it was the one army which had entirely replaced the horse with motor transport, but some of its recently arrived divisions were only partially equipped and incompletely trained. The French armies in the extreme north were generally of good quality, but those in the centre were largely made up of lower-grade formations, many of whom consisted of conscripts with just one year's training. While the French outnumbered the Germans ten to seven in artillery, many of their weapons were 1914–18 vintage and were horse-drawn. When it came to tanks, the Dutch had none and the Belgians a mere ten, but the French and British had 3,370 available, compared to 2,445 German. The German tanks were concentrated, however, the bulk being with Army Group A, which was to make the decisive Ardennes thrust. True, the French had by this time formed three armoured divisions, but while their heavy Char Bs and fast Somuas looked impressive, absence of tank radios meant that these formations lacked the flexibility of the Panzer division. Furthermore, the bulk of the French tanks were dedicated to infantry support and, as such, split up into penny packets. As for the one British armoured division, it was still not ready to cross to France, and the 310 British tanks available were mainly light reconnaissance types dispersed among the infantry divisions.

ARDENNES, MAY 1940

The plunge of Heinz Guderian's XIX Panzer corps through the heavily wooded Ardennes, May 1940. Believing that the Germans would not send armour through here, the Allies merely had light screening forces defending the region. Guderian and his fellow Panzer corps commanders, Reinhardt and Hoth, were helped by special force members dressed in civilian clothes, who posed as tourists and were able to neutralize demolitions on bridges and defiles.

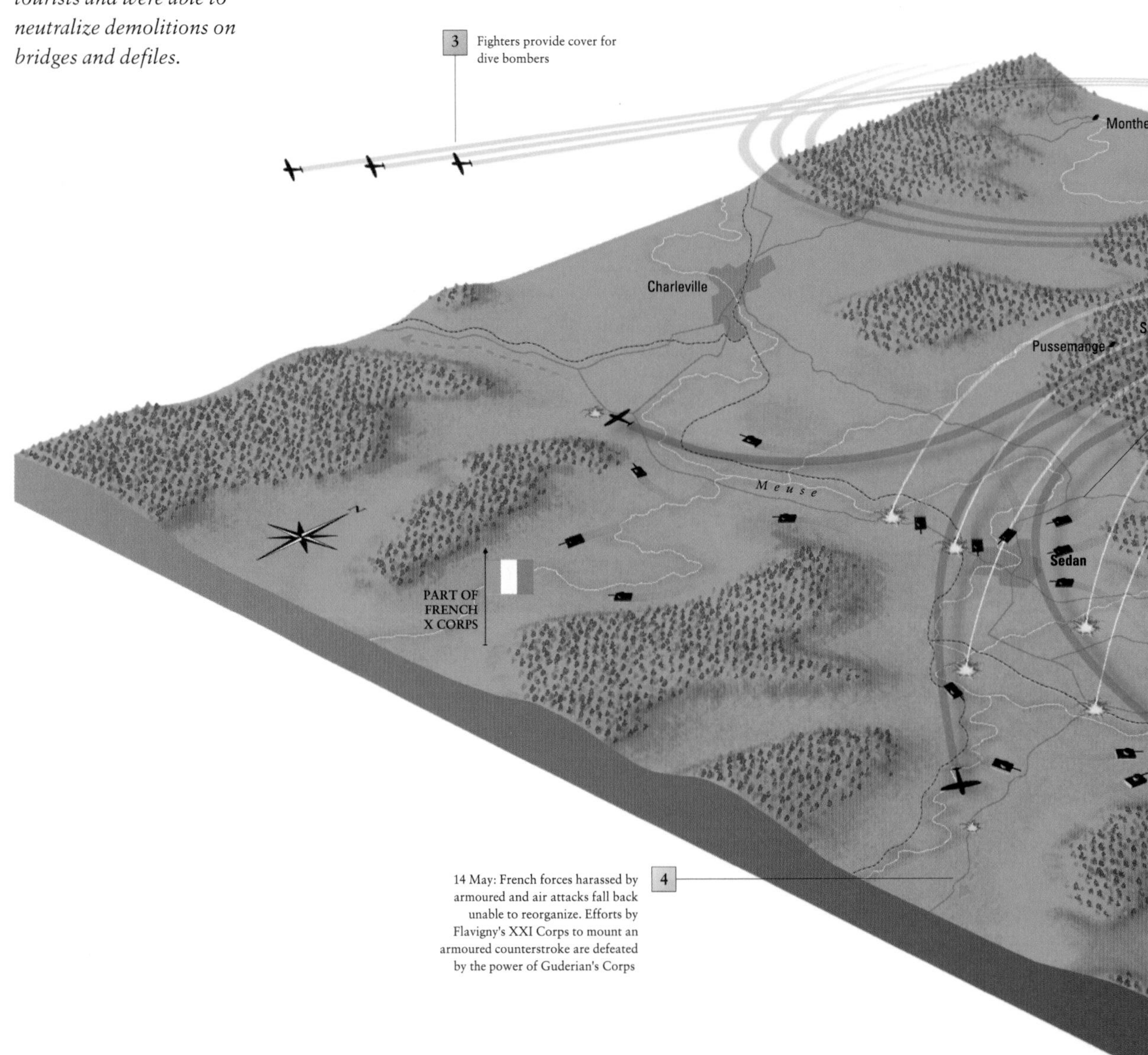

When it came to the situation in the air, the scales came down even more heavily on the German side. The Luftwaffe had some 4,000 operational aircraft, almost all modern combat-proven types. The Allies possessed just over 3,000, but many were obsolescent. In addition, while the Germans had spent the winter drawing on the lessons of Poland to hone co-operation between air and ground forces, the Allies were still only paying lip-service to this vital aspect of modern war.

But the greatest Allied weakness was that they were structured to fight a static defensive campaign and this was reflected in their cumbersome chain of command, especially in the critical northern region of France. The French commander-in-chief, Maurice Gamelin, totally reliant on the civilian telephone system, had delegated the conduct of operations to a subordinate headquarters, that of the Commander-in-Chief North-East Front, General Alphonse Georges. This was even though Gamelin had drawn up the plan of campaign himself, and he and Georges did not

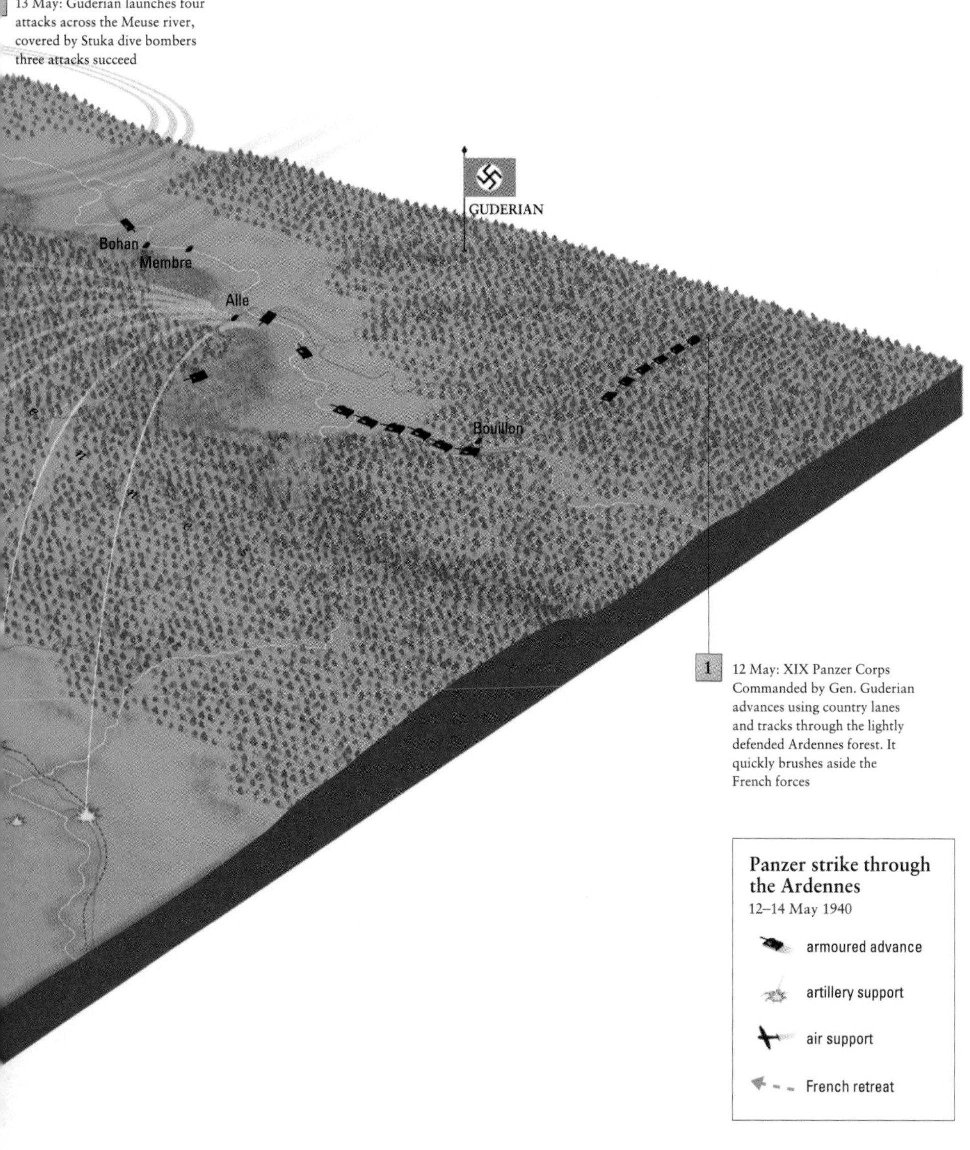

Panzer strike through the Ardennes
12–14 May 1940

Invasion of the West

The decisive German blow was the armoured thrust through the Ardennes. Once the Panzers were across the River Meuse, they were able to split the Allied forces in two. Having defeated the northern Allied armies, the Germans turned south to overcome the remainder of France (Plan Red).

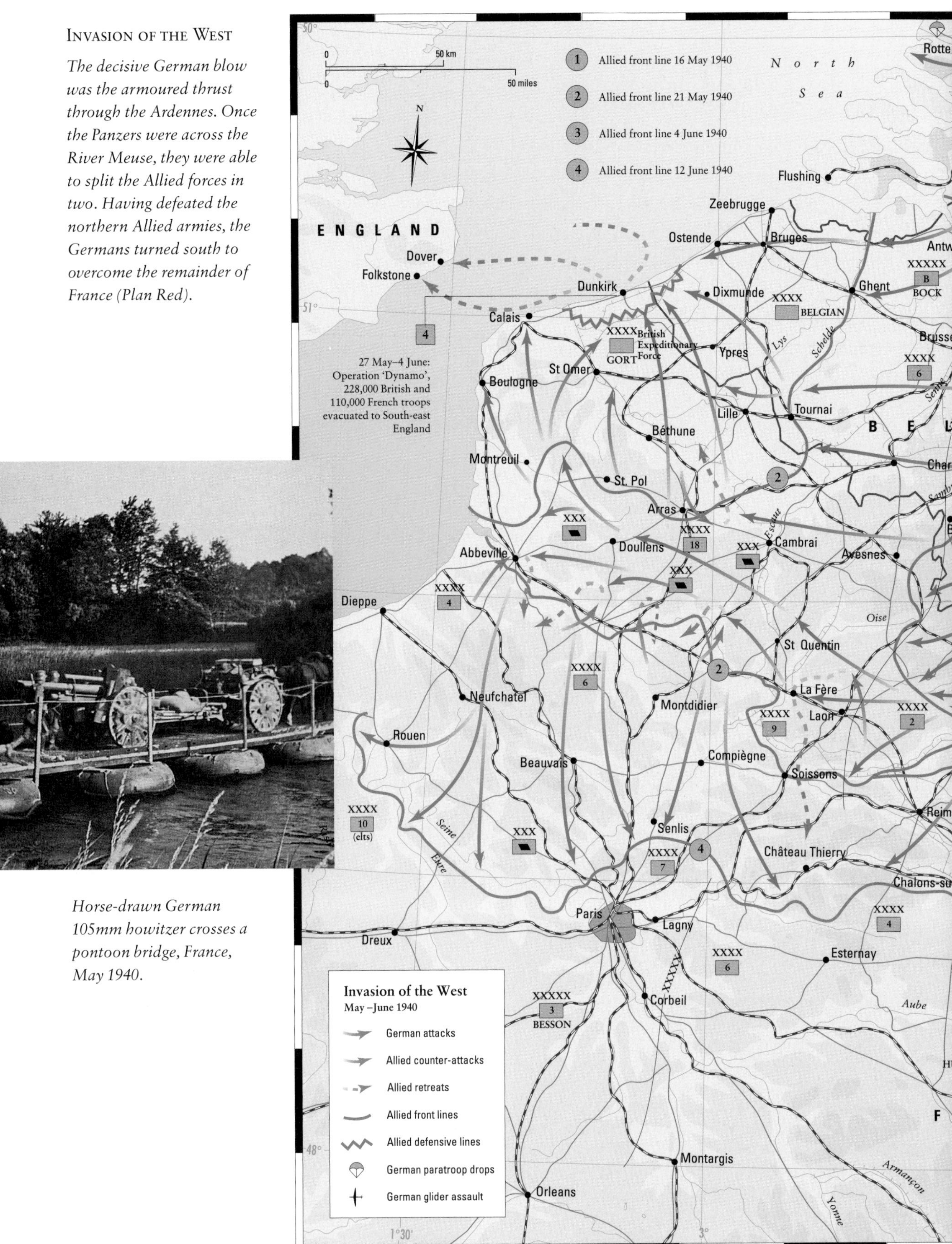

Horse-drawn German 105mm howitzer crosses a pontoon bridge, France, May 1940.

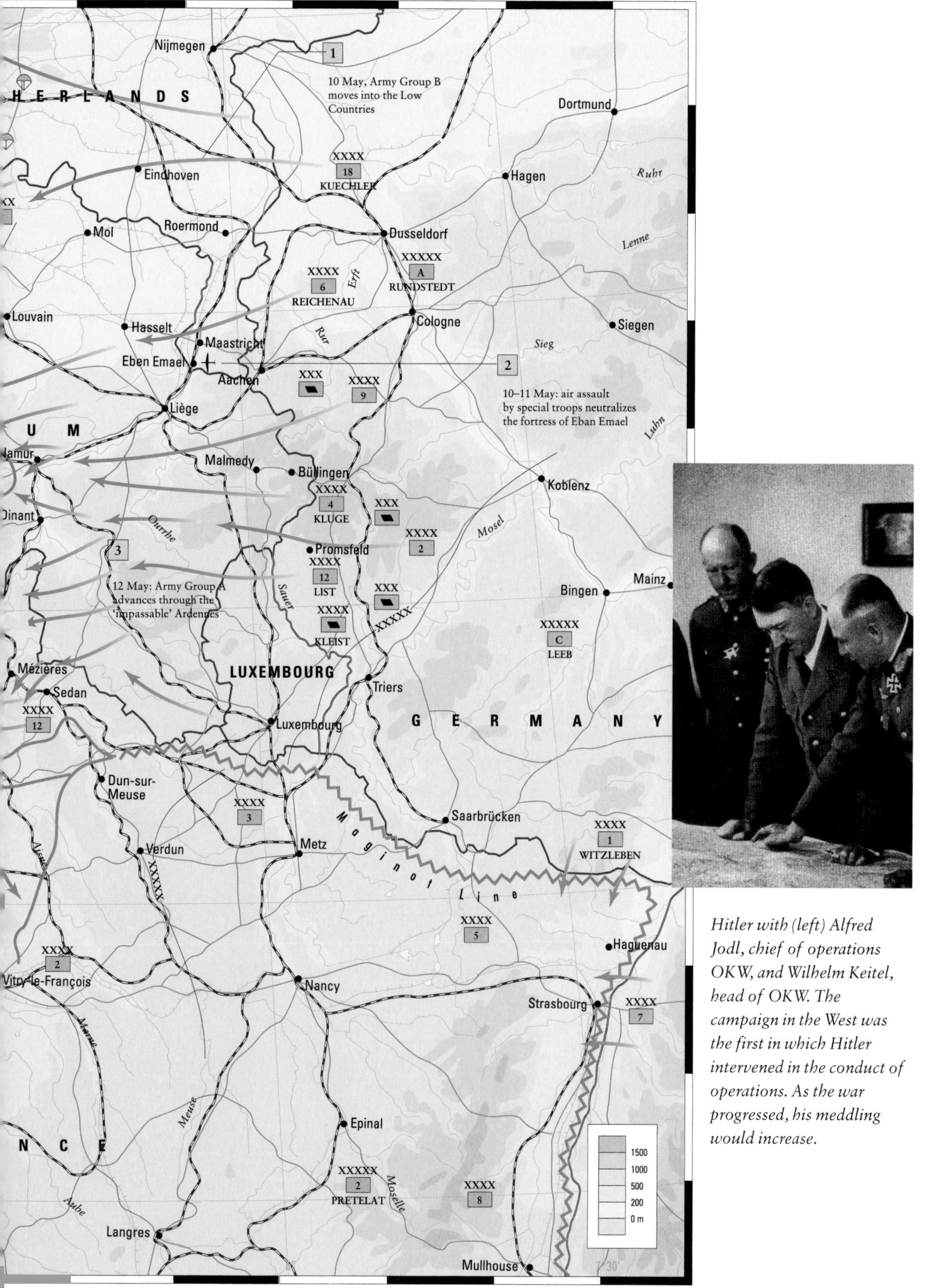

Hitler with (left) Alfred Jodl, chief of operations OKW, and Wilhelm Keitel, head of OKW. The campaign in the West was the first in which Hitler intervened in the conduct of operations. As the war progressed, his meddling would increase.

personally get on with one another. Georges had two French army groups under his command, as well as the BEF, whose commander, Lord Gort, had the right of appeal to the British government. But while Gamelin commanded all ground forces, he had no direct control over the French air force; this had two headquarters, which sometimes gave out conflicting orders.

The German attack was opened by the Luftwaffe, determined as always to catch the Allied aircraft on the ground. There were also a series of airborne operations. These were used in Holland to secure vital bridges and an airfield, where reinforcements were brought in by air. In Belgium there was a spectacular glider *coup de main*, which secured the key to the Belgian defences, the seemingly impregnable fortress at Eben Emael. These attacks were followed by the Panzer spearheads. Meanwhile, the northern Allied armies moved into northern Belgium according to plan, little realizing what was about to take place to the south.

Von Rundstedt's Army Group A included a Panzer group of seven divisions, which were organized in three corps. Behind them came five motorized infantry divisions, and then the main body of infantry, still reliant on its feet. The Panzer divisions plunged into the Ardennes, easily brushing aside the light Belgian screening forces, which were all that had been deployed there. In just two days they reached the River Meuse and prepared to cross it in the face of the French defences on the far bank.

Panzer grenadiers dismount from Sd Kfz 251 halftracks. This vehicle served the German Army well and by the end of the war existed in twenty-one variants, ranging from command vehicle to mobile flak guns. During the French campaign, however, the majority of Panzer grenadiers relied on trucks for transport. Not until 1941 were they fully equipped with these armoured personnel carriers.

In Holland the bemused Dutch stood little chance. They were forced to surrender after just five days. A significant part of the main port of Rotterdam was also destroyed by air attack after its garrison hesitated to hand it over to the Germans. Allied efforts to stem the German advance in Belgium through air attacks on bridges failed, with casualties in aircraft being high. Yet the Dyle Line was holding.

Much helped by close air support, the Panzer divisions punched their way across the Meuse in less than a day. Indeed, the Ju87 proved itself to be a highly effective aerial artillery weapon, with its siren, switched on when it began its dive, having a significant demoralizing effect on the French defenders. The French now attempted a counter-attack, using Flavigny's XXI Corps, which included an armoured division. The slow passage of orders and the time taken by the tanks to refuel meant that they arrived too late and the attack never took place. The Allies then tried to destroy the bridges which the Germans had thrown across the Meuse by air attack. As in Belgium this failed, with an even heavier loss in aircraft.

The Panzers now broke out of their bridgeheads and thrust westwards. Recognizing the danger to the Allied forces on the Dyle, the order to withdraw back into France was given. This was disillusioning for the troops, who believed they had been giving a good account of themselves. Their frustration was made worse by the growing number of refugees heading in the same direction. Rumours, too, began to abound of a German fifth column operating behind the lines. This stemmed in part from the impact of the German airborne assaults of the first day.

The next two weeks saw Panzergruppe von Kleist cut a broad swathe from the Meuse to the English Channel. Allied attempts to mount armoured counterstrokes against its flanks largely failed because the higher command was unable to react quickly enough. One, however, did demonstrate what might have been achieved. Two British infantry tank battalions struck at the flank of Erwin Rommel's 7th Panzer Division and the SS Totenkopf Division outside Arras on 21 May. It did knock them off balance, but the attack was on too small a scale to have any more

than a momentary effect. Even so, the same higher command nervousness as in Poland over allowing the Panzers to get too far ahead was displayed, much to the chagrin of Guderian, the most thrusting of the German armoured commanders. Yet, as the days passed, the wear and tear on men and vehicles increased, and halts had to be called so that crews could rest and the supply system, especially the fuel trucks and mobile workshops, could catch up.

By 22 May the Panzer divisions had reached the Channel and now turned north to seize the ports of Boulogne and Calais. Under increasing pressure from Army Group B and cut off from the French forces south of the Somme, the northern Allied armies, including the Belgians, were being hemmed in, with their backs to

A dramatic shot of a German 88mm anti-tank gun and the two French Somua tanks that it has just knocked out. The '88' was undoubtedly the most powerful anti-tank gun of the war and was later mounted in the PzKw VI Tiger tank. It was also one of the main weapons of the Luftwaffe-controlled flak arm and was originally designed as an anti-aircraft weapon.

the Channel coast. The following day, concerned at the state of the Panzer divisions, von Rundstedt ordered them to halt for twenty-four hours. Hitler personally approved this decision. This gave the Allied forces within their contracting perimeter a respite of sorts. On the 25th, however, the Belgian high command, whose forces were fighting next to the BEF, warned that they could not hold out for much longer, especially since virtually the whole of their country was now overrun.

To Lord Gort this was grave news indeed, especially since a Belgian surrender would leave the BEF in the air. He believed that, for his country's sake, it was more important to save what he could of his army than to continue to fight on with his allies and face inevitable destruction. Churchill agreed to his request and the evacuation of the BEF from Dunkirk began on 26 May. In the meantime, Goering declared that his Luftwaffe could complete the destruction of the Allied pocket. Hitler agreed, making the Panzer halt order permanent so that they could prepare for the second phase of the operation, the overrunning of the remainder of France.

The Dunkirk evacuation began just in time, since, on 27 May, the Belgians surrendered. For the next week ships of all sizes and descriptions ploughed back and forth across the Channel. Home-based RAF fighters struggled to keep the Luftwaffe off them. Even so, many ships were lost. Yet they managed to bring no fewer than 220,000 British and 120,000 French and Belgian troops off the beaches and back to Britain. Goering's boast had proved an empty one.

On 5 June the German armies turned south, assaulting the hastily prepared French defences on the Rivers Somme and Aisne. Within twenty-four hours they had broken through and the Panzers were once more running amok. Many of the French troops who had been evacuated to Britain returned to their motherland, only

French and British troops, some of them wounded, who failed to get off the Dunkirk beaches. They faced the prospect of becoming prisoners of war, in the event, for five years.

to be caught up in the growing confusion. The British tried to send a second BEF to help their beleaguered ally, but after the advance parties had landed at Cherbourg it became clear that the situation was hopeless and it was withdrawn.

On 10 June Mussolini announced that he would declare war on Britain and France the following day, thus finally honouring his pledge to Hitler of months before. The French made Paris an open city so that it would not suffer the fate that befell Warsaw. German troops entered the capital on the 14th. By this time Army Group C had begun to attack the Maginot Line, which was coming under threat from the rear. Prime Minister Reynaud resigned on the 16th and the French put their fate into the hands of that old hero Marshal Henri Pétain. He immediately sought

The meaning of German occupation – a round-up of suspected Polish Jews. Initially most would be confined in ghettoes, where they slowly starved to death. From 1942, the Nazis adopted a policy of wholesale extermination of the Jewish race. The result was the death camps such as Auschwitz and Treblinka.

an armistice with the Germans. On 20 June Italian troops invaded southern France. Two days later, in the same railway carriage in which the fighting had been brought to an end in November 1918, a Franco-German armistice was signed. That with Italy came into effect on 24 June.

In the course of just six weeks the Germans had overrun western Europe at a cost of just 40,000 killed and missing. The rest of the world stood stunned, but the secret of the German success was simple – the pace at which they had conducted their operations enabled them to seize the initiative from the outset and retain it throughout. The Allied command, control and communications systems were unable to cope and timely reaction to German moves proved ever more impossible.

Britain now stood alone and few thought that she would survive for long without making peace with Hitler. He himself assumed the same. Yet Churchill had made it clear immediately after Dunkirk that Britain and her empire would fight on. But the means to do so were slender. Manpower was not a problem. Indeed, many men were still waiting to be conscripted into the armed forces – the government did not want to repeat the mistake of 1914 when there were no weapons and equipment for many of the thousands of volunteers who flocked to the colours. More care had also been taken to ensure that those working in critical industries were not conscripted. Indeed, to an extent the opposite to 1914–18 happened, with men being conscripted to work in the coalmines so that production could be increased. Women, too, were expected to do war work of some sort, whether in the armed forces, industry, on the land, or in other government service. Only mothers of young children were totally exempted.

These measures, and the pre-war setting up of 'shadow' factories, which could quickly switch to munitions production, were not enough to make up for the lost years of the 1920s and early 1930s. Truth was that the army in particular was woefully short of modern weapons, and this was aggravated by the fact that the BEF had been forced to leave its heavy weapons behind in France. The RAF had also suffered serious losses in fighters, especially over Dunkirk. Yet, almost relieved not to be encumbered by continental allies, the British, inspired by Churchill's speeches, were determined to resist.

While the British were aiming for total mobilization of their country for war, Germany was still, in many respects, on a peacetime footing. True, there was a degree of food rationing, as there was in Britain, but the economy did not undergo the dramatic change of gear needed to wage a long war of attrition. Instead, there was merely a gradual increase in munitions production. Yet, in the midsummer of 1940, most Germans thought that the hostilities were at an end and that they could enjoy the fruits of victory. That Hitler actually disbanded seventeen army divisions after the fall of France seemed to confirm this. At the same time, however, he had do something about the British refusal to accept the facts.

On 1 July 1940 Hitler ordered plans to be drawn up for the invasion of Britain, but no date was set for it. This decision was confirmed by a directive he issued just over two weeks later, which did give a provisional date of 15 August. The Germans had virtually no experience of amphibious operations and the planners regarded the exercise as merely a river crossing on a larger scale. This failed to take into account the reputation of the English Channel as one of the more contrary seas. They called for an invasion on a wide front, but the German navy made strong objections. They would have to secure the English Channel against the Royal Navy and doubted their ability to do so. Consequently, the frontage was reduced, but it was still wider than that of the Allies when they landed in Normandy four years later. Germany possessed no landing ships or craft to transport the army across the Channel, and so a massive operation to gather up barges from the waterways of western Europe was got under way. All agreed, however, that no invasion would be possible until the Luftwaffe had gained air supremacy over southern England.

OPPOSITE: *A Waffen-SS recruiting poster. 'You can join them on your 17th Birthday', it reads. During the Polish and French campaigns the Waffen-SS lacked discipline and were guilty of battlefield war crimes. Later they became highly effective in combat.*

Goering began his operations in mid July by trying to draw the RAF's fighters out over the Channel through attacks on convoys. These had to be rerouted, but the RAF was not to be drawn. At the same time, Hitler made one final attempt to bring the British to the peace table, an offer which was immediately rejected. At the end of July he realized that 15 August was too ambitious, and postponed the invasion date to 15 September, stressing that Sealion, as the operation was code-named, was dependent upon the Luftwaffe's success. This now intensified its efforts in what became known as the Battle of Britain. The British pre-war development of radar now came into its own, giving sufficient warning for the RAF fighters to get airborne before the attack arrived. This, together with the quality of the Hurricane and Spitfire, combined with the limited range of their main adversary, the Messerschmitt Me109, made it an uphill struggle for the Luftwaffe. At the same time, British bombers began to attack the concentrations of barges in Channel and North Sea ports. As summer turned to autumn, and with the RAF still showing as much fight as ever, Hitler was forced to make a further series of postponements. Eventually, on 17 September, he postponed Sealion indefinitely and turned his eyes eastwards, leaving his adversary to suffer the wholesale bombing of cities by night which became known as the Blitz. Unlike Napoleon in 1805, however, Hitler did not immediately march his army away from the Channel coast leaving just its smouldering camp-fires. Thus, in British eyes, the threat of invasion remained throughout the winter.

A Type VII U-boat. After the fall of France Hitler mistakenly believed that the twin threat of these and his Luftwaffe would be sufficient for Britain to sue for peace.

Britain had survived, and Churchill believed that she could hold out indefinitely

©ANTON
WAFFEN-SS
EINTRITT NACH VOLLENDETEM 17. LEBENSJAHR

against Hitler. Yet, on her own, she was not strong enough to defeat him, especially since she was now committed to a campaign against Italy in the Mediterranean and North Africa, and could not afford to lower her guard in the Far East in the face of an increasingly militant Japan. Britain must have a powerful ally and this could only be the United States.

President Franklin Roosevelt had every sympathy with Britain's plight, but US public opinion in the late summer of 1940 was still firmly against entering the war – polls indicated that only 8 per cent of Americans were prepared to do so. Nevertheless, Roosevelt was a realist and knew that sooner or later his country would be drawn in. The United States must not be as ill prepared as she had been in 1917. Consequently, he initiated a massive expansion of the munitions industry, including a major shipbuilding programme. He also obtained Congress consent for the National Guard and reservists to be called up for one year's active duty and for limited conscription to be introduced.

Members of an SS Einsatzgruppe escort Polish Jews to a concentration camp. In 1939 Poland had the largest Jewish population in Europe. Over half were murdered by the Nazis.

With regard to his dealings with Britain, Roosevelt was more cautious, especially since another presidential election was due in November 1940. In August, however, he and Churchill agreed that, in exchange for the lease of British naval bases in the Caribbean, the US navy would hand over fifty elderly destroyers. These were badly needed as convoy escorts, since the German U-boats, now operating from French Atlantic ports, were seriously threatening Britain's crucial Atlantic lifeline. This was the only active step that Roosevelt took, although reports from American correspondents based in Britain during the Blitz were slowly changing the US public's perception that her defeat was inevitable.

Roosevelt's caution paid off and he won another term as president. That Christmas he told the American people that the war was being fought for four essential freedoms – of speech and religion, and from fear and want. To support these, America must become 'the arsenal of the democracies'. He followed this up in January 1941 by introducing his LendLease bill, which became law two months later. The principle of this was that America would provide arms for the democracies, who would pay for them in kind after the war; Roosevelt likened it to lending a neighbour a garden hose to put out a fire. The first two beneficiaries of this were Britain and China.

At the same time, the secret ABC (America, Britain, Canada) talks took place in Washington, DC. The object was to draw up a joint strategy to be followed in

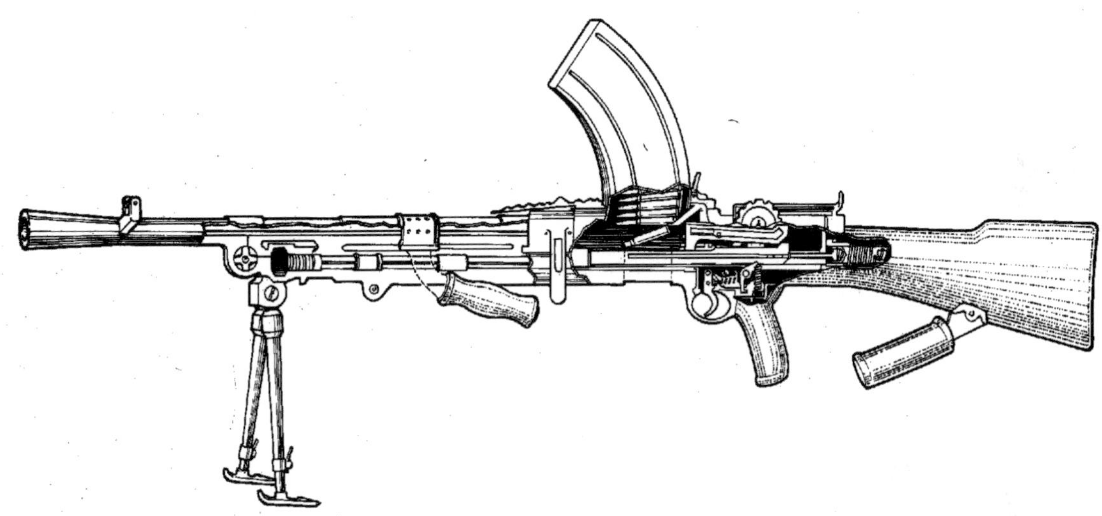

BRITISH BREN GUN

The British Bren gun, one of the most successful light machine-guns of the war. The original design was Czech, and the name 'Bren' comes from the Czech town of Brno, whose armaments factory was responsible for its development and the British Enfield armament factory. Introduced into service in 1938, it served the British Army faithfully through 1939–45 and for many years beyond.

the event of American entry into the war. The crucial decision made was that, even if hostilities with Japan took place, the defeat of Germany was to be given priority. While none of the three countries was formally bound by this policy, it at least gave the Americans a realistic strategic framework in which to draw up their military plans.

Britain was now sustaining several governments-in-exile from the countries of German-occupied Europe. This included equipping and arming the volunteers who had managed to find their way to Britain – the so-called 'Free Forces'. Within occupied Europe itself, the Germans installed a variety of governments. The majority were, at least on the surface, civilian based, but Belgium and occupied northern France, because of their geographic proximity to Britain, had military governments. France was unique in that the southern half of the country was allowed autonomy under Pétain's Vichy regime, which also controlled the French African and Far East territories. It had, however, little control over foreign policy.

Within these countries there were generally three attitudes to the occupiers. At one extreme were those, like Vidkun Quisling of Norway, who held strong right-wing views and saw the German occupation as the dawn of a new Europe. Some

OPPOSITE: *German troops march down Paris's Champs-Elysees. That they just failed to reach the French capital in 1914 made entry of it in June 1940 that much more satisfying.*

even enlisted in the foreign legions of the Waffen-SS after Hitler's invasion of Russia, seeing this as a crusade to crush Bolshevism. Anti-Semitism, too, caused many to turn a blind eye to German persecution of the Jews, and some actively assisted in it. The broad middle ground of people concentrated on getting on with their lives as best they could under the restrictions imposed on them. If this meant a degree of passive collaboration with the occupying power, then so be it.

At the other end of the spectrum were those who were determined to resist the Germans. Resistance could be active or passive. The latter took the form of industrial strikes, demonstrations, and the production of propaganda through underground newspapers, leaflets and wall slogans. Active resistance encompassed intelligence gathering, aiding escaped Allied prisoners of war and shot-down aircrew, sabotage, and direct armed action against the Germans. Resistance was never the province of any particular social class or political grouping, but encompassed a complete cross-section of each country. While the majority of the population, trying to live as near normal a life as possible, provided a necessary cloak for its activities, the Resistance was constantly under threat from German intelligence, collaborators and informers, with torture and death often the penalty for being caught.

German troops check the identity papers of French civilians. The Occupation meant a severe restriction of personal liberties. In order to get by, the vast majority were forced into a degree of passive collaboration.

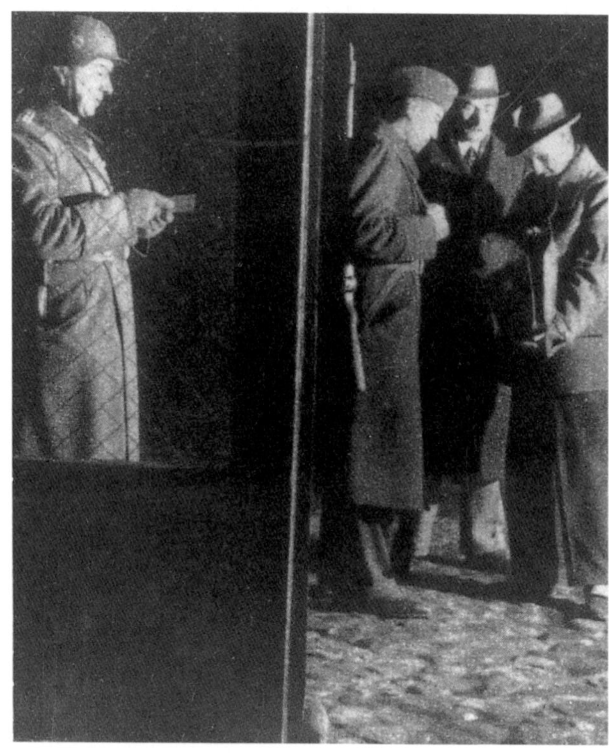

The Resistance movements could never have survived, let alone developed, without external support. It was with this in mind that Churchill ordered the setting up of the Special Operations Executive (SOE) in July 1940. In his words, its mission was to 'set Europe ablaze', and SOE was to do this by establishing proper Resistance networks within each occupied country and then co-ordinating their operations, ensuring that they conformed to the overall Allied plan. This was done largely through the insertion of agents, who also organized the supply of weapons and explosives, usually delivered by aircraft. The Resistance also needed to believe in eventual liberation, and the part played by the BBC in fostering this cannot be overstated – by the end of 1943 it was broadcasting in forty-five languages.

Another factor which helped to give the peoples of occupied Europe hope was the RAF. The only way in which Britain could hit back directly at Germany was through air attack. The noise of RAF bombers overhead by night, and the BBC's reports of their raids, gave some comfort to those suffering under the Nazi yoke. Even so, during the winter of 1940–41 the prospect of liberation seemed a long way off. Indeed, the only British ground forces taking an active part in the war were doing so away from Europe and across the other side of the Mediterranean.

CHAPTER THREE

Mussolini's Dream: The Mediterranean Theatre (1940–41)

ITALIAN INFANTRY in one of their fortified camps just inside Egypt, September 1940. The war in North and East Africa was initially just between the British and the Italians. While the Italians enjoyed overwhelming numerical superiority, their general standard of training and the quality of their weapons was below that of their adversary. Once Rommel and his combat-hardened Afrika Korps arrived on the scene, the British found that they had a much more formidable enemy. This was not helped by the fact that the British were forced to fight several simultaneous campaigns.

THE MEDITERRANEAN THEATRE 1940–41

The desert became littered with knocked-out and burning tanks, and full of smoke and dust; the brigade was taking a severe battering. So the battle raged: parry and thrust , with no hope of reinforcements, as each unit was engaged in its own life-and-death struggle, and they were too far apart to assist one another ... Shellfire caused what I can only describe as huge dust spouts, and between them one could see the infantry going forward in extended order, while here and there a tank was visible and a few Bren carriers. It wasn't long before the whole weight of enemy artillery fire caused the whole scene to be almost blotted out, and one could only wonder whether anyone would come out of such an inferno alive.

BRITISH TANK DRIVER, SIDI RIZEGH AIRFIELD, 22 NOVEMBER 1941

MUSSOLINI'S OVERALL STRATEGY up until he brought Italy into the war in June 1940 remains a matter of debate among historians. During the 1930s he flirted with the western democracies almost as much as he did with Hitler. His presence at Munich during the Czech crisis and the part he played in those last days of August 1939 cast him in the role of international mediator. Then again, his prevarications during the first nine months of the war indicate that perhaps he just wanted to be on the winning side. Yet, given the similarities between Fascism and National Socialism, and Mussolini's strategic ambitions for Italy, it was probably inevitable that he would in time honour the Pact of Steel.

Mussolini's grand design was twofold. He wanted to create a major colonial empire in north-east Africa. He had made a significant start to this with his subjugation of Abyssinia, but to consolidate the empire he needed to weld Libya physically to Abyssinia and Eritrea, as well as take over the whole of the Horn of Africa. Standing in his way were Egypt, Sudan and British Somaliland, all firmly under the British umbrella. Britain also blocked him in the Mediterranean, which he regarded as *Mare Nostrum*, her mighty Mediterranean Fleet a formidable competitor to the Italian navy.

In June 1940 it seemed, on paper at least, that Mussolini had a relatively straightforward task. Britain herself was now on her own and under imminent threat of invasion. She could hardly be in a position, therefore, to reinforce the Mediterranean theatre. The British Mediterranean fleet had its main base at Malta, which was within easy air-striking distance from Sicily. Force it to withdraw and the Royal Navy would be confined to the periphery, being reduced to operating from Gibraltar or Alexandria, while Italy controlled the central Mediterranean.

On land the picture looked even brighter for Italy. The British Commander-in-Chief Middle East, General Sir Archibald Wavell, had 63,000 troops in Egypt, Palestine and Iraq. These had not only to defend these territories against external threat, which now included Vichy French Syria, but also to police them. Indeed, in

Palestine the Arabs had resorted to violence in their protest at the influx of Jewish refugees and the situation had only been brought under control on the very eve of war after a three-year counter-insurgency campaign. In contrast, in Libya alone there were 250,000 Italian and indigenous troops. To the south, Italy could field a further 300,000 troops in the Horn of Africa, while the British garrisons in Sudan, British Somaliland and northern Kenya numbered a mere 10,000. In the air, the situation was the same. The Italians had nearly 500 aircraft based in Africa, with a further 1,200 which could be deployed from Italy. The RAF, on the other hand, had a total of a mere 370 in Egypt, Palestine and East Africa, and almost all of these were obsolete types.

Yet, unlike Hitler's strike against Poland, Mussolini launched no immediate blitzkrieg. Instead, the opening of the war in the Mediterranean was marked by a few scattered air attacks by both sides. He did, however, have plans to invade Egypt from Libya, but these were temporarily frustrated by the death of his supremo in

An Italian supply convoy in Libya. The desert provided the opportunity for rapid advances, but inevitably these would outrun supplies, forcing them to a halt. This was the main reason why the pendulum of fortune swung so dramatically backwards and forwards during the campaign in Egypt and Libya.

Libya, the internationally renowned aviator Italo Balbo, who was shot down by his own anti-aircraft guns during a tour of inspection. This lack of positive activity did, however, encourage the British screening forces in Egypt to maintain a policy of aggressive patrolling, which included the capture of two Italian frontier forts. In retaliation, the Italians took frontier posts in southern Sudan, but did not penetrate further, while at sea the two navies had their first major clash on 9 July. After its flagship was hit, the Italian navy remained in port for the next few weeks.

In August the pace began to quicken. The Italians quickly overran British Somaliland, threatening the entrance to the Red Sea. At the same time the exiled Emperor Haile Selassie organized a revolt within Abyssinia. Churchill, too, made a crucial decision. He had already agreed to the reinforcement of the Mediterranean Fleet and now ordered 150 precious tanks to be sent from Britain to Egypt via South Africa so as not to risk their loss in the Mediterranean. They had, however, not arrived when the long-awaited Italian invasion of Egypt began on 13 September.

The British plan was to withdraw from contact and not to offer battle until the Italian advance reached Mersa Matruh, where defences had been prepared. The reason for this, and one that would dominate thinking during the desert campaign, was that east of here there would always be an open southern flank, which could be easily turned. At Mersa Matruh, however, any defensive position could always be anchored on the impassable Qattara Depression to the south. Yet, to the surprise of the British, the Italian advance was hesitant from the outset and came to a halt after just three days. Now, sixty miles into Egypt, the Italians constructed a series of fortified camps, while they brought up more supplies.

A few days later the tank reinforcements from Britain finally arrived and Wavell ordered a counter-attack to be planned. The Italian commander, Marshal Rodolfo

Graziani, realizing that the British now had superior tank strength, both in numbers and quality, decided not to risk a further advance, in spite of Mussolini's urgings, and remained in his fortified camps.

The focus of attention now switched to the Balkans. Mussolini was envious of Hitler's success in northern Europe and noted that he was now looking to the south-east. The evidence for this was the affinity between Germany and the Horthy regime in Hungary and German economic interests in Romania, notably the Ploesti oilfields. Romania, however, had been forced to cede territory to the Soviet Union in June 1940. This encouraged Bulgaria and Hungary to make demands on Romania. Fearful that they might block his supply line from Ploesti, Hitler forced Romania to hand back Transylvania, which had been taken from Hungary after the Great War. In return he guaranteed the security of the remainder of Romania. The immediate result was a coup in the country. King Carol was forced to abdicate and another right-wing 'strong man', General Ion Antonescu, came to power, placing Romania even more firmly under Berlin's umbrella.

Now, with apparent deadlock in Africa, Mussolini resolved to attack Greece with his forces stationed in neighbouring Albania. His generals complained that it was too late in the year and that the troops were insufficiently prepared, but he refused to listen. On 28 October he met Hitler in the Brenner Pass and told him that he had that day invaded Greece. Hitler was furious at this unilateral decision, but there was nothing he could do about it. The Italian forces penetrated through the mountains, but the Greek forces, ill prepared as they were, soon flung them back into Albania. The Italian plight was then aggravated by the onset of winter.

It was now that Churchill's 1914–18 Balkan ambitions resurfaced. He offered to send British forces to assist the Greeks. The Greeks were chary since they feared that the British wanted to bring them into the war against Germany, but did accept five RAF squadrons and agreed that an infantry brigade be sent to Crete to relieve Greek forces stationed there. These troops and the aircraft had to come from Wavell's already stretched command.

Italian troops arrive by air in Libya. Although most reinforcements and supplies were sent by sea from Italy, these were under threat from the British Mediterranean Fleet. Because of similar threat, the main British supply route to Egypt avoided the Mediterranean in favour of the much longer route round South Africa.

Mussolini's self-imposed Balkan distraction did, however, provide added promise for Wavell's planned counter-offensive in Egypt. This was launched in the early hours of 9 December 1940 under the strictest secrecy – the troops taking part thought that they were merely carrying out a deployment exercise. Wavell could only spare two divisions – 7th Armoured, which had been formed in Egypt on the eve of war, and 4th Indian – and needed to send the latter to Eritrea to open offensive operations in East Africa. Consequently, he saw Operation Compass as merely a five-day raid. Yet its initial success was dazzling. The Italians were totally taken by surprise and their fortified camps quickly overrun.

Wavell now ordered 4th Indian Division to Eritrea, but a division was just arriving from Australia to take its place. He therefore ordered the offensive to continue. Assisted by the guns of the Royal Navy, the Western Desert Force, as it was called, began to advance up the coast road, crossed into Libya, and invested the port of Bardia. This fell to the Australians on 5 January.

The Balkans factor now intervened once more. Churchill was determined to cement an alliance with Greece and warned Wavell that the deployment of more British forces here was to take priority over further advances in North Africa. Churchill's concern was reinforced during January by the receipt of intelligence of a German build-up in Romania and Bulgaria. This was largely thanks to Ultra, the

EAST AFRICAN CAMPAIGN

Fought on several fronts and in largely inhospitable terrain, the campaign proved a severe test of the logistics systems of both sides.

code name for the deciphering of top-secret German radio traffic generated by the Enigma encoding machine. The groundwork for this had been done by the Poles, who brought their knowledge to France after the fall of their country. Thereafter the operation had moved to Britain, where it became the major focus for the government Code and Cypher School at Bletchley Park in the English Midlands. As the code-breakers became ever more adept, Ultra was to play an increasingly significant role in the conduct of the war.

The Greeks, however, continued to resist Churchill's pressure. Even so, Wavell was conscious that he probably only had limited time to complete his operations in Libya. Consequently, he pressed on. The important port of Tobruk was captured on 22 January and Wavell now began to use this to compensate for his rapidly lengthening supply lines across the desert from the Nile Delta. His field commander

The final Italian surrender in Abyssinia at Gondar on 27 November 1941. They were allowed to march out with colours flying and their weapons – the traditional way of paying respect to a defeated enemy.

in Libya, General Richard O'Connor, now mounted a bold operation totally to destroy the Italian Tenth Army in Libya. While 6th Australian Division continued to advance along the coast road, 7th Armoured Division was to thrust across the base of the 'Cyrenaican bulge', the Jebel Akhdar, and block the Italian withdrawal. It was a 'close-run thing'. The British tanks reached the coast road south of Benghazi on 6 February and immediately found themselves embroiled with Italians retreating from the town, which the Australians entered on the same day. After two days'

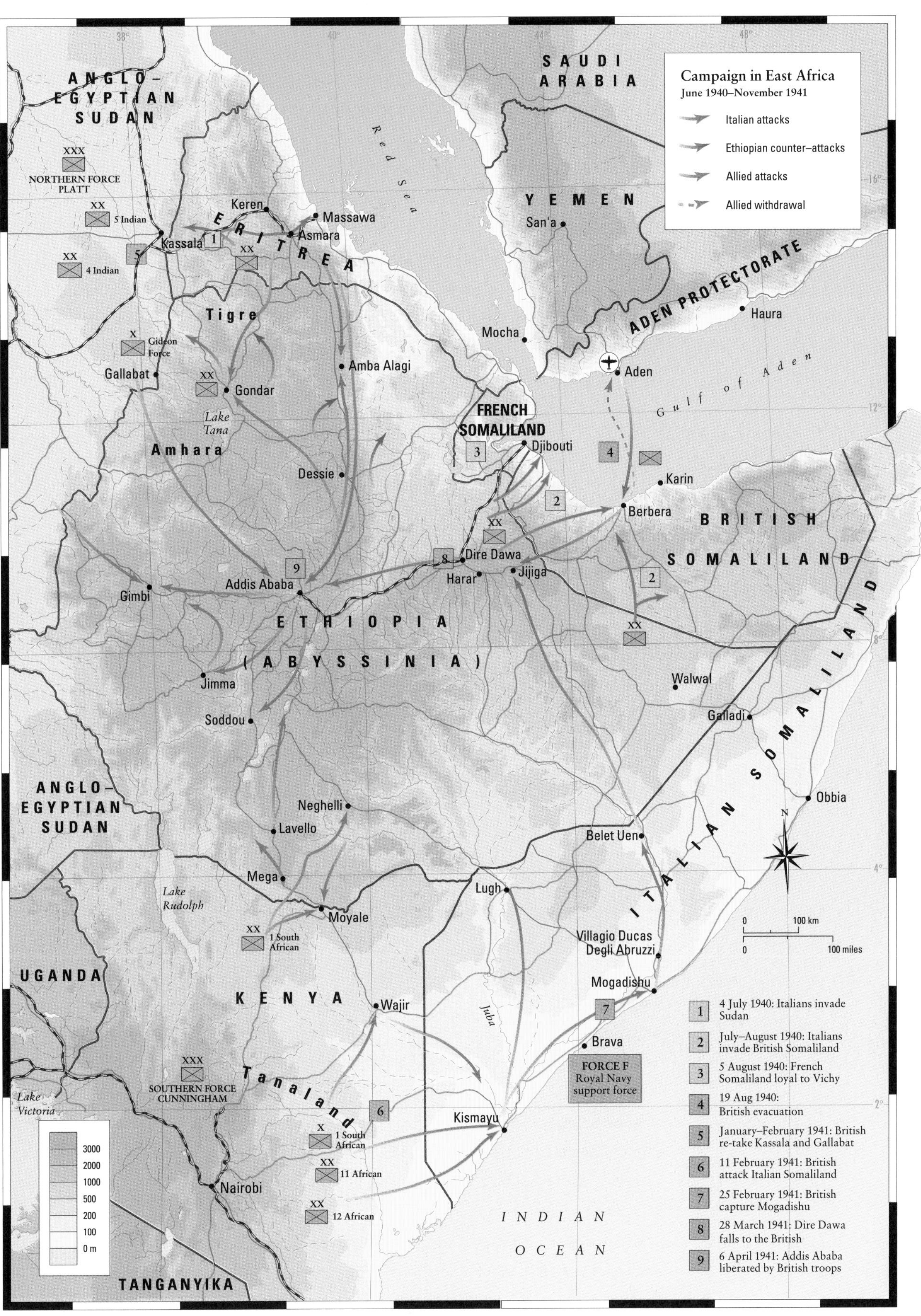

Campaign in East Africa
June 1940–November 1941
Italian attacks
Ethiopian counter-attacks
Allied attacks
Allied withdrawal
ANGLO-EGYPTIAN SUDAN
SAUDI ARABIA
YEMEN
ADEN PROTECTORATE
ERITREA
FRENCH SOMALILAND
BRITISH SOMALILAND
ETHIOPIA (ABYSSINIA)
ITALIAN SOMALILAND
KENYA
UGANDA
TANGANYIKA
Red Sea
Gulf of Aden
INDIAN OCEAN
NORTHERN FORCE PLATT
5 Indian
4 Indian
Gideon Force
SOUTHERN FORCE CUNNINGHAM
1 South African
11 African
12 African
FORCE F Royal Navy support force
Keren
Massawa
Asmara
Kassala
Tigre
Gallabat
Gondar
Amba Alagi
Lake Tana
Amhara
Dessie
Djibouti
Mocha
San'a
Aden
Haura
Karin
Berbera
Dire Dawa
Harar
Jijiga
Addis Ababa
Gimbi
Jimma
Soddou
Walwal
Galladi
Obbia
Neghelli
Lavello
Mega
Moyale
Lake Rudolph
Belet Uen
Lugh
Villagio Ducas Degli Abruzzi
Mogadishu
Brava
Wajir
Juba
Tanaland
Kismayu
Nairobi
Lake Victoria
0 100 km
0 100 miles
3000
2000
1000
500
200
100
0 m
1 4 July 1940: Italians invade Sudan
2 July–August 1940: Italians invade British Somaliland
3 5 August 1940: French Somaliland loyal to Vichy
4 19 Aug 1940: British evacuation
5 January–February 1941: British re-take Kassala and Gallabat
6 11 February 1941: British attack Italian Somaliland
7 25 February 1941: British capture Mogadishu
8 28 March 1941: Dire Dawa falls to the British
9 6 April 1941: Addis Ababa liberated by British troops

fighting the Italians surrendered and the whole of the province of Cyrenaica was now in British hands. The two months' campaign cost the Italians some 150,000 killed and captured, 400 tanks and 800 guns, while the British suffered just 2,000 casualties.

Simultaneously, Wavell was also on the offensive in East Africa. On 19 January British forces invaded Eritrea and the following day Haile Selassie at the head of his Patriots crossed the Sudan–Abyssinia border. Shortly afterwards, African forces entered Italian Somaliland from Kenya. This southern offensive proceeded rapidly, with the port of Mogadishu falling on 25 February before the advance swung north-west into Abyssinia. In the north, the mountainous terrain of Eritrea was blocked by the fortress of Keren. The Italian forces here held up the British for two months in what became a grim battle fought in almost impossible conditions of heat and thirst. In March a further British force crossed the Red Sea and re-entered British Somaliland, quickly liberating it. Troops from the southern offensive entered Addis Adaba in early April and Haile Selassie returned to his capital in triumph a month later. Keren had been finally captured towards the end of March and the advance continued south to the final significant Italian position at Amba Alagi, which surrendered on 18 May. This, to all intents and purposes, marked the end of the East African campaign, although the final Italian resistance in Abyssinia was not overcome until November 1941. Yet British success in this campaign was being simultaneously counterbalanced by crises on the shores of the Mediterranean.

British infantry under artillery fire in the Western Desert.

No sooner had Wavell completed the conquest of Cyrenaica than the expected order from Churchill to send troops to Greece arrived. With growing evidence of a German build-up in the Balkans, the Greeks had at last succumbed to British pressure. W Force, consisting of the equivalent of four divisions, was assembled under General Maitland Wilson and began to cross to Greece in early March. This did, however, have one consolation in that it drew the Italian fleet out of harbour and enabled the Royal Navy to engage it in battle off Cape Matapan, resulting in a decisive British victory. Otherwise, the Greek distraction left Wavell in a parlous state, especially in Cyrenaica. Here the now veteran 7th Armoured and 6th Australian Divisions had to be withdrawn to refit after the rigours of the recent campaign. Their place was taken by the newly arrived and unblooded 2nd Armoured and 9th Australian Divisions, but the former had to pass a brigade to W Force. Such was the paucity of fit tanks that some of its remaining units had to be equipped with inferior captured Italian types. This was all the more serious since Hitler had now decided to take an active part in the Mediterranean theatre.

In autumn 1940 Hitler had begun to woo the Spanish dictator General Franco to join the Axis with an eye to seizing Gibraltar, which was crucial to British naval operations in the Mediterranean. Given the parlous state in which the ravages of the civil war had left his country, Franco was unwilling to comply and managed to resist Hitler's overtures. Irrespective of this, however, were the Italian reverses at the end of the year and Hitler decided that he must help Mussolini out in both North Africa and Albania. Luftwaffe units were also sent to Sicily to assist in the crushing of Malta and made their first attacks on British ships in early January.

Mussolini declined the offer of help in Albania, but did accept that for Libya. Consequently, on 12 February 1941 Erwin Rommel arrived in Libya as commander of what was called the Deutsches Afrika Korps (DAK). He had been given two recently formed divisions, 5th Light and 15th Panzer; both contained a high percentage of veterans of the Polish and French campaigns. The DAK was placed under Italian command, but Rommel had the right to refer to Berlin if he was unhappy over the way his command was being handled. After their recent defeat in Cyrenaica, the Italian forces needed time to gather their strength and the intention was to remain on the defensive at least until the DAK was complete in theatre. The British gained knowledge of this through Ultra and considered that there was no immediate threat to Cyrenaica. Indeed, Churchill was able to use this to allay Wavell's fears over the dispatch of W Force to Greece. But both British and Italians reckoned without Rommel.

Crusader tanks await the order to advance, summer 1941. This tank was armed with a 2pdr (40mm) gun. While it had a good turn of speed, its armour was thin. Pennants were flown on the radio aerials as a recognition signal. Their position was changed each day.

Although an infantryman by trade, Rommel's command of 7th Panzer Division (which became known as the Ghost Division because of the rapidity of its advance)

Vickers machine-gun. This first entered British Army service in 1912 and was not declared obsolete until 1968. The barrel was surrounded by a jacket through which water was passed to keep it cool. It had a high reputation for reliability and seldom suffered from mechanical problems.

in France had convinced him that swift attack was the key to victory. The longer the Axis forces waited, the stronger the British defences in Cyrenaica would become. He therefore obtained both German and Italian agreement for a limited offensive, with Agedabia as the initial objective and a possible subsequent thrust up to Benghazi if this went well.

On 24 March, less than two weeks after the last elements of 5th Light had arrived at Tripoli, Rommel struck. He was supported by Luftwaffe elements transferred from Sicily. He quickly drove back the British screening forces and then clashed with 2nd Armoured Division. The two-day battle that followed revealed that the British cruiser tanks and captured Italian types were no match for the PzKw IIIs and IVs, and that the German tactics were superior. The British withdrew and Agedabia fell into Axis hands on 2 April. Such was the ease with which Rommel had driven the British back that he decided to take advantage of their confusion and advance to the Egyptian frontier. He achieved this by the end of April in a thrust that was even more spectacular than that by the British a few months earlier. Indeed, there was only one blemish – Rommel failed to secure Tobruk, which remained in British hands, although isolated.

The loss of Cyrenaica was a serious blow to British fortunes in the Mediterranean, all the more so since it left Malta outside combat aircraft range from

North Africa and put the island at the mercy of Axis air power. In consequence, much of the British naval effort in the Mediterranean had to be tied up in ensuring that Malta was given sufficient supplies to enable it to hold out against the constant air bombardment to which it was now subjected.

In the eastern Mediterranean the situation became just as grim. Hitler's growing interest in the Balkans had been largely motivated by the need to secure his southern flank for what he regarded as his ultimate campaign, the invasion of Russia. He had little difficulty in getting Hungary and Romania to join the Tripartite Pact, which had been signed by Germany, Italy and Japan in September 1940. Bulgaria prevaricated for a little while and then, in spite of British pleas, also joined. Hitler now began to apply pressure to Yugoslavia, demanding right of passage for German forces in exchange for the port of Salonika and part of Macedonia once Greece had been subjugated. The Yugoslav government succumbed on 25 March, but two days later a group of air force officers mounted a *coup d'état*, overthrowing the regent and establishing a government of national unity, which promptly renounced the pact.

Hitler was furious and ordered the immediate launching of Operation Marita. This involved a multi-pronged invasion of Yugoslavia and Greece by German, Italian and Hungarian forces. They struck on 6 April. Yugoslavia's long borders precluded any coherent defence and the country was overrun in another devastating blitzkrieg campaign in a mere three weeks. Greece proved a slightly harder nut to crack. The British and Greek forces in the eastern part of the country had prepared defences close to the Bulgarian border – the Aliakmon Line – but, for political reasons, this did not cover the Yugoslav border. Thus, the Greek forces in the west were less well prepared to face the initial attack, which came through the extreme south-east of Yugoslavia. Furthermore, they were threatened in the flank by an Italian counter-offensive from Albania. Inevitably, the pressure proved too much and they were forced to withdraw, thus exposing the flank of the Aliakmon Line. This made the outcome inevitable. On 22 April the Royal Navy arrived to begin evacuating W Force, which took a week, with some troops being taken back to Egypt and others sent to reinforce the garrison on Crete. Greece eventually surrendered at the end of the month and the only remaining British toehold in the northern part of the eastern Mediterranean was Crete.

Reverses in Libya and Greece in April 1941 were compounded by a revolt in the British mandate of Iraq. A pro-German group seized power, with the intention of allowing the Luftwaffe to base aircraft there. A division was sent from India by brigades, but the Iraqis laid siege to the important RAF base at Habbaniyah. In early May Wavell sent a force into Iraq from Palestine. This raised the siege of Habbaniyah and brought the situation under control by the end of May, with the coup leader, Raschid Ali, fleeing to Persia.

As if Wavell did not have enough on his plate, Churchill was urging him to drive Rommel back. Accordingly, on 15 May he launched Operation Brevity, which lived up to its name. Although Halfaya Pass, Sollum and Capuzzo were captured on the first day, Rommel mounted a counter-attack, driving the British forces back

A German Junkers Ju52 shot down over Crete, 20 May 1941. The German losses of transport aircraft during the invasion deterred them from mounting any further large-scale airborne operations.

to their start line. Wavell's worries were further compounded by intelligence received from Ultra at the end of April that the next German target was Crete. Furthermore, the Vichy French in Syria were intending to allow the Luftwaffe use of their airfields. Churchill urged Wavell to invade, but with all his other commitments, he simply did not have the immediate forces to spare for this.

He was determined to defend Crete and appointed General Bernard Freyberg to command the garrison, now considerably strengthened by troops evacuated from Greece. To gain maximum surprise, the Germans planned to assault the island from the air with airborne forces, and then bring in reinforcements and heavy weapons by sea. Unfortunately, although Ultra provided clear intelligence on the German plan, Freyberg was convinced that the main landings would be from the sea and did not give the defence of Crete's airfields (the primary German objectives) the priority that he should have done. Furthermore, the RAF view was that Crete was not worth the sacrifice of valuable fighters that were needed elsewhere in the theatre. Consequently, after the first few days of German air attacks the RAF withdrew its remaining aircraft, allowing the Germans total supremacy in the air.

Yet, when the attack did come on 20 May the Germans suffered heavy casualties and a significant number of their transport aircraft were lost to anti-aircraft fire from

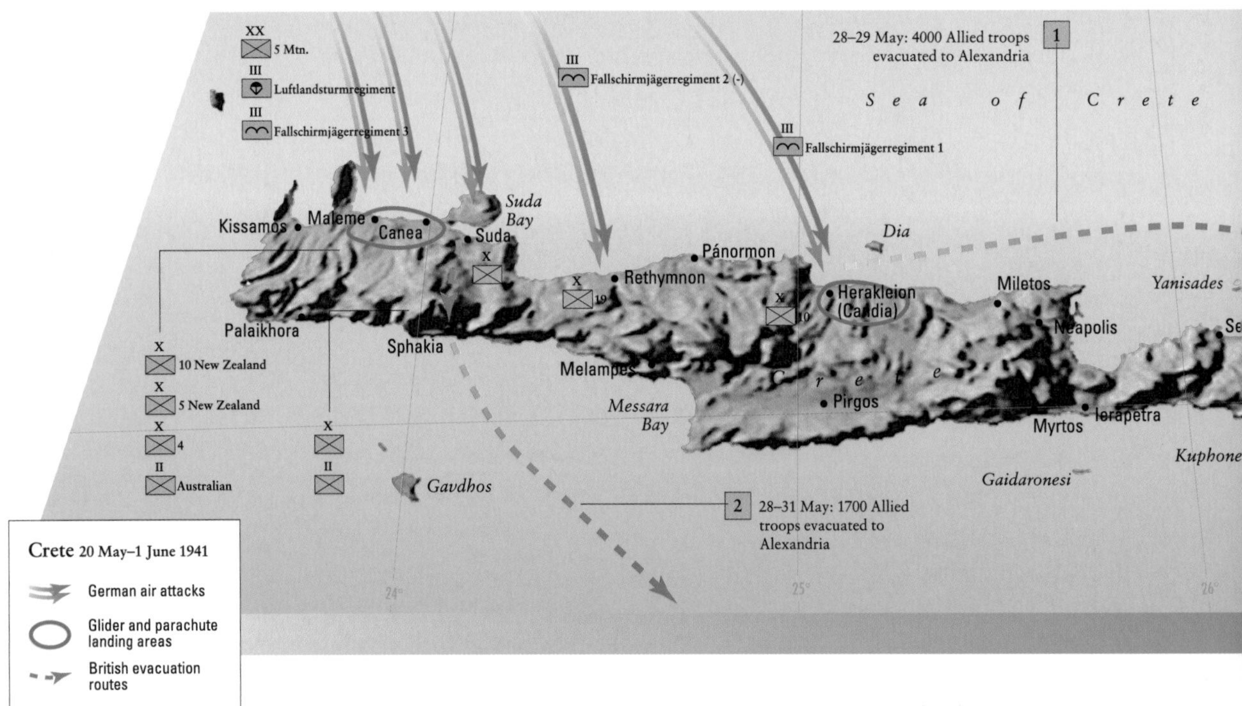

The Balkans
6–30 April 1941
German attacks
Allied evacuation
German front line
Allied fortified line
AUSTRIA
HUNGARY
ROMANIA
YUGOSLAVIA
BULGARIA
ALBANIA
GREECE
ITALY
TURKEY
Budapest
Graz
Szeged
Zagreb
Karlovac
Banda Luka
Travnik
Sarajevo
Uzice
Belgrade
Bucharest
Dubrovnik
Nis
Sofia
Plovdiv
Skopje
Erdirne
Bitola (Monastir)
Berat
Edessa
Sérrai
Drama
Xanthi
Komotine
Alexandroupolis
Kilkis
Salonica
Kozani
Katerine
Larisa
Tonnena
Trikkala
Arta
Lamia
Missolonghi
Khalkis
Marathon
Athens
Patrai
Corinth
Pyrgos
Tripolis
Kalahai
Monemyasia
Brindisi
Corfu
Thasos
Samothrace
Lemnos
Lesbos
Khios
Andros
Tinos
Naxos
Crete
Carpathians
Sava
Danube
Adriatic Sea
Ionian Sea
Aegean Sea
XXXX 2 WEICHS
XXX XLVI
XXX XLIX
XXX LI
XXXX 3 HUNGARIAN
XX 8
XX XLI
XX 14
XX 16
XXXX 2 ITALIAN AMBROSIO
XX 11
XXX L
XXXX 12 LIST
XXX XI
XXXX 1 Panzer KLEIST
XXX XIV
XX 5
XX 16
XXX XL
XXX XVIII
XXX XXX
XXXX 9 ITALIAN
XXXX 11 ITALIAN
XXXX 2 GREEK
XXXX W WILSON
XX 2
XXXX 1 GREEK
XX 5
XX 5
1 German front line 16 April
2 German front line 20 April
3 German front line 23 April
4 British evacuation 22–28 April
N
0 100 km
0 100 miles
2000
1500
1000
500
200
0 m
18°
22°
46°
38°
35°

the ground. The higher command wanted to abort the operation and it was only the conviction of General Kurt Student, who had planned it, that allowed it to continue. The next day, largely thanks to a breakdown in communications, the German paratroops captured the airfield at Maleme and were able to fly in reinforcements. Freyberg, with many of his troops still defending Crete's northern coast, was unable to mount an effective counter-attack. The adverse air situation compounded his problems and, after three days' fighting, he decided that Crete could not be held. The Royal Navy, which had already destroyed the German seaborne element, was once more called in to evacuate the army. This was completed on 1 June, but at the cost of a significant number of ships, victims of air attack, and well over 10,000 men had to be left behind.

In spite of this additional reverse, Churchill persisted in his demands that Wavell take offensive action, both to relieve Tobruk and to deal with the Syrian problem.

A column of PzKw IIIs of 15th Panzer Division en route for the front in Libya, summer 1941. This joined 5th Light (later 21st Panzer) Division to form Rommel's Deutsches Afrika Korps.

He complied, launching an attack, which included Free French troops, against Syria on 15 June. The Vichy French were embittered by a 'perfidious Albion', which had not only deserted them in June 1940, but had then gone on to bombard the French fleet in its North African ports, where it had withdrawn after the armistice, to prevent it falling into German hands. They also considered Charles de Gaulle, leader of the Free French who had hoisted his banner in Britain before the armistice with the Germans was signed, a traitor. Consequently, they offered sometimes fierce resistance and it was not until mid July that the fighting ceased. Even then, many Vichy French chose to return to France rather than accept the invitation to join the Free French.

A week after the strike into Syria, Wavell mounted Operation Battleaxe in the Western Desert. The aim was to break through the Axis defences on the Egyptian border, relieve Tobruk, and advance into the Cyrenaican Bulge. The offensive fell, however, virtually at the first hurdle. Although the British once more captured Capuzzo, Rommel, with the DAK now reinforced by 15th Panzer Division, had little difficulty in repulsing the attack. This was primarily due to one weapon – the 88 mm anti-tank gun. This far outranged the British tank guns, which also fired only solid shot. Consequently, the British armour had to rely on artillery to engage the German anti-tank guns. This was a cumbersome and often ineffective method of taking on such pinpoint targets. The result was that on the first day of Battleaxe the British lost ninety-one tanks, as opposed to just twelve German tanks destroyed, and were driven back to their start line by the end of the day.

The failure of Battleaxe was the last nail in Wavell's coffin as far as Churchill was concerned, and he was replaced by Sir Claude Auchinleck, an Indian army soldier whose active service in this war had been confined to the abortive Norwegian campaign. Wavell had faced an almost impossible situation during the first year of

A knocked out 88mm anti-tank gun, Western Desert, 1941. This could penetrate 83mm of armour – thicker than that on any British tank of the time – at 2,000 yards. The Germans often used their tanks to draw the British armour on to the 88s.

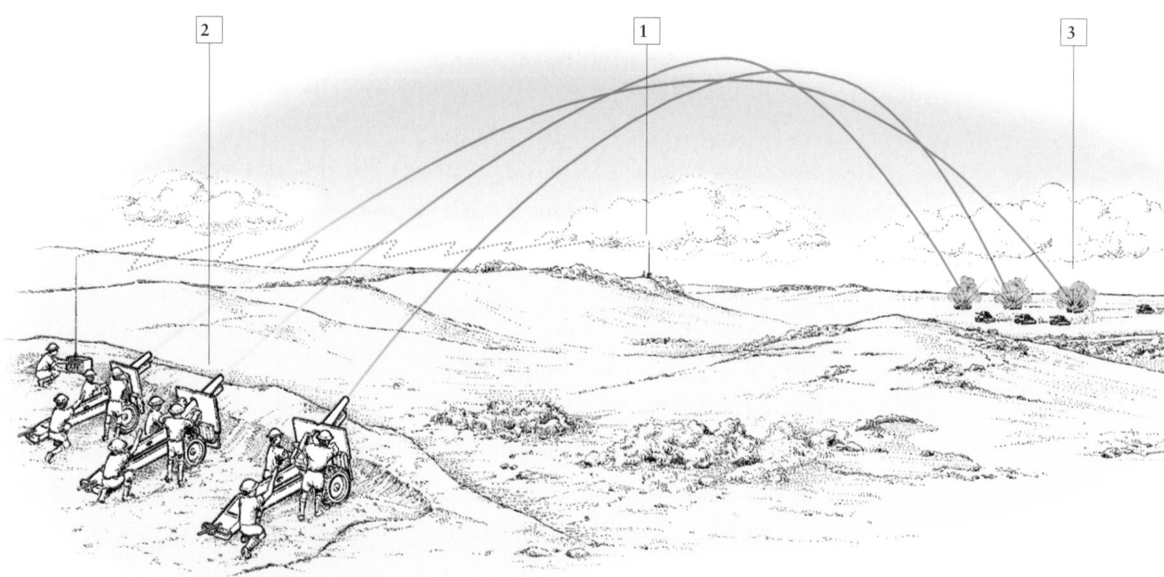

BELOW: *Artillery (2) could not usually see the target (3) it was firing at. Its fire was therefore controlled by a forward observation officer equipped with radio (1). The technique was to bracket the target and then make a series of standard range corrections to bring the fire on to it. Radio gave the artillery much greater flexibility than the field telephone and cable of 1914–18.*

Operation Crusader, November 1941. A Crusader passes a 'brewed-up' PzKw IV. Fire was and still is the tank crewman's greatest fear. It was usually the gunner, who was down in the hull, and the driver who had the most difficulty in evacuating the tank.

the war in the Middle East. With always limited resources, he had found himself having to conduct simultaneous campaigns at all points of the compass. While his early success in Libya had been negated and there had been failure in Greece and on Crete, Wavell had destroyed Mussolini's East African empire, crushed the Iraqi revolt, and dealt with the Vichy French problem in Syria. It was not a bad record.

On 22 June 1941 the Germans invaded Russia. Thereafter every other theatre of war in which their forces were engaged was regarded as a sideshow, not least North Africa, the only other region in which the *Wehrmacht* was actively engaged. In contrast, North Africa remained Britain's only ground campaign. The height of the Egyptian summer brought with it a lull in operations, however. Tobruk still held out, resupplied entirely by sea, although the Australians holding it had to be relieved at the insistence of their government and were replaced by a composite division. Churchill reiterated his insistence on its early relief, but Auchinleck refused to move until he had built up his forces.

In the meantime, the Middle East, especially on the British side, was becoming a breeding ground for what became known as Special Forces. Churchill himself had provided the spur for this, when he called for the raising of the Commandos in June 1940 to harry the German coastal defences in occupied Europe. An equivalent, the Middle East Commandos, was formed shortly afterwards. The long open desert flank invited infiltration and to this end the Long Range Desert Group was created for deep reconnaissance behind the Axis lines. They themselves had an equivalent, the Italian Auto-Saharan Group, which was responsible for the defence of southern

Libya. Other British Special Force units were also formed and became a haven for those who had become bored by conventional soldiering. Among them was the Special Air Service (SAS), the brainchild of a young officer recovering in hospital from a parachute injury; its original role was raiding Axis airfields. With SOE also establishing itself in the Middle East, there was soon a plethora of these units, but, in the early days at least, their operations were ill-coordinated and often did not conform to the overall operational plan.

In August 1941 there was a short and virtually bloodless campaign to close another Middle East back door to the Axis. The Shah of Persia had adopted an anti-British stance and, although he emphasized his country's neutrality, he was employing German military advisers. In the light of the continuing success of the German drive into Russia, the prospect of a future German offensive into the Middle East from the Caucasus could not be ruled out. Consequently, the British decided to occupy the country. This was done in conjunction with the Russians, who

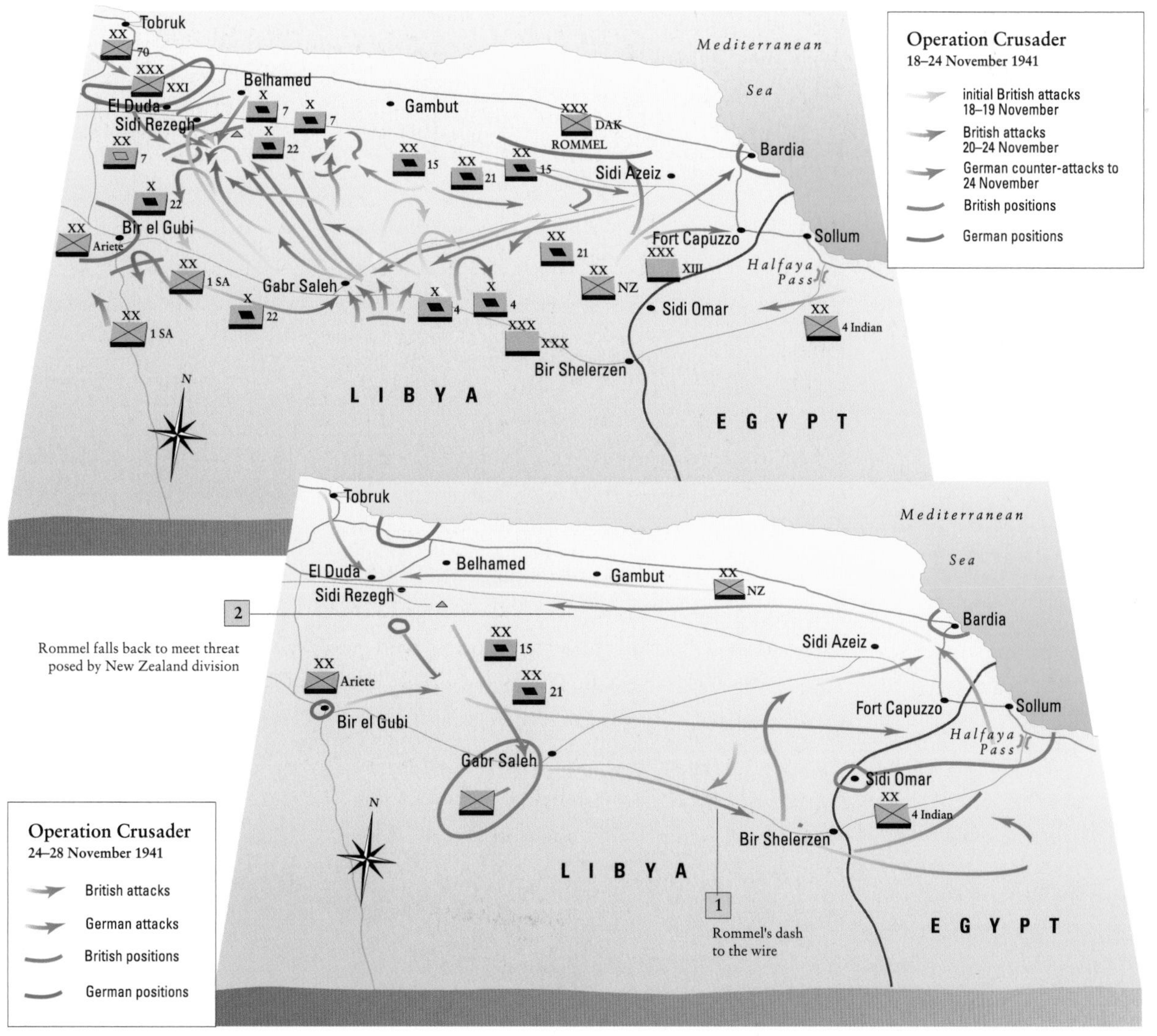

Operation Crusader

This was one of the most desperately fought battles of the Desert Campaign. The British armour suffered a serious mauling at Sidi Rizegh, but Rommel overreached himself in his 'dash to the Wire'.

were also concerned over this potential threat from the south. Not only did this operation secure the Abadan oilfields for the British, it also provided a physical link with their new ally. Persia, too, was to become a vital conduit for the supply of LendLease to Russia.

With Persia taken care of, Auchinleck could turn his full attention to his projected offensive in the Western Desert. He had received substantial reinforcements and at the end of September the Western Desert Force was renamed Eighth Army, with two other armies (Ninth and Tenth) to command the troops in Palestine, Iraq and Persia. The Axis, too, had received reinforcements, with Rommel now commanding the mobile forces, which consisted of two Panzer divisions (5th Light

Erwin Rommel contemplates his next move. He was often impatient and preferred to be up with his leading troops rather than back at his headquarters. While this often better enabled him to sense how the battle was going, it could prove difficult for his staff, especially if they needed urgent decisions from him.

had now become 21st Panzer) and the newly arrived 90th Light Division, together with the Italian XX1 Corps.

Detailed planning of Operation Crusader, as the British offensive was code-named, was undertaken by Sir Alan Cunningham, the commander of the Eighth Army. The plan was that XXX Corps, which contained the bulk of the British armour, was to engage and destroy the Axis armour, while XIII Corps advanced up the coast towards Tobruk, whose garrison would then break out when the time was ripe.

The attack opened at dawn on 18 November, taking the Axis forces by surprise. Misreading the British intentions, Rommel sent the DAK dashing off towards Bardia, enabling XXX Corps to advance to Sidi Rizegh, just ten miles south-east of Tobruk; XIII Corps also enjoyed some success and on 20 November the Tobruk garrison was ordered to begin its break-out. It was premature, since Rommel, realizing his mistake, brought the DAK and Italian armour back to Sidi Rizegh. For two days a desperate tank battle raged here, centred on the airfield, with the wreckage of Axis aircraft littering it. At the end of it Rommel had halted XXX Corps. Always ready to seize the chance to turn the tables on his adversary, Rommel then personally led the DAK on a dash to the Egyptian frontier, to cut off the Eighth Army from its forward supply depots. In the meantime, XIII Corps had continued its steady advance.

However, Rommel's precipitous move had thrown the Eighth Army into confusion – the 'fog of war' had truly descended. Cunningham, fearful of being cut off, wanted to abort the operation and withdraw, but Auchinleck overrode him, putting his own chief of staff, Neil Ritchie, to command in Cunningham's place. But Rommel, too, had his problems. Tenuous radio communications meant that he was largely out of touch with his main headquarters and consequently was unclear as to the overall situation. His thrust appeared to be striking into thin air and was also being harried by the Desert Air Force. He was also running short of fuel. Therefore he turned on his tracks.

Meanwhile, XIII Corps had linked up with the Tobruk garrison and Rommel now tried to restore the siege, but without success. On 7 December the Axis forces withdrew from Tobruk, intending to hold the Eighth Army at Gazala. The threat of being outflanked did not, however, make this a viable option. Rommel therefore decided to cut his losses and, reeling in his supply lines, withdrew westwards out of Cyrenaica. Thus, the British found themselves back where they had been the previous February. But, as then, their forces were worn down by the recent intense operations and their supply lines grievously stretched.

The pendulum of fortune had swung violently in the Mediterranean theatre during 1941, but the end of the year brought a dramatic development on the wider stage. The surprise Japanese attack on the US Pacific Fleet base at Pearl Harbor had finally brought America into the war. Hitler, hoping to persuade the Japanese to join in his war against Russia, declared war on the United States. Thus Britain now had the ally she had long wanted. But the Herculean struggle on the Eastern Front had caused the campaign in North Africa to pale into insignificance.

CHAPTER FOUR

Hitler Turns East: Russia (1941–3)

German infantry, *supported by tanks, fight their way into a Russian town during Operation Barbarossa, as the invasion of the Soviet Union was code-named. After its successes in Poland, Norway, France, the Low Countries, and the Balkans, the German Blitzkrieg machine was well honed by mid 1941. The fact that invasion took the Russians by almost complete surprise increased the prospects for success. But the very vastness of the Soviet Union, combined with its weather, would deny the Germans ultimate victory.*

RUSSIA 1941–3

Attacks in undiminished violence ... Frightful conditions in the city area proper where about 20,000 unattended wounded are seeking shelter among the ruins. With them are about the same number of starved and frostbitten men, and stragglers, mostly without weapons ... Heavy artillery pounding the whole city ... Tractor works may possibly hold out a little longer ...

RADIO MESSAGE HQ GERMAN SIXTH ARMY, TRAPPED AT STALINGRAD, TO HQ ARMY GROUP DON, 24 JANUARY 1943

HITLER'S ULTIMATE OBJECTIVE had always been to the East. Apart from his loathing of Russian Bolshevism, he saw western Russia as a means of providing the German people with the necessary additional living room (*Lebensraum*), which would enable them to consolidate their domination of

Bemused Russian peasants watch a horse-drawn German supply column go by. The deeper into Russia the Germans advanced, the greater their logistics problems. The relative paucity of good roads and railways, which were of a different gauge to those in Poland and Germany, aggravated the situation.

Europe. Nevertheless, accommodation with Moscow in August 1939 had served to make his immediate aims more attainable. Indeed, the only one of these that he failed to achieve was peace with Britain, but there was little that Europe's offshore island could do to hinder his plans for the Soviet Union.

Although he had intimated his thoughts to various of his military commanders in the previous weeks, Hitler first made his intentions generally known to them at a conference held at his alpine retreat on 31 July 1940. The decision on whether to invade Britain in September or postpone it until 1941 was dependent on the Luftwaffe's success in gaining air superiority over southern England. But regardless of this, Hitler saw the Soviet Union as Britain's last hope of salvation, he told the meeting. Destroy Russia and Britain would surely collapse. He then presented his outline plan. It would involve 120 divisions, part thrusting through the Ukraine to the River Dnepr, while the remainder advanced through the Baltic states and then on to Moscow. He estimated that it would take five months to achieve and needed to be completed before the onset of the Russian winter.

Captured Russian troops being marched westwards, away from the fighting. During the first eighteen days of the German invasion the Soviet Western Front alone recorded nearly 420,000 casualties out of an initial strength of 625,000 men. Prisoners of war accounted for the vast majority of the casualties.

Poland was to be the main mounting base for Operation Barbarossa, but as an essential preliminary the Balkan flank had to be secured. With this in mind, Hitler ordered the transfer from the west of two Panzer and ten infantry divisions to Poland towards the end of August 1940 with orders to be prepared to secure the Romanian oilfields. He then set about his diplomatic assault of the Balkan nations (see Chapter 3). Hitler also secured his northern flank through an agreement made with the Finns in September 1940 by which he was able to pass supplies through their country to the German forces in northern Norway. This enabled German troops to be stationed in Finland, a step which worried Moscow.

In November 1940 Soviet foreign minister Vyacheslav Molotov visited Berlin to raise the issue of the German presence in Finland. Hitler tried to fob him off by inviting the Soviet Union to join the Tripartite Pact. Moscow would only consider this if the German forces were removed from Finland and if Bulgaria, the Dardanelles, and the Persian Gulf were incorporated in the Soviet sphere of interest, conditions which were unacceptable to Berlin. But, in spite of this, the two countries signed a fresh treaty in January 1941. This recognized the existing spheres of influence and also renewed trade agreements through which German machine tools were exchanged for Russian food, especially grain.

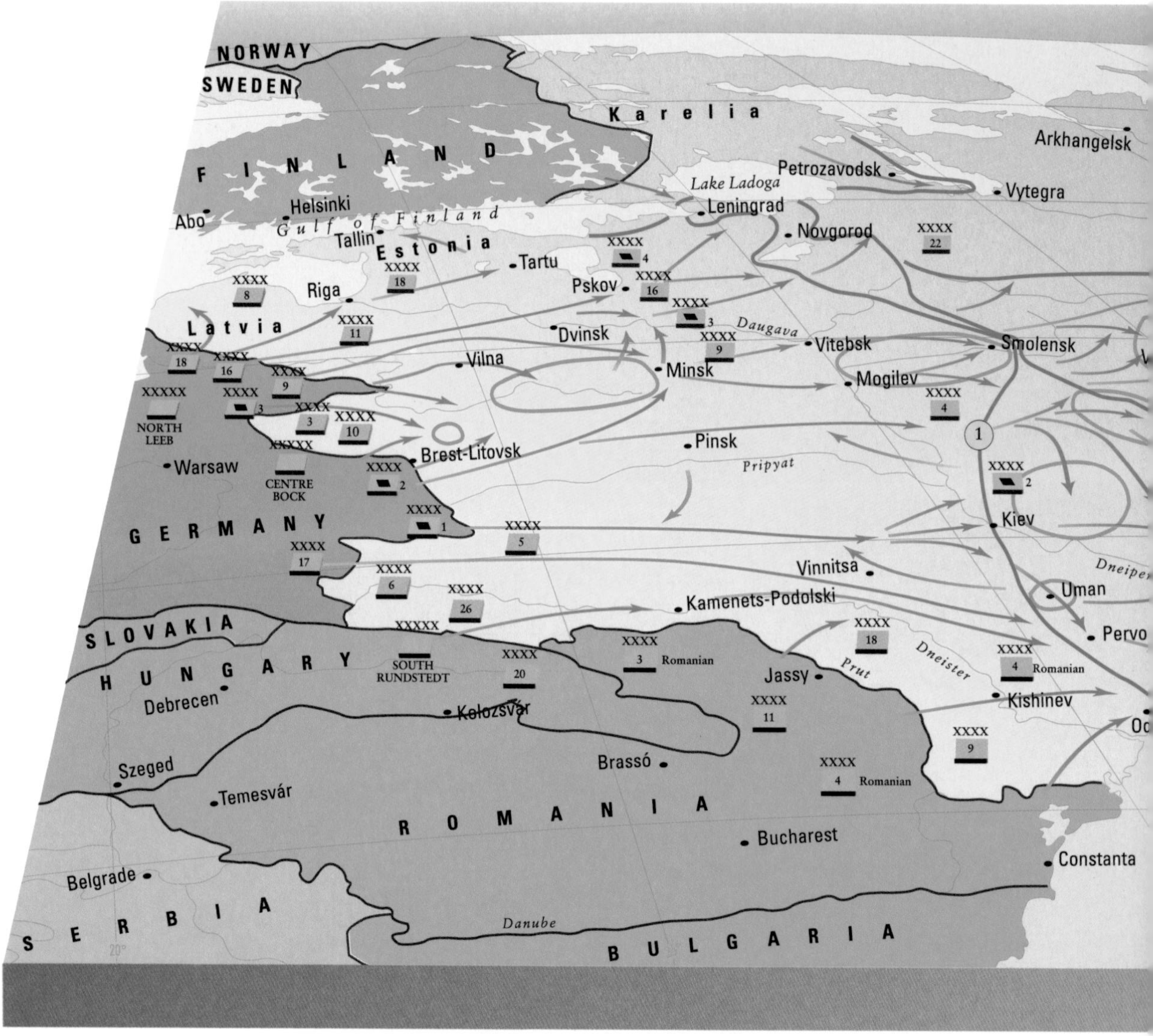

NORWAY
SWEDEN
FINLAND
Karelia
Arkhangelsk
Petrozavodsk
Lake Ladoga
Vytegra
Abo
Helsinki
Gulf of Finland
Leningrad
Novgorod
Tallin
Estonia
Tartu
Pskov
Riga
Latvia
Dvinsk
Daugava
Vitebsk
Smolensk
Vilna
Minsk
Mogilev
NORTH LEEB
CENTRE BOCK
Warsaw
Brest-Litovsk
Pinsk
Pripyat
GERMANY
Kiev
Dneiper
Vinnitsa
Uman
Kamenets-Podolski
SLOVAKIA
HUNGARY
SOUTH RUNDSTEDT
Debrecen
Kolozsvár
3 Romanian
Jassy
Prut
Dneister
Pervo
4 Romanian
Kishinev
Od
Szeged
Brassó
4 Romanian
Temesvár
ROMANIA
Bucharest
Constanta
Belgrade
SERBIA
Danube
BULGARIA

Meanwhile, the Barbarossa plan had been refined and was the subject of a Hitler directive issued in December. He now considered that the key to its success was the destruction of the Soviet forces. To achieve this there would now be three rather than two thrusts. The northern axis would pass through the Baltic states and then on to Leningrad, where the Finns, keen to reclaim the territory they had lost in March 1940, would co-operate in the seizure of the city. The centre thrust was to play the main part in the destruction of the Soviet forces. To this end it was allocated two Panzer groups compared to the one each earmarked for the north and south. These were to trap the Soviet forces through huge encircling movements.

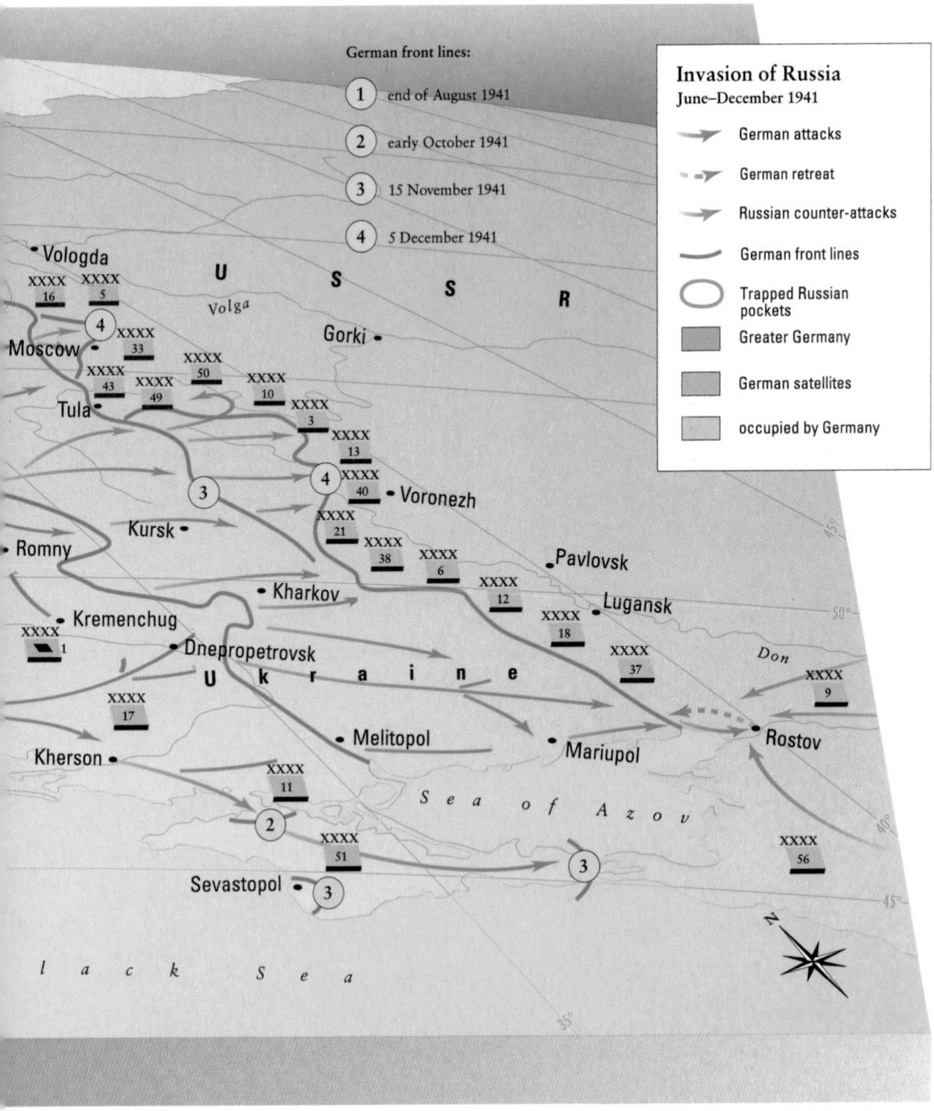

German front lines:
1 end of August 1941
2 early October 1941
3 15 November 1941
4 5 December 1941

Invasion of Russia
June–December 1941

German attacks
German retreat
Russian counter-attacks
German front lines
Trapped Russian pockets
Greater Germany
German satellites
occupied by Germany

Vologda
USSR
Volga
Moscow
Gorki
Tula
Voronezh
Kursk
Romny
Pavlovsk
Kharkov
Lugansk
Kremenchug
Dnepropetrovsk
Ukraine
Don
Rostov
Melitopol
Mariupol
Kherson
Sea of Azov
Sevastopol
Black Sea

OPPOSITE: *This striking shot of a German infantryman appeared on the cover of the* Wehrmacht *journal* Signal.
ABOVE: *Not all Russian units were prepared to surrender. Here a wounded Russian officer directs the defence of a position.*

Operation Barbarossa

The German invasion involved no less than 134 divisions (17 Panzer, 12 motorized, 120 infantry), supported by 2,000 aircraft. In the period up to the German advance grinding to a halt in front of Moscow in early December, the Red Army lost over 2,800,000 men killed, captured and missing, representing a quarter of its overall strength.

Simultaneously, the southern thrust would secure the Ukraine, Russia's 'granary', as originally planned. The invasion was to take place in May 1941.

To deploy the almost 3.6 million men, 3,600 tanks and 2,700 aircraft taking part in Barbarossa under the tightest possible security was an enormous challenge. It was a tribute to the German movement staffs, in particular, that it was achieved without any major problems occurring. But two significant factors prevented the invasion from being mounted on time. One was the decision to invade Yugoslavia and Greece. Some historians argue that since the German forces involved were follow-up troops, this did not affect the timing of Barbarossa. On the other hand, the diversion of supplies to the Balkans would have acted as a brake. More noteworthy, however, was the fact that the Russian spring thaw came late in 1941. As the attack could not be mounted until the ground had dried out, it was not until 21 June that the codeword *Dortmund* was issued to the three army groups taking part. It meant that the attack would start in the early hours of the following morning.

The open Russian steppes were ideal terrain for tanks, but the maps the Germans used had little detail and were often inaccurate. This made navigation difficult.

The Soviet attitude to the storm about to be unleashed on them is still a subject of puzzlement and conflicting theories. Moscow certainly had prior warning of the invasion. The German build-up of forces in Poland could not be wholly disguised. The British had obtained sufficient intelligence of Hitler's intentions from Ultra and other sources and had passed it on to Moscow. The Russians also knew of it from their own sources, notably Richard Sorge, press attaché to the German Embassy to Tokyo, and one of the most successful spies of the war. He became privy to the invasion through German attempts to persuade the Japanese to renounce their five-year non-aggression pact with the Soviet Union, which they signed in April 1941, and to attack from Manchuria. But Japanese ambitions lay to the south and they were not to be moved.

Yet the Russians took no obvious steps to prepare themselves for the imminent onslaught. Some have proposed that Stalin was preparing a pre-emptive strike on Germany and that to adopt a defensive posture would conflict with this. An opposing and more generally accepted theory argues that the Soviet forces were not ready for renewed conflict and that Stalin did not want to do anything to provoke Hitler. Certainly, the armed forces were still very much in the throes of the reformation and reorganization following their poor showing in the war against Finland. As it was, not until the very eve of the offensive, after a German deserter had warned that it would take place the following morning, did Stalin issue an alert.

At 2 a.m. on 22 June 1941 a Soviet grain train chugged across the River Bug at Brest-Litovsk, one of many that had taken this route during the past few months under the German–Soviet trade agreements. Seventy-five minutes later the German artillery commenced a short sharp bombardment. Overhead there was a steady drone of aircraft, as the Luftwaffe set about its priority task of destroying the Red Air Force. Then the Germans attacked on a 500-mile front.

The first two weeks of the campaign were dazzling in their success for the Germans. Wilhelm von Leeb's Army Group North rapidly overran the Baltic states. In the centre Fedor von Bock used his two Panzer groups to create a huge pocket in the area of Bialystok. When this was finally reduced on 3 July it yielded no less than 290,000 prisoners, 2,500 tanks, and 1,500 guns. Only von Rundstedt's Army Group South, physically separated from the other two army groups by the Pripet marshes,

A supply column passes exhausted German infantry snatching a brief rest before they continue their march. Their endurance was severely tested as they strove to catch up the Panzers.

met any significant resistance. This was largely because General Mikhail Kirponos, commanding the South-west Front, had his troops on a higher state of alert than elsewhere. He also pursued a more energetic defence, mounting a series of attacks into the flanks of the German advance which did cause some temporary dislocation. It was during these attacks that the Germans met the formidable T-34 tank for the first time. But Kirponos's attacks became increasingly disjointed and the pace of Army Group South's advance quickened.

Stalin remained strangely silent during the first few days of the German onslaught. Not until 3 July did he broadcast to the Soviet people, exhorting them to defend until the last. By this time the Red Air Force in western Russia had been

Troops of Army Group North enter a Latvian town. The Baltic states were annexed by the Russians in the summer of 1940. The ruthless purges instituted by Moscow caused the majority of the people of the three states to welcome the Germans.

virtually destroyed and the ground forces had lost over 600,000 men, representing almost a third of their total strength in the theatre. The catastrophe grew as the Panzer divisions thrust ever deeper across the open steppe. Here, maps were sometimes of little use in the often featureless terrain and the tank commanders relied for guidance on the explosions of the Stukas' bombs as they struck enemy positions ahead. Such was the pace of the advance that the Panzers were sometimes as much as ten days' march ahead of the main foot-marching infantry body. Once the tanks had trapped Soviet forces, they would have to pause to await the arrival of the main body, which would then carry out the reduction of the pocket. These waits, however, did enable the Panzer formations to draw breath and allow their logistics to catch up with them.

As July wore on, the opposing dictators began to take an increasing hand in the operations. Hitler had appointed himself supreme commander of the *Wehrmacht* prior to the war and operated through the *Oberkommando der Wehrmacht* (OKW), with the obsequious Field Marshal Wilhelm Keitel as its chief of staff. At the outset of Barbarossa Hitler established OKW in a forest outside Rastenburg in East Prussia and spent almost all his time there. Increasingly, he breathed down the neck of the army commander-in-chief, Walter von Brauchitsch, who was nominally responsible for the conduct of operations through his own headquarters, the *Oberkommando des Heeres* (OKH). Hitler's increased meddling began to confuse von Brauchitsch and his army group commanders. He believed that Moscow should be the prime objective, in that Stalin would be prepared to sacrifice much in defence of the capital and that this was therefore the best way of achieving the destruction of the Red Army. On 19 July, however, Hitler laid down that Leningrad and the Ukraine were

now the priorities and Army Group Centre was ordered to hand over both its Panzer groups once the huge pocket they had created at Smolensk had been reduced. Moscow would merely be bombed into submission.

Apart from the fact that the Luftwaffe, lacking heavy bombers, was ill equipped to mount a strategic bombing offensive against the Russian capital, Army Group Centre was achieving the best results. To rob it of its armour was to ignore the basic military tenet of reinforcing success. But von Brauchitsch found it difficult to argue against Hitler, especially since Hitler could point to numerous instances in previous campaigns when his generals had been shown up as doubting Thomases.

Conscious of the increasing annihilation of his armies, Stalin, too, decided to take direct control of operations, making himself Commissar for Defence. Since the purges, the Communist Party already had a strong grip on the armed forces, with political officers at the elbow of commanders at every level. Now the party strengthened its grip on all aspects of life in the Soviet Union. Stalin set up a general headquarters, the Stavka, under his own command, to direct military operations. Rather than visit subordinate headquarters, as Hitler was prepared to do, Stalin came to rely on troubleshooters, reliable senior officers who were attached to the Stavka, whom he would send out to points of crisis to take charge of the situation. He also instituted a series of draconian measures. Many of the generals who had faced the initial German blitzkrieg were relieved and executed. This gradually bred tough and ruthless commanders, who could be relied on to obey orders, whatever the cost in casualties. Stalin also issued, among his edicts, an order that troops were to fight to the last man, and that the families of those who surrendered would be deprived of all their rights. Indeed, even those who escaped

During the first half of the war the Germans used Czech 38t tanks to partially equip some of their Panzer divisions. This was because domestic tank production was unable to match the rapid expansion of the Panzer arm.

OPPOSITE: *210mm German railway gun in action. The Germans developed a number of types of railway gun, with the largest calibre being 520mm. They were used to shell Britain from France and also in the sieges of Leningrad and Sevastapol. This particular model had a range of some 70 miles.*

or were liberated from German captivity often found themselves posted to penal battalions.

Harshness on the German side was directed at the Russian people, whom Hitler regarded as subhuman (*Untermenschen*). Captured Soviet soldiers were not treated according to the Geneva Convention, unlike those of the western Allies. During the first few days after surrendering this was sometimes understandable, since the German armies did not have sufficient food and shelter immediately available to provide for the sometimes hundreds of thousands trapped in the great pockets. But thereafter, once they were in proper POW camps, their treatment did not change. Indeed, it became worse, with most captured Russians being employed as slave labour.

Hitler had two specific targets among the Soviet population. One was members of the Communist Party, whose fate was enshrined in his infamous Commissar Order, issued before the invasion took place, and which called for the summary execution of all political officers. The Russian Jews were also to be rooted out. This task was given to the SS Einsatzgruppen (Special Groups) following up behind the armies, who were literally extermination squads. While the *Wehrmacht* tried to distance itself from their activities, it was drawn in, even if this was merely witnessing mass executions carried out by the Einsatzgruppen.

The crew of a PAK36 37mm anti-tank gun engage Russian tanks. Each German infantry regiment (two or three battalion structure) had a company of these guns.

Yet many Russians in the overrun territories, especially in the Ukraine, where desire for total autonomy had always been strong, welcomed the invader. They believed that the Germans had come to liberate them from the Communist yoke. Fed with Nazi racial doctrine, the Germans failed to grasp the significance of this, even though, as their casualties mounted, they did recruit a sizeable number of Russian POWs into their army. These were known as *Hiwis* (*Hilfswillige*, or 'voluntary helpers'). But soon many others, once they realized the true nature of their occupiers, turned against the Germans and an increasing number joined the bands of partisans being formed in the forests and marshes by soldiers who had evaded capture. Soon these were to become an increasing thorn in the flesh of the German lines of communication. But the resolve of the Russian people was also stiffened when Stalin began to appeal directly to their patriotism rather than exhorting them to defend Marxist-Leninism.

Yet, while the Soviet Union was galvanizing itself, the military situation grew ever bleaker. True, the advance of Army Group North had been slowed by heavily wooded terrain and growing troop

exhaustion. Even so, it reached Leningrad at the beginning of September. The Finns, meanwhile, had declared war on the Soviet Union and had launched an offensive down the Karelian peninsula. This threatened Leningrad from the north. While they refused to advance beyond their 1939 frontier, the Finnish operations were sufficient to place Leningrad under siege; its only remaining access to the rest of the country was by water, across the south part of Lake Ladoga. Before it had to surrender its Panzer groups, Army Group Centre created and reduced another massive pocket in the Smolensk area. This yielded a further 310,000 prisoners. Moscow also suffered its first air attack on 22 July, with 127 aircraft taking part. The Luftwaffe would mount a further seventy-five attacks on the capital before the end of the year, but such were the demands of the ground forces for its support that none of these exceeded sixty bombers in strength.

With the help of Guderian's Panzer group, now transferred from Army Group Centre, von Rundstedt created a vast pocket around the Ukrainian capital, Kiev. When this was finally eradicated on 10 September, a further 600,000 Russians fell into German hands. The bulk of these losses was borne by the South-west Front, which in two months' fighting lost over 80 per cent of its numerical strength. Thereafter, Army Group South continued to press towards the River Donets and also entered the Crimea, where the Black Sea Fleet's base at Sevastapol was put under siege.

Soviet poster exhorting defence of the Motherland. It was this message, rather than defending Marxist-Leninism, which appealed to the majority of the Soviet people.

On 5 September 1941, however, Hitler had another change of heart. Moscow was once more to have priority. Army Group North was to hand over its armour and air assets to Army Group Centre, and, once the Kiev pocket had been reduced, Army Group South was also to return the Panzer group it had been loaned. The redeployment again took time to complete, and von Bock was not ready to begin his drive on Moscow until the end of the month. Yet on the 27th the first of the autumn rains fell, the precursor to the Russian winter. Moscow was still almost 200 miles away from Army Group Centre. To seize it before the snow came would require another lightning advance.

Von Bock launched his offensive, code-named Typhoon, on 30 September. He quickly created two large pockets, but this time most of the Russians within that at Bryansk managed to break out to fight another day. They were also well aware of the threat to their capital. Unlike 1812, when the Russians made no attempt to defend Moscow and allowed Napoleon to enter it, Stalin was determined to hold it and on 10 October appointed his main troubleshooter, Georgi Zhukov, to organize its defence with the newly created West Front. Zhukov initiated the digging of anti-tank ditches to the west of the city and arranged for the transfer of reinforcements from Siberia. Yet in the face of the German advance, albeit slowed by the rains, panic did set in. Many Muscovites fled and several of the organs of government, as well as foreign embassies, were moved to east of the Urals. Stalin, however, remained in the capital.

Hitler now decided that, instead of a direct thrust on Moscow, it was to be taken by double envelopment. The autumn mud was, however, taking its toll. The German

Finnish snipers in action. The Finns eagerly joined in Barbarossa to recover the territory they had lost after their winter war of 1939–40 with the USSR. They helped to cut Leningrad off from the north. Having regained their lost territory in the Karelian isthmus, they halted their offensive operations.

supply system broke down and the tanks ground to a halt through lack of fuel. The replacement system was unable to cope with the increasing casualties and many units were down to half strength. At the end of October a temporary halt had to be called. This gave the Russians a vital breathing-space and by mid November Zhukov had some eighty divisions, many of them from Siberia, deployed in Moscow's defence. The temperature had now dropped, the rain turned to snow, and the ground hardened. The German advance could resume, but the troops themselves were ill equipped to face the Russian winter, with no provision having been made for the issue of warm clothing.

The final advance to Moscow – German infantry and tanks cautiously approach a Russian village. The temperature would soon drop further, leading to much suffering among the troops. Overstretched supply lines meant that it would be some time before they received suitable winter clothing.

Meanwhile, Army Group South had captured Kharkov and overrun the whole of the Crimea, apart from Sevastapol. Finally, towards the end of November it reached and captured Rostov-on-Don, gateway to the Caucasus.

The Moscow operation resumed on 15 November and after eight days the northern prong had reached a point just thirty miles from the capital. Now the Germans began to close up to the defences protecting the city. But on the night of 4/5 December the temperature suddenly plummeted to –35°C. The following morning tank engines would not start, weapons were frozen, and frostbite ravaged the German ranks. Moscow had been saved.

Hitler reluctantly agreed that local withdrawals to more defensible terrain could be made in front of Moscow. But he was furious at von Rundstedt for withdrawing his forces, which were out on a limb, from Rostov in the face of a Russian counter-attack, and removed him from command. He was replaced by von Reichenau, who then promptly suffered a fatal heart attack. In front of Moscow, the Russians now mounted a series of counter-attacks. Although they made limited progress, such was the pressure that von Brauchitsch sanctioned further withdrawals. Hitler countermanded these and sacked the army commander-in-chief, announcing that he himself would take von Brauchitsch's place. At the same time, von Bock, worn out by the battle for Moscow, was placed on the sick list and succeeded by Gunther von Kluge.

Early in October, Hitler had publicly boasted that the Soviet Union was broken and would never rise again. Now, just over two months later, nothing could be further from the truth, as the German people had begun to realize. Their suspicions were strengthened that all was not well on the Eastern Front when, just before Christmas, propaganda minister Josef Goebbels broadcast an appeal for winter clothing for the troops. This served to reinforce the contrast with Christmas 1940, when no German soldiers were actually in combat. Now, especially with America in the war, the German people had begun to realize that they were in for a long struggle.

In the Soviet Union the situation remained grim, in spite of the fact that the Germans had at last been halted. Virtually the whole of western Russia was now under Nazi domination. Conditions in Leningrad were bad and growing worse, with starvation already beginning to stalk the streets. True, a tenuous supply route had been established across the now frozen Lake Ladoga, but it could bring in only a fraction of the food that the city needed. Efforts to relieve the siege in January 1942 failed. However, the Soviet war industry was being relocated beyond the Urals and out of range of the German bombers. During 1942 its expansion would be greater than that of any of the combatant nations other than the United States. This was partly achieved by offering better rations to those working in heavy industry. However, the loss of the Ukraine badly affected food production, and rationing became so stringent that the daily number of calories allowed for the average Russian became dangerously low.

Women in Russia were mobilized to a greater extent than elsewhere. Unlike the other warring nations, Soviet women served in the front line as machine-gunners, snipers and tank crews. They even provided a complete bomber regiment.

During the first months of 1942 Soviet counter-attacks were mounted along almost the whole front. Although these showed that the Red Army was not yet ready to go over to the offensive, the pressure was such as to keep the Germans off balance. Even so, in spite of the intensity of the Russian winter, German resistance was fierce. In early February the Russians created their first pocket when they trapped 90,000 Germans south of Lake Ilmen at Demyansk. The Luftwaffe was called in and successfully kept the pocket supplied until those inside it could be relieved. Hitler became insistent that there should be no further withdrawals and sacked von Leeb when he asked permission to withdraw. In March, however, came the spring thaw, which forced a temporary halt to active operations.

Both sides now drew up fresh plans. Stalin's strategy was to build on the active defence that he had been operating during the early months of 1942. He expected

A German MG34 light machine-gun. It had a very high rate of fire (850 rounds per minute). It was partially replaced by the MG42, which was easier to mass-produce.

the Germans to make another attempt to capture Moscow and believed that pre-emptive attacks would prevent them from doing this. At the same time, he sent Foreign Minister Molotov to visit Britain and America to urge them to create a second front on mainland western Europe. Stalin had also by now instituted the new level of command – the theatre – with Zhukov's West Theatre controlling the northern half of the 1,200 mile front, while fellow Stavka member Semyon Timoshenko's South-west Theatre was responsible for the remainder. This additional command level proved to be cumbersome, however, and was abolished after a few months.

Stalin was right in believing that the Germans would resume the offensive, but Hitler was looking elsewhere than Moscow. The brunt would now be borne by Army Group South and the strategic objective was the Caucasus oilfields. Not only would this draw in much of the Red Army in defence of a vital commodity, but it would also increase German oil resources. At the time these were largely dependent on Romania, although a synthetic oil industry was being set up within the Reich itself, one that would soon provide more fuel than Ploesti. The mechanics of Operation Blue were grandiose. Army Group South was to be subdivided into two army groups, A and B. Army Group A was to attack north of Kharkov and then strike south-east between the Donets and the Don. Army Group B would strike at the junction of these two rivers and link up with Army Group A, whereupon the axis of advance would swing south towards the Caucasus. A subsidiary drive would now secure Stalingrad on the Volga so as to provide flank protection to the main advance. A deception plan was also put in place to encourage the Russians to believe that Moscow was the main objective.

A Soviet counter-attack. T-34 tanks carrying infantry storm into the attack. Lacking armoured personnel carriers, the Russians often transported infantry about the battlefield in this way. However, they did interfere with the tank commander's vision and also the turret traverse, so once fire was opened on the tanks, the infantry would have immediately to bail out.

Stalin's policy of pre-emptive attacks took an interesting turn when on 12 May Timoshenko launched an offensive south of Kharkov. This caught the German Sixth Army in the midst of preparing to eradicate the very salient from which the Russians mounted their attack. Consequently, the offensive initially made good progress, forcing the Sixth Army back across the River Orel. But then the German armour struck the increasingly extended Russian flanks. The Soviet South-west Front, which was leading the attack, was totally cut off and virtually destroyed. This augured well for Blue.

Simultaneously, Erich von Manstein's Eleventh Army had begun to clear the Russians from the eastern Crimea, which they had regained during the winter, and prepared to secure Sevastapol. The garrison of the port continued to offer bitter resistance and it did not finally fall until the beginning of July, and then only after a massive bombardment by aircraft and heavy artillery. Nevertheless, Hitler was delighted and sent von Manstein north to deal with Leningrad.

The interrupted preparations for Blue continued, with Hitler flying to von Bock's headquarters to approve formally the final plan. But on the eve of the operation the complete details fell into Russian hands after a light aircraft was shot down. While

Russian infantry with PPSh-1941G sub machine-guns. The drum magazine held seventy-one rounds, which was just as well, as the rate of fire was 900 rounds per minute.

the Russians believed that the papers were authentic, they remained convinced that Blue was merely a subsidiary operation and that the main objective was still Moscow.

The offensive itself was launched on 30 June. While the advance towards the Don proceeded rapidly, attempts to trap the Red Army in pockets largely failed; it had learnt lessons from the previous year and slipped away eastwards rather than allow itself to be encircled. Hitler became increasingly frustrated and eventually sacked von Bock and disbanded HQ Army Group South, a clear indication that he was taking personal control. He was convinced that sizeable Soviet forces remained to be trapped in the Rostov area and tasked Army Group A with this, passing much of Army Group B's armour and air support to it. Once Siegmund List had destroyed the Russians in the Rostov area he was to secure the Black Sea coastline of the Caucasus, as well as the Maikop oilfields and Grozny, before advancing to Baku. In the back of Hitler's mind a grandiose scheme was forming. With Rommel then hammering at the gates of Cairo, Hitler thought that his Caucasus thrust could subsequently be directed to the Middle East and link up with the Axis forces in North Africa, thus totally destroying the British hold.

List broke out of his bridgeheads over the Don on 25 July and quickly shattered

German infantry with a PzKw III. This has spare fuel in a container mounted on its rear decks.

THE DRIVE INTO THE CAUCASUS

Army Group A was initially very successful, but as Hitler directed increasing resources to support Army Group B's drive on Stalingrad so the offensive began to lose momentum. Eventually, Army Group A was left dangerously extended.

the Soviet South Front. Thereafter he advanced rapidly southwards, entering Maikop on 9 August, but only to find that the Russians had destroyed the oil installations. In the meantime, Friedrich Paulus's Sixth Army was advancing towards Stalingrad. Still missing Hermann Hoth's Fourth Panzer Army, which had been lent to List, although it was now in the process of being returned, Paulus attempted to bounce the Don west of Stalingrad, but was repulsed. With additional air support switched from Army Group A, he tried again, was successful, and reached the outskirts of Stalingrad on 10 August. Hoth had still not joined him when he began to attack the city nine days later.

The drive into the Caucasus had now reached the mountains, but the Russian defence began to congeal. This was especially so on the Black Sea coast. List's long lines of communication were also reducing the momentum of his advance. Furthermore, Hitler was now stripping him of further air support. His attention was becoming fixed by the city that bore Stalin's name. It was a fixation shared by his opponent, who gave orders on 24 August that Stalingrad must be held, sending Zhukov to co-ordinate its defence.

Paulus now began to break into Stalingrad. Street fighting is a slow and costly business, with every building capable of being turned into a strongpoint. Stalingrad was no exception. Gradually, however, the Germans drove Vassili Chuikov's Sixty-second Army back towards the Volga, which divides the city in two, but found it an increasingly uphill struggle as their casualties grew. Paulus and his superior commander, Maximilian von Weichs, were also becoming concerned about their flanks. Not only were these long, but they were held largely by troops from Germany's allies.

Hungarian, Romanian, and Slovakian troops had taken part in the initial invasion of Russia as part of Army Group South. A few weeks later Mussolini sent a corps, which by summer 1942 had grown into an army. Franco, too, maintained his pro-Axis sympathies. Although he was still determined to keep his country out of the war, especially since the British were allowing Spanish imports of essential raw materials to breach their stringent naval blockade, he did send volunteers to Russia to fight with the Spanish Blue Division. The forces of these nations were not as well equipped as the Germans and their fighting calibre was generally not as high. They tended, therefore, to be used in secondary roles. At Stalingrad, however, every available German soldier was drawn into the battle for it; hence the employment of allied forces to guard the flanks of the deep salient.

As autumn drew on, the battle for Stalingrad became ever more remorseless. The Russians had reinforced on the east bank of the Volga and eventually the situation reached stalemate. It was the same in the Caucasus, where Army Group A finally came to a halt at the beginning of November. The fighting of the summer and autumn had extended the length of the Eastern Front to over 2,000 miles, which left the numerically inferior German forces more stretched than their opponents, whose manpower resources now enabled them to switch to the offensive.

The Russians had noted the vulnerability of the flanks of the Stalingrad salient

The Caucasus
June–November 1942
German attacks
German retreat
German front line
Russian retreat
oilfield
2000
1500
1000
500
200
0 m
U S S R
UKRAINE
Kazakhstan
GEORGIA
AZERBAIJAN
ARMENIA
TURKEY
Tula
Kursk
Eletz
Tambov
Penza
Voronezh
Saratov
Svoboda
Belgorod
Pavlovsk
Kharkov
Kamishin
Izyum
Stalingrad
Lugansk
Baskunchak
Novo Cherhassk
Rostov
Mariopol
Yeisk
Astrakhan
Elista
Ulan Erge
Kerch
Taman
Krapotkin
Krasnovar
Armavir
Stavropol
Novorossiisk
Maikop
Georgiyevsk
Tuapse
Piatigorsk
Kisliar
Sochi
Mozdok
Grozny
Ordzhonikidze
Makhach Kala
Sukhum
Poti
Kutais
Tiflis
Batumi
Don
Donets
Khoper
Medvedista
Volga
Kuban
Kuma
Sura
Sea of Asov
Black Sea
Caspian Sea
Caucasus Mountains
XXXXX VORONEZH FRONT GALIKOV
XXXXX SOUTHWEST FRONT VATUTIN
XXXXX DON FRONT ROKOSSOVSKY
XXXXX STALINGRAD FRONT YEREMENKO
XXXXX NORTH CAUCASUS FRONT BUDENNY
XXXXX TRANS-CAUCASUS FRONT TYULENEV
XXXXX B WEICHS
XXXXX SOUTH BOCK
XXXXX A LIST
XXXX 60
XXXX 2
XXXX 40
XXXX 6
XXXX 2 HUNGARIAN (elts)
XXXX 1 Guards
XXXX 5
XXXX 21
XXXX 65
XXXX 24
XXXX 66
XXXX 8 ITALIAN
XXXX 3 ROMANIAN
XXXX 6 PAULUS
XXXX 62
XXXX 64
XXXX 57
XXXX 51
XXXX 4 HOTH
XXXX 4 ROMANIAN
XXXX 28
XXXX 17 RUOFF
XXXX 11 (-)
XXXX 47
XXXX 56
XXXX 12
XXXX 1 KLEIST
XXXX 9
XXXX 44
XXXX 18
XXXX 37
XXXX
50°
45°
40°
German front lines:
1 June 1942
2 23 July 1942
3 November 1942
N
0 100 km
0 100 miles

The fighting in the suburbs of Stalingrad. A 75mm infantry gun and a PAK38 anti-tank gun engage Russian positions.

and, as Paulus continued to hammer away at the city itself, planned a riposte. On 19 November the Southwest and Don Fronts struck at the northern flank of the salient, which was defended by the Third Romanian Army. Next day the Stalingrad Front struck at the Fourth Romanian Army in the south. Subjected to concentrated bombardments followed by mass attacks of tanks and infantry, the Romanians soon broke and on 23 November the two Soviet prongs linked up, cutting off the German Sixth Army and part of Fourth Panzer Army. Goering, recalling the Luftwaffe's success in maintaining the Demyansk pocket the previous February, declared that he could do the same at Stalingrad. Hitler, with the city so nearly in his grasp, therefore ordered Paulus to stay put and not to attempt a break-out. He also organized a relief force, Army Group Don, under von Manstein, to break through the Soviet defences and relieve Paulus.

Von Manstein wanted to mount this operation,

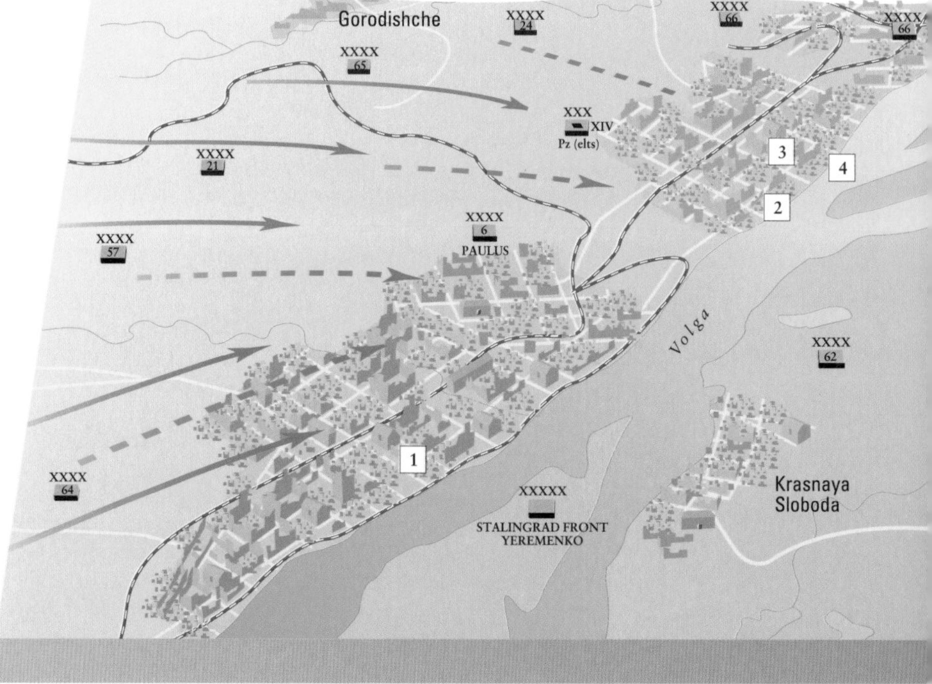

code-named Winter Storm, at the earlier possible opportunity, since any delay would enable the Russian defences to grow ever stronger. But continued Soviet pressure on Army Group B forced him to commit some of his reserves, and not until 12 December was he able to unleash his attack. In the meantime, the Russians had attempted to cut the Stalingrad pocket in two, but called off their attacks after five days' virtually fruitless effort. On 16 December, they launched a fresh attack, this time against the Italians, who were holding the northern part of Army Group B's front. The Italians soon broke and this rolled back Army Group B's northern flank. Meanwhile, von Manstein had reached a point sixteen miles from the pocket before being frustrated by strong defences on the River Myshkova. He suggested to Paulus

THE GERMAN ASSAULT ON STALINGRAD

By mid-November 1942 the Germans had forced the Russian 62nd Army into a narrow pocket on the west bank of the River Volga. The Grain Elevator and Red October Factory were the scenes of the bitterest fighting of the battle.

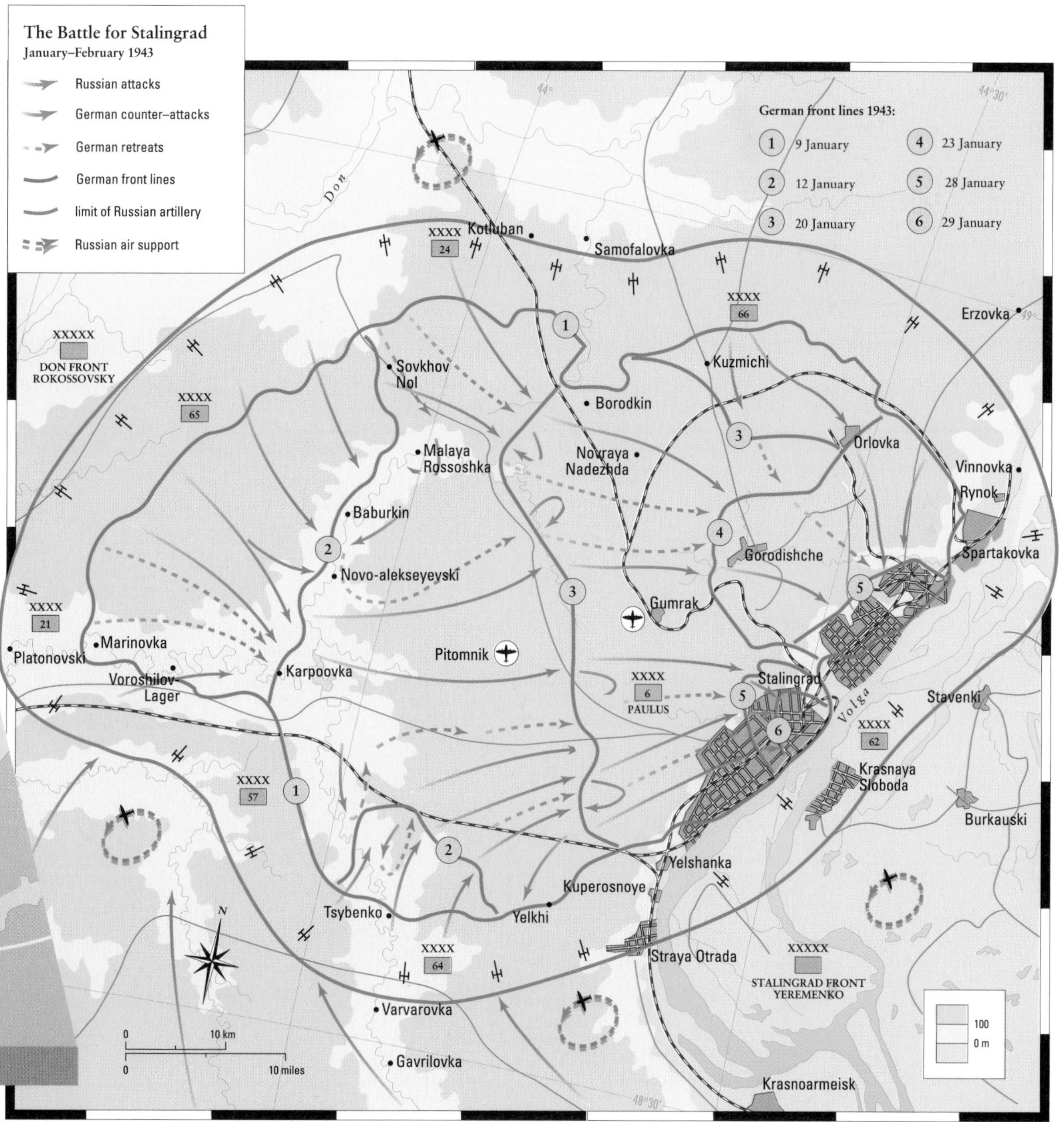

that he break out, but the latter refused, conscious of the Führer's order to hold on at Stalingrad. The Russians now attacked the Romanian Fourth Army once more, on the southern part of Army Group B's front. It now seemed that the whole of this and Army Group Don might be encircled. Hitler therefore sanctioned a general withdrawal.

This left Paulus separated by 125 miles from the main German forces and made the Luftwaffe's task of resupplying him even less feasible. To maintain the pocket Paulus needed 750 tons of supplies per day, but the best that the Luftwaffe achieved was 250 tons. Now it dropped to a daily average of 80 tons, with transport aircraft continually being lost. The Russians steadily increased their pressure on the pocket, where conditions became ever more desperate. One after another, the airfields within it were overrun. Yet Hitler continued to forbid any break-out, although such was the pitiful state of the German troops in the pocket that they were no longer capable of offensive action.

In Germany the propaganda machine painted Stalingrad as an epic struggle against the Bolshevik hordes which would serve to inspire generations to come.

The Nazi propaganda machine portrayed the last days of the Sixth Army's struggle in Stalingrad as a heroic crusade against impossible odds.

Paulus's last message to Hitler, sent on his birthday, 30 January 1943, echoed this, with its indication that he would never surrender. Hitler promptly rewarded him with promotion to field marshal, but privately hoped that Paulus and his senior officers would do the honourable thing and fall on their swords. By this time the Sixth Army had been reduced to two small pockets within Stalingrad itself. Paulus himself surrendered the following day, while the northern pocket held out for just two more days.

The Germans suffered 110,000 killed in the fighting for Stalingrad and a further 90,000 were made prisoner, the vast majority of these never seeing their homes again. Paulus and some of the other generals were so embittered by Hitler's treatment of the Sixth Army that they became willing tools of the Soviet propaganda machine. As for the Red Army, it lost nearly 500,000 men in the defence of Stalingrad, but not only had it thwarted the Germans, it had decisively defeated them. From now on the German armies in the east were to be on the defensive. Stalingrad was, indeed, a major turning-point of the war. The tide was also turning against the Axis in the west.

The reality of Stalingrad was that 90,000 half-starved German soldiers went into captivity. Only 5,000 of them would ever see their homeland again.

CHAPTER FIVE

SECOND FRONT: WESTERN EUROPE AND THE MEDITERRANEAN (1942–3)

US TROOPS have their first sight of Britain. The December 1941 Washington conference agreed that, as an essential preliminary to the defeat of the Axis powers, the British Isles should be built up as an arsenal. But, throughout 1942 and the early part of 1943 there was a fierce strategic debate between the British and Americans over how best to achieve victory. The Americans wanted to mount a cross-Channel invasion as soon as possible, but the British favoured a more circumspect approach, with priority being given to the Mediterranean. The Americans accepted that a cross-Channel invasion was not possible in 1942, but President Roosevelt wanted US troops in action in the European theatre before the end of 1942 so as to uphold his 'Germany first' policy to the American people. Consequently, he was forced to accept the British view.

WESTERN EUROPE AND THE MEDITERRANEAN 1942–3

I have visited the clearing station and surgical hospital daily. The men like to see me. Few of them are suffering and all but a couple are cheerful. The treatment of the wounded is much better than the last war, and the food is good. They give all the men a shot in the arm before they take the ambulance ride. Every soldier has three hypos, a bottle of sulpher nilimade [sic] pills and some powder. He can give himself a shot and then take a pill every five minutes until the bottle is empty. He dusts some of the powder on the wound. The blood plasma is fine too. Lots of the belly wounds are curing.

GENERAL GEORGE S. PATTON IN A LETTER TO HIS WIFE, TUNISIA, 25 MARCH 1943

One of the first American soldiers to arrive in Britain under Bolero ashore in Northern Ireland, 26 January 1942. The aim was to deploy 100,000 men per month and for one million Americans to be in Britain by the end of the year.

WHEN HITLER AND MUSSOLINI declared war on the United States on 11 December 1941 they did President Roosevelt an enormous favour. The attack on Pearl Harbor had drawn him into war with Japan, but did this give him the justification for declaring war against her European allies? Roosevelt had his doubts that the American people would wear it. Now the die was cast and America found herself at war on two widely separated fronts. The question was which should take priority.

On 13 December Churchill and his military advisers set sail from Britain to meet his new ally. The subsequent talks held in Washington, DC under the code name Arcadia were to be the first of many such conferences at which Allied strategy for the next phase of the war was to be decided. Churchill himself was convinced that defeat of Germany must take priority over that of Japan and could point to Plan ABC-1, which had been agreed at the beginning of the year, as an outline blueprint. On the other hand, the US Navy, smarting under the destruction of much of its Pacific Fleet, pressed for offensive action against Japan. Roosevelt overruled his admirals, pointing out that the navy would be in no position to undertake offensive operations in the Pacific for some time to come. Thus the policy of 'Germany First' was adopted.

It was now a question of how to achieve victory in Europe. Both sides agreed that this could only be done by invading the continent of Europe and that Britain must be the mounting base for this.

Consequently, American ground and air forces would be deployed here under the code name Bolero. Indeed, the first American troops arrived in Britain before the end of January 1942. The conference also had no difficulty in agreeing to continue the naval blockade and strategic bombing of Germany. It was essential to keep the Soviet Union in the war and the supply of American and British weapons would help in this. Three supply routes were established – by land through Persia, by air from Alaska to Siberia, and by sea from Britain to the northern ports of Archangel and Murmansk.

Where to strike first in Europe proved more problematical for the conference. The American instinct was to mount a cross-Channel invasion of occupied France as early as possible in 1943. The British, who had been considering this problem for the past year, blanched at this. The spectre of the Dardanelles in 1915 still haunted them and an operation, in conjunction with de Gaulle and his Free French, against Vichy Dakar on Africa's north-west coast in September 1940 had proved an embarrassing failure. Pinprick raids by Commandos against hostile coasts had served only to highlight the complexity involved in amphibious operations, especially the need for large quantities of specialized shipping. Nevertheless, they had already recognized that some form of early operation against occupied western Europe might become necessary and the conference left this on file under the code name Sledgehammer, as it did the American proposal for a cross-Channel invasion (Round Up) in 1943.

Valentine tanks of a newly raised armoured division on exercise somewhere in Britain, 1942. They were, in fact, designed for infantry support, but a shortage of cruiser tanks forced them to be used for training the new armoured formations. Valentines fought as infantry tanks in North Africa and Tunisia during 1942–3.

The British, however, did have an alternative proposal. At the time of Arcadia they were driving the Axis forces out of Cyrenaica and were keen to clear the whole of north Africa of the Axis presence. This could be accelerated by Anglo-US landings in French North-west Africa. The American reaction to this was one of suspicion. They had always taken an adverse view of British imperialism and believed that the British had an underlying motive in North Africa. Even so, Gymnast, as this plan was code-named, was also left on the table. To examine these unresolved issues Churchill and Roosevelt agreed on the setting up of the Combined

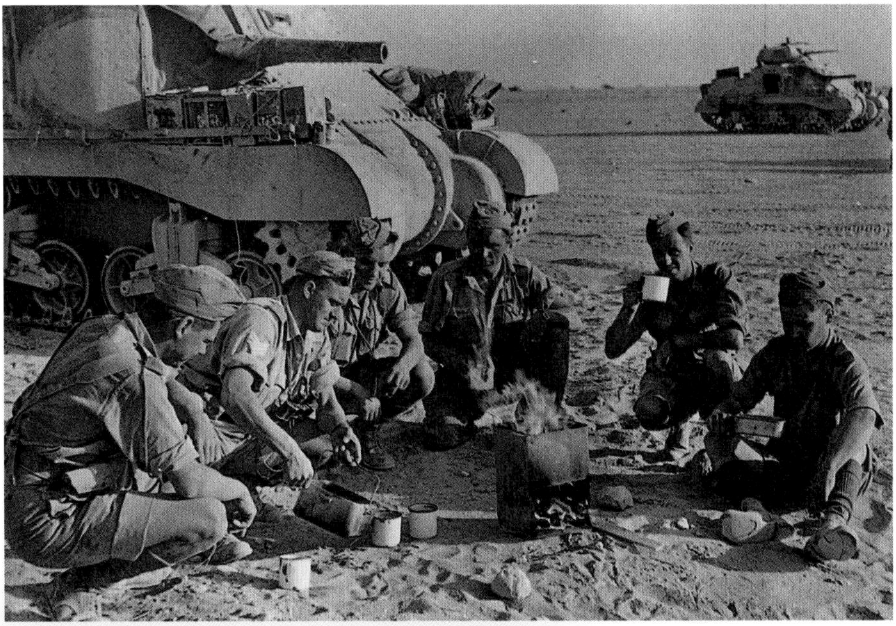

The British crew of a US-supplied General Grant tank enjoy a break for tea, Western Desert 1942. This tank was armed with a turret-mounted 37mm gun and hull-mounted 75mm. Its high silhouette was a disadvantage.

ROMMEL'S 1942 OFFENSIVES

Rommel consistently out-generalled the British. He was only stopped at el Alamein by the exhaustion of his troops and his overstretched supply lines.

1 21 January: Rommel feints toward Mechili while the bulk of his forces head for Benghazi

2 29 January: Rommel reaches Benghazi

3 26 May: the Battle of Gazala

4 21 June: Rommel takes Tobruk

5 28 June: Rommel reaches Mersa Matruh

6 30 June: Rommel poised to take El Alamein

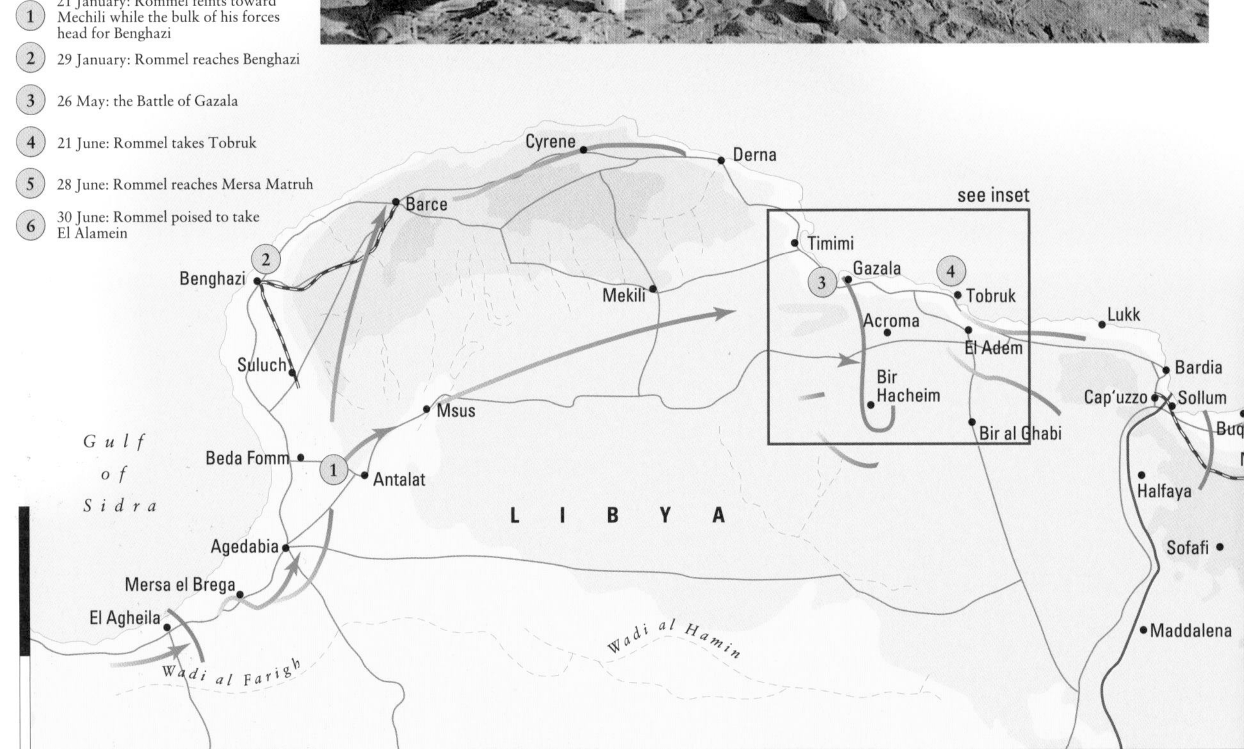

Chiefs of Staff. This body was to be based in Washington and made up of the US Chiefs of Staff Committee and permanent representatives of the British chiefs of staff.

North Africa remained the only theatre in which the ground troops of the western Allies, at least those of Britain and the Dominions, were actively engaged. In January 1942 the British were once more masters of the eastern Libyan province of Cyrenaica and were now preparing for a further offensive into Tripolitania. Rommel, however, was determined to take advantage of their extended lines of

GAZALA

The battle starkly demonstrated two characteristics of the Desert war – the problem of the open flank and the British failure to concentrate their armour.

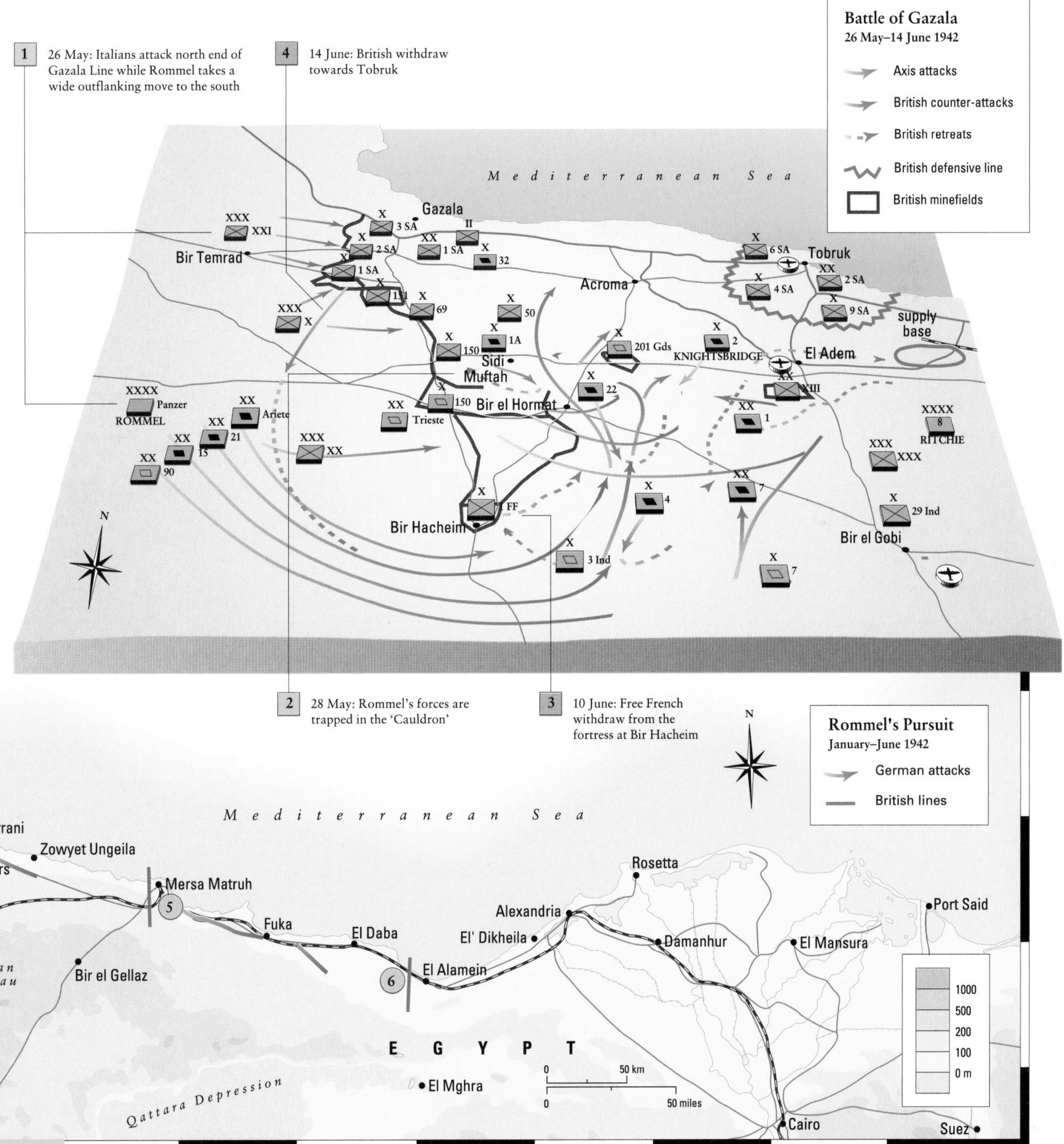

communication, which were aggravated by the fact that the port of Benghazi was riddled with mines and unusable. Lax British radio security also told him that British tank unserviceability was high, while he himself had just received forty-five replacement tanks. But Rommel also had a new master, Albert Kesselring, whom Hitler had appointed Commander-in-Chief South so as to improve co-ordination with the Italians. Both he and the Commando Supremo wanted to rebuild the Axis strength in Libya before mounting further offensive operations, but Rommel, whose command was now retitled Panzerarmee Afrika, chose to ignore them.

On 21 January 1942, in an operation which mirrored his first foray into Cyrenaica almost a year earlier, Rommel attacked, quickly throwing the inexperienced British 1st Armoured Division into confusion. After two days the Italians ordered him to withdraw, refusing to allow their troops to penetrate further into Cyrenaica. Rommel's reaction was to press on with just the Afrika Korps. He recaptured Benghazi on the 29th and drove the confused British back to Gazala. Here the Eighth Army had hastily thrown up defences. Not strong enough to penetrate these, and with his tanks almost out of fuel, Rommel halted. What he had done, however, was once more to put Malta out of range of British aircraft and the island was again under close aerial siege.

Deeply concerned by this, Churchill pressed Auchinleck to attack once more. But the Commander-in-Chief Middle East wanted to improve his logistics before launching another offensive. This included extending the Egyptian coastal railway to Tobruk and building up sizeable forward stocks of supplies. Auchinleck also wanted to create a strong armoured fighting force and strengthen the Gazala defences to deter another pre-emptive Axis attack. Therefore he would not be ready to attack before June. Churchill was displeased and the argument between the two men rumbled on. Eventually, the prime minister threatened to remove part of the Desert Air Force to India to assist in countering the Japanese offensive in Burma. Auchinleck now agreed to bring his offensive forward to mid May, but then changed his mind and put it back to mid June.

In contrast, the Axis powers were trying to restrain their commander on the ground. They decided in March that the primary objective for summer 1942 was to be the capture of Malta so as to secure their supply lines to North Africa: Operation Herakles called for an intensified air offensive against the island, followed by a joint air and sea assault. Rommel, however, argued for a continuation of the offensive in Libya, believing that, with additional German reinforcements, he could drive the British back across the Suez Canal. Hitler, in the midst of planning the drive into the Caucasus, would not countenance further troops being sent to Libya. Even so, on 1 May Rommel was granted a concession. He would be allowed to mount a limited attack to capture Tobruk. If this was successful, he could advance to the Egyptian frontier, but would have to halt here, since much of his air support would be needed for Herakles. At some later stage, dependent on the degree of success in the Caucasus, Rommel could continue across the Suez Canal.

The British defences in the Gazala Line were fundamentally flawed. They

Montgomery speaks to troops of the Eighth Army before the attack at El Alamein. It was part of his command style to ensure that every man was made to feel that his role in the forthcoming battle was vital to gaining victory.

consisted of a series of brigade-sized 'boxes' stretching forty miles south of Gazala to Bir Hacheim. These were wired in and protected by minefields. Unfortunately, they were too far apart to be mutually supporting. The British armour was positioned behind the Gazala Line. Auchinleck wanted it to be kept concentrated so that it could strike a decisive blow at any Axis attempt to take advantage of the line's open desert flank. The Eighth Army commander, General Ritchie, was, however, worried about his forward supply dumps, which had been prepared for his own offensive, and dispersed the armour to protect them. This was also to prove a mistake.

Rommel began his approach march on the evening of 26 May. His intention was to use the Italian infantry to mask the Gazala Line, while he took his armour on a hook to the south. Ritchie spotted this move, but was certain that it was a feint, being convinced that the main assault would be against the line itself. Early the following morning Rommel swung round Bir Hacheim, which was held by a Free French brigade, and started to advance north-eastwards. Some of the British armour was taken by surprise and one armoured division HQ was overrun, but the remainder gave as good as it got during the next two days. Gradually, however, Rommel pushed it back. Fuel, though, was now becoming a problem and he decided that he must punch through the Gazala Line in order to establish a supply route. Consequently, on 31 May the Italians began to attack one of the brigade boxes from the west, while elements of the DAK did so from the east. In the aptly called three-day battle of the Cauldron the box was destroyed.

Ritchie tried to mount a counter-attack into the Cauldron, but lack of co-ordination meant failure. Consequently, he established a new line facing south and running eastwards from Gazala and awaited Rommel's next attack. This came on 11 June, the same day that Bir Hacheim, which had held out for over two weeks, finally fell. The subsequent battle of Knightsbridge saw most of the surviving British armour destroyed. Ritchie therefore began to order his forces to begin to withdraw to the Egyptian frontier. Auchinleck countermanded him, hoping to continue to hold west of Tobruk. It was too late.

There would be no second siege of Tobruk. The defences had been allowed to deteriorate and the South African division sent to hold the port had no time to prepare itself before Rommel arrived. He entered Tobruk on 21 June, but allowed himself little respite before resuming the pursuit of the now disorganized Eighth Army. Ritchie's intention was to make a last stand at Mersa Matruh, but Auchinleck believed that preservation of the Eighth Army was now the priority. He therefore took command of it himself and, leaving a rearguard at Mersa Matruh, withdrew the remainder to El Alamein, where the Qattara Depression comes closest to the coast. If he could not hold Rommel here he would withdraw his army across the Suez Canal and give battle there.

By 30 June the 'brave but baffled' Eighth Army was back on the El Alamein Line and Rommel had closed up to it. Auchinleck knew from Ultra that he would attack next day. The Axis forces were equally exhausted and at the end of an overstretched supply line, even though they had captured a number of British dumps.

The subsequent month's fighting on the El Alamein Line can be likened to that of two exhausted heavyweight boxers trading ever weaker punches. First Rommel attacked, but made few gains. The British then counter-attacked with similar lack of success. The armies literally fought themselves to a standstill and by the end of July both had had enough.

The summer of 1942 witnessed the most protracted period of intense combat in the Western Desert. Once more it showed that the German tactics were more flexible and fluid. One of the secrets of their success was the *Kampfgruppe* (battle group), an ad hoc formation of tanks, mechanized infantry and guns, which could be formed at a moment's notice to suit a particular tactical situation. The British were more rigid in their approach and the co-operation between the various arms was not as close. Their continued tendency to piecemeal their armour also acted to their disadvantage. Co-operation between the Desert Air Force and the Eighth Army also demonstrated that they still had much to learn from the German example.

Maintenance on a Curtiss P-40 Kittyhawk of the Desert Air Force at a forward landing ground. The Kittyhawk was a fighter-bomber used for tactical support of ground forces.

While the two sides licked their wounds in Egypt, the Anglo-US strategic debate continued. Much of it was coloured by Soviet demands for a second front to be opened in western Europe, which was supported by left-wing agitation in Britain. In addition, Roosevelt feared that, unless the Allies took some positive action in 1942, the American people would demand that priority be switched to the Pacific.

An American delegation visited London in April and Churchill went to Washington in June. The result was a perplexing number of options. There was Sledgehammer, which now would involve six divisions, with its aim of establishing a lodgement in France if Russia seemed on the point of collapse. Gymnast, too, was still on the table. In addition, Churchill proposed a landing in Norway (Jupiter) and another possibility was the Iberian peninsula. The British had also drawn up plans for a twenty-four-hour raid on the French port of Dieppe. What both sides did agree was that Round Up should still take place in 1943 and, to this end, Bolero must be maintained. The western Allies also recognized that amphibious shipping was still in short supply and that any operation mounted in 1942 must not be to the detriment of Round Up. The British believed that Sledgehammer would not meet this criterion and continued to press hard for Gymnast, to which Roosevelt eventually agreed towards the end of July. Churchill then visited Moscow and, after much acrimonious discussion, got Stalin to accept that there would be no second front in Europe in 1942.

En route to Moscow, Churchill visited Egypt. He decided that Auchinleck, even

An American Torch convoy in mid Atlantic. It was bound for Casablanca on the Atlantic coast of French North-West Africa. It was a measure of the effective security surrounding Torch that the landings took the Germans and Italians completely by surprise.

though he had eventually succeeded in frustrating Rommel, had lost the confidence of his troops and that fresh blood was needed. In his place as C-in-C Middle East Churchill appointed the urbane Harold Alexander, who had recently supervised the British retreat from Burma. Command of the Eighth Army was given to Bernard Montgomery, but only after the original appointee, desert veteran 'Strafer' Gott, had been killed in an air crash on his way to assume this post.

Montgomery's brash self-confidence very quickly permeated to the men of the Eighth Army. He told them that there would be no withdrawal from El Alamein; they would repulse Rommel's next attack where they stood. Ultra had told him that Rommel would attack again, at the end of August, once he had received additional fuel and ammunition. The convoy carrying these across the Mediterranean was intercepted and they never arrived. In the meantime, Montgomery took another significant step when he had the headquarters of the Desert Air Force collocated with his own. This would make it very much more responsive to the needs of the army.

Rommel duly attacked on 30 August. Harried by the Desert Air Force, he tried for two days to seize the vital Alam Halfa ridge, but without success. He then withdrew behind his own minefields, forced to go over to the defensive. Montgomery now set about preparing to drive the Axis forces back. He did not intend to launch an offensive until he had built up a sizeable superiority in men and weapons. To this end he relied on Alexander's charm to mollify the always impatient Churchill.

Back in Britain, the Americans continued their steady build-up of air power and ground troops. They were given a warm welcome by the long-beleaguered British. Indeed, with their smart uniforms, high rates of pay, nylons, chewing-gum and swing music, they added a distinct element of glamour to the grimness and grime of wartime Britain. Misunderstandings were inevitable. The British found it difficult to comprehend the strict racial segregation that existed in the US armed forces, while the GIs, coming from the most modern industrialized society in the world, were continually puzzled by the seemingly old-fashioned British approach to life. There was, too, the matter of being 'divided by a common language'.

The problem of language was also felt in the higher echelons, as British and American staffs struggled to hammer out a common strategy. There was initially mutual suspicion. Some Americans thought the British patronizing, or, as one writer put it, 'pipe-smoking blue-eyed bastards, with that elegant manner, and no manners at all'. The British, on the other hand, found many Americans to be unexpectedly naïve and ignorant of the world at large, especially in their belief that any problem could be solved provided enough money was thrown at it. Nevertheless, this initial friction was worn down with time and the joint Anglo-US staffs became highly effective. Indeed, the planning for Gymnast, or Torch, as it later became known, went surprisingly smoothly.

The final plan called for simultaneous landings on Morocco's Atlantic coast, and at the Algerian ports of Oran and Algiers. The Moroccan operations would be conducted by US forces sailing direct from America, while the other two assaults would be mounted from Scotland. These would also be made up of American ground forces, apart from at Algiers, where the British would provide Commandos as part of the spearhead, as well as follow-up forces. These would then advance into Tunisia and eventually link up with the British Eighth Army. In recognition of the fact that Torch was largely an American operation, the overall commander was to be Dwight D. Eisenhower, then Commanding General of the European Theatre of Operations (ETO) in Britain.

Apart from the need to get American troops blooded in combat and be seen by the American people to be carrying out positive action in ETO, a major reason for US predominance in Torch was the French. Encouraged by the Germans, anti-British feeling had been maintained in Vichy France. It had, however, no axe to grind with the United States, which had enjoyed diplomatic relations with it and in February 1941 had even set up a trade agreement with French North Africa, where a US representative, Robert Murphy, continued to reside during 1942. He was now to play an important role in persuading the Vichy forces to come over to the Allied side. They needed a figurehead, however, and this was found in the person of General Henri Giraud, who had escaped from German captivity and reached Vichy France, from where he was extracted by the Allies on the eve of Torch. All this had to be done, however, without the knowledge of the Free French leader in London, Charles de Gaulle, whose name was still anathema to many Vichy French.

In spite of having secured Giraud, there was still a problem. This was Admiral François Darlan, Pétain's foreign minister and potential successor, who spent much time in North Africa and was known to be opposed to any deal with the Allies. Eventually, through Murphy's offices, Eisenhower's deputy, General Mark Clark, was taken secretly by submarine to a rendezvous on the Algerian coast to meet one of the senior French army officers, General Charles Mast. He assured Mark Clark that the army would offer only token resistance, but could give no guarantees for the navy. That done, the amphibious task forces set sail from America and Scotland.

Across the other side of North Africa dramatic events were now taking place. On the night of 23/24 October, 900 British guns opened fire on the Axis defences at El Alamein. It was certainly the largest bombardment fired by the British so far in the war, but did not compare to the massive trench bombardments of 1916–17 or those now being fired by the Red Army on the Eastern Front. Even so, it impressed all who witnessed it. Then began the break-in of the now formidable Axis defences. For, with the Qattara Depression prohibiting an open desert flank, a frontal assault was the only option available to Montgomery.

He attacked in both the north and the south, but progress was slow, especially after Rommel, who had been on sick leave in Europe, resumed command on 25 October. He used the DAK as a mobile reserve, switching it to whichever part of the line was most under threat. After five days' intense battle, Montgomery was forced to regroup and amend his plan. He now concentrated on the northern part of the defences, using his armour to ward off the DAK. By now the Axis forces were desperately short of fuel and, in spite of orders from Hitler to defend until the last, Rommel began to withdraw his forces on the evening of 2 November. Two days later, Montgomery finally broke through, but his efforts to trap the withdrawing Axis forces failed. Slow passage of information and problems in getting replenishment through to the tanks were the two main reasons for this. Then, on 6 November, two days' rain further slowed progress. Rommel was therefore able to continue to withdraw intact across Cyrenaica and into Tripolitania, his rearguards turning on the Eighth Army every so often to make it keep its distance. Nevertheless, Rommel's defeat at El Alamein was significant. It also marked the last victory by British arms alone in the European and Mediterranean theatres.

On 8 November 1942 the Torch landings took place. Although U-boats had made several sightings on the Allied convoys en route, the general Axis view was that the objective was either Dakar or to reinforce Malta. They were thus largely taken by surprise. On the other hand, the French resistance to the landings was stiffer than expected, especially at Algiers. Nevertheless, the fighting ceased after three days and the French in Morocco and Algeria signed an armistice. In retaliation, German forces moved into Vichy France.

The next step was to secure Tunisia and General Kenneth Anderson's euphemistically titled First British Army – it consisted of hardly more than a division's worth of British and American troops – set off to do this. British and US paratroops and the Commandos were used to secure the port of Bône and forward airfields. The Axis reacted very quickly. As early as 9 November, the day after the original landings, German paratroops had landed at an airport outside Tunis and Axis aircraft and submarines attacked shipping off Algiers. After establishing an air bridge from Sicily, the Axis also began to bring troops in by sea.

The first clash of arms in Tunisia came on 17 November, when a lightly armed British force confronted a *Kampfgruppe* commanded by Rudolf Witzig, the officer who had led the daring *coup de main* on the Belgian fortress of Eben Emael in May 1940. The British, outgunned, were forced to withdraw. Problems now arose. The Allied supply line depended on a single antiquated railway and matters were made worse by the arrival of the autumn rains. Allied air power relied on grass fields which quickly turned to mud, while their opponents were operating from metal airstrips in Tunisia. As a result the Axis enjoyed air superiority. Even so, after a

pause, Anderson pressed forward and by the beginning of December his troops had reached a point just twenty miles from Tunis before being thrown back. After further fruitless attempts to push forward, they were forced to go over to the

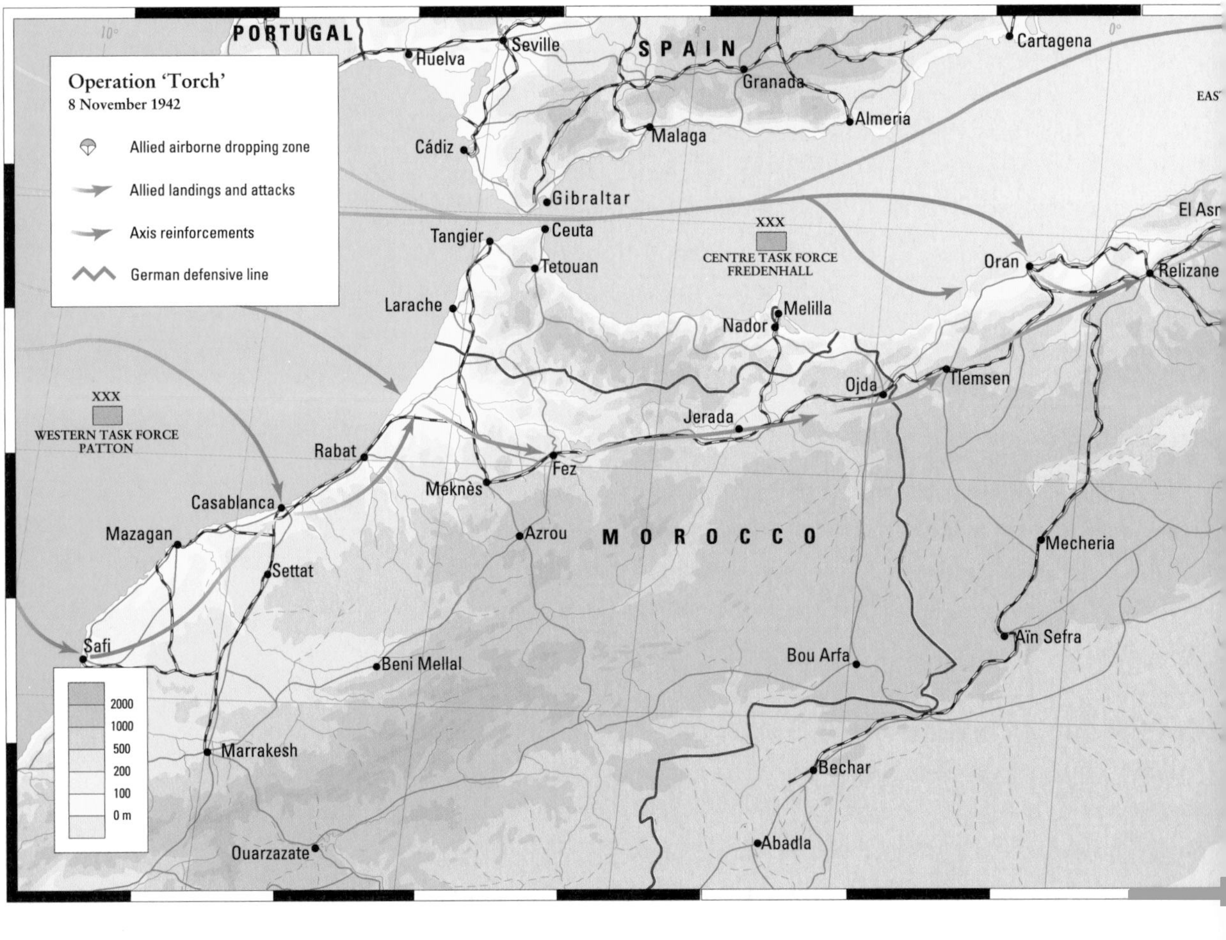

Operation 'Torch'
8 November 1942

Allied airborne dropping zone
Allied landings and attacks
Axis reinforcements
German defensive line

PORTUGAL
SPAIN
Huelva
Seville
Granada
Almeria
Cartagena
Malaga
Cádiz
Gibraltar
Ceuta
Tangier
Tetouan
XXX
CENTRE TASK FORCE
FREDENHALL
Oran
Relizane
El Asr
Larache
Melilla
Nador
Ojda
Tlemsen
XXX
WESTERN TASK FORCE
PATTON
Jerada
Rabat
Fez
Meknès
Casablanca
Mazagan
Azrou
MOROCCO
Settat
Mecheria
Safi
Aïn Sefra
Bou Arfa
Beni Mellal
Marrakesh
Bechar
Abadla
Ouarzazate
2000
1000
500
200
100
0 m

defensive. The Allies had to accept that the closer they got to Tunis the more the Axis forces were able to concentrate against them and the more tenuous their lines of communications became. Thus, the end of the year found both sides occupying a long front in western Tunisia, each with too few troops to do anything other than aggressive patrolling.

This situation continued throughout the first half of January 1943, as both sides reinforced. Meanwhile, across the other side of Tunisia, Montgomery had continued his pursuit of Rommel through Tripolitania. Eventually, on 23 January the Axis forces crossed into Tunisia, while Montgomery halted at Tripoli in order to open up the port for resupply before advancing further.

With Torch and the British victory at El Alamein, as well as the increasing Russian success at Stalingrad, it was time that the Allies agreed the next phase of their strategy. Churchill proposed a meeting of the Big Three (himself, Roosevelt, and Stalin) in Iceland, but Stalin said that he was too busy, although he pressed fo assurances that Round Up would be mounted in 1943. Consequently, Churchill and Roosevelt, together with their respective military staffs, met at Casablanca in mid January 1943. It was to be the pivotal conference in shaping the strategy of the western Allies in Europe.

The critical decision was that ultimate victory would only come with the

OPPOSITE: *German paratroops move up to the front, Tunisia, December 1942. Both sides used mules in the hilly terrain. They would do the same in Italy.*

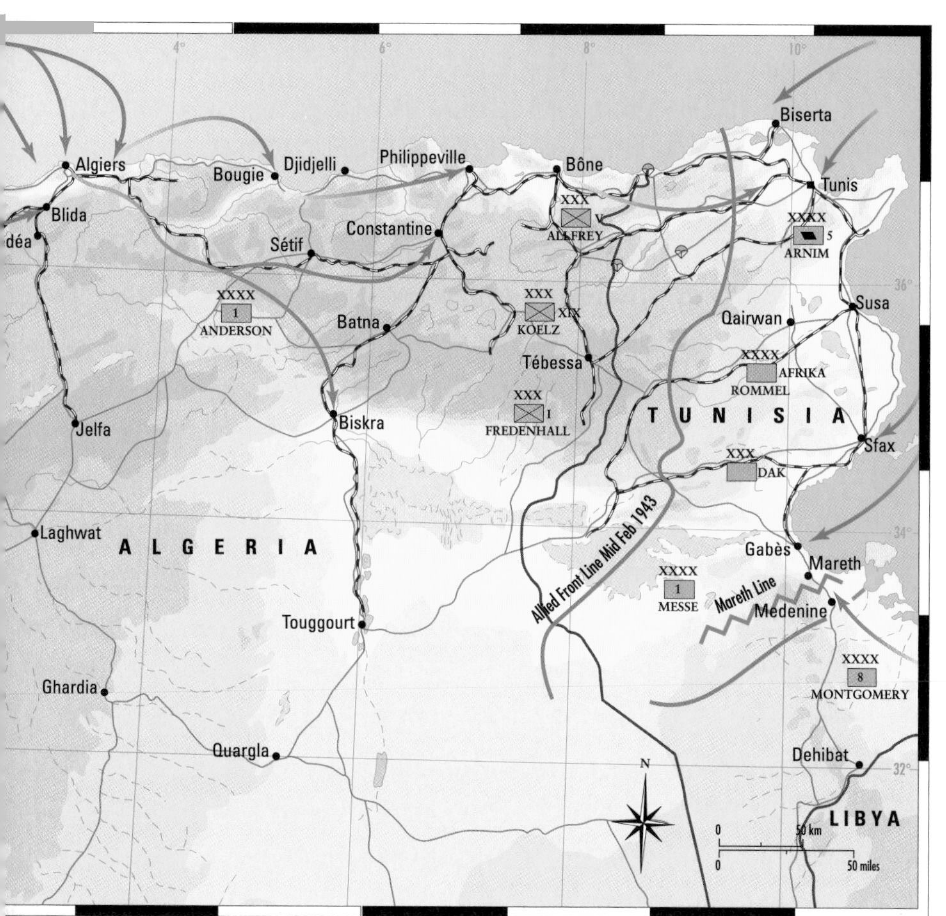

FRENCH NORTH-WEST AFRICA WINTER 1942–3

The advance of the First Army into Tunisia from the west initially went well, but the rapid Axis deployment of troops across the Mediterranean, the inexperience of the Allied troops, and ever more tenuous supply lines, together with the onset of winter, denied them the prize of Tunis.

unconditional surrender of Germany, Japan, and Italy. There must be no question of their militaristic regimes being allowed any chance to rise again, as had happened in Germany after 1918. The 'Germany first' policy was reaffirmed, with Britain agreeing to increase her military contribution in the Far East and Pacific after the war in Europe had been won. Before entering Fortress Europe, the two allies agreed on essential preparations in the air and at sea. Firstly, the U-boat scourge must be removed from the Atlantic if the US build-up in Britain was to be maintained. Also, the Anglo-US strategic bombing forces were to mount an offensive against Germany, the priorities being her war industries and the morale of her people.

When it came to deciding where the Allied ground forces should strike next, the differences of the previous year resurfaced. The Americans regarded Churchill's Mediterranean strategy as peripheral and maintained their suspicion that he had a hidden agenda. They therefore continued to press for Round Up as the main operation for 1943. The British argument was that this might have been feasible if Tunisia had been secured before the end of 1942. As it was, given the success of the Axis deployment to the country, it was clear that the campaign here was likely to continue until the spring. The increasing Allied commitment to Tunisia was to the detriment of Bolero and by the time the troops and amphibious shipping were returned to Britain and retrained it would be too late to mount Round Up before the autumn, when the weather and tides would not be favourable. Instead, they proposed that the primary objective for 1943 should be to knock Italy out of the war. As a first step, Sicily should be invaded in July.

The American chiefs of staff realized that the truth of the matter was that their more experienced opposite numbers were better briefed and had the arguments at their fingertips. They were forced to accept the British view. As a sop to the Americans, it was agreed that there should be a major cross-Channel raid during the summer to inflict damage on Germany's Atlantic defences in France. A plan would also be drawn up for the seizure of the Cotentin peninsula in north-western France. Casablanca taught the US chiefs of staff a bitter lesson. From now on they would be briefed as comprehensively as the British. In addition, as more American forces crossed the Atlantic, they would come to be in the majority, enabling them to dictate to their ally. Such are the vagaries of coalition warfare.

By mid January the Axis had built up sizeable forces, including 100,000 German troops, in western Tunisia. These came under the umbrella of Hans-Jürgen von Arnim's Fifth Panzer Army. In eastern Tunisia, and safely back behind the French-built defences of the Mareth Line, was Rommel and his Panzerarmee Afrika. This was renamed First Italian Army, and the Italian General Vittorio Ambrosio appointed Supremo over both armies, although it was still Kesselring in Rome who was pulling the strings. Montgomery continued to regroup on the other side of the Tunisan border, while First Army in Tunisia now had three corps in line – British, US, and a poorly equipped French corps. They were holding a 150-mile front running down through the Eastern Dorsale to Fondouk.

The Axis strategy in Tunisia was to be one of active defence through pre-emptive attacks. The first of these spoiling operations was mounted by von Arnim. Designed to secure all the passes in the Eastern Dorsale, it was a successful blow against the still ill-equipped French. Meanwhile, in the southern part of the front, American troops carried out raids with varying success. Von Arnim struck again at the end of the month and drove the French out of Faid. In mid February came a more ambitious Axis operation. Montgomery had begun his advance from Tripoli on 7 February, but was slowed by heavy rains. Rommel therefore took his armour to strike at the Americans in the Gafsa area, while von Arnim attacked further north astride their boundary with the French. The still inexperienced US forces were thrown into confusion and lost the vital Kasserine Pass through the Western Dorsale. British forces were sent down from the north and succeeded in preventing further Axis exploitation.

During this time Eisenhower had had his hands full, not just with the campaign in Tunisia, but also dealing with the political problems of French North Africa. After Torch, Admiral Darlan, who happened to be in Algiers at the time, was made high commissioner, with Giraud as commander of the French forces. Darlan was assassinated by a young French royalist on 25 December and Giraud took his place. De Gaulle, furious at not being given prior information about Torch, now made approaches to Giraud, who rebuffed them. At the Casablanca Conference the Allies

A Sherman tank of the Eighth Army during the advance to the Mareth Line. During 1943 this became the most commonly used tank by both the Americans and the British. Well armoured and equipped with a 75mm gun, it also had an excellent automotive performance. Its one disadvantage was that the ammunition stowage was such that it often caught fire when hit. For this reason the crews called it the 'Ronson lighter'.

agreed that the two men must co-operate, but their mutual antipathy and arrogance made them difficult bedfellows, and much of Eisenhower's time was spent smoothing their ruffled feathers. In order to lighten his burden, Alexander was appointed to command 18th Army Group to co-ordinate the operations of the First and Eighth Armies.

While von Arnim continued to mount spoiling attacks in western Tunisia, Rommel prepared to strike at the British Eighth Army, which had now crossed from Libya. Ultra told Montgomery of Rommel's intentions and the First Italian Army was rebuffed at Medenine on 6 March. It was Rommel's last flourish, for he left Africa three days later. Montgomery prepared to attack the Mareth Line; US II Corps, now under command of George S. Patton, who had commanded the Moroccan Torch landings, began to attack in western Tunisia. After almost a week's fighting, Montgomery succeeded in outflanking the Mareth Line and advanced north to the next Axis defensive line at Wadi Akarit. Simultaneously, Patton continued to press foward into the Eastern Dorsale.

By now the Axis supply lines across the Mediterranean had been almost severed by air and sea attack. Yet their forces in Tunisia, whose terrain favoured the defence, continued to fight tenaciously. Montgomery broke through at Wadi Akarit on 6 April, but was unable to prevent the First Italian Army from withdrawing to yet another defensive position further north, this time at Enfidaville. Two weeks later von Arnim launched further spoiling attacks against First Army, but was repulsed. Montgomery was unable to break through at Enfidaville and Alexander decided that the main offensive should now be undertaken by First Army, with some of the Eighth Army's armour transferred to it. After a number of preliminary attacks, the final offensive was launched on 6 May. Five days later the Axis forces surrendered, no fewer than 240,000 of them going into captivity.

Tunisia has often been regarded, at least in British eyes, as almost a footnote to the desert campaigns, but it proved to be a prolonged and grim struggle, especially during the winter months. As Stalingrad was the turning-point on the Eastern Front, so Tunisia was in the West. For, with North Africa now cleared of Axis forces, the assault on western Europe itself could finally begin. Tunisia was also the first campaign of 1939–45 in which the forces of Britain and America fought side by side. Furthermore, there were significant lessons to be learnt for the future. Not the least of these concerned armour.

In 1940, after the success of the German blitzkrieg in the west, both Britain and America began a vast expansion of their tank forces. Indeed, the US army aimed to create no fewer than fifty armoured divisions. The hilly Tunisian terrain highlighted the need for infantry–tank co-operation, however, and, recognizing that even closer countryside was likely in Europe, emphasis was placed on getting the right balance between the two arms within the armoured divisions. There was renewed realization that the infantry divisions also needed plenty of dedicated tank support. The result was to slow and even halt the creation of further armoured divisions, especially since the Allies came to believe that their primary role was break-out and pursuit.

For the assault on Sicily the Allies were faced with another major amphibious operation. The inhibiting factor was landing-craft availability, and it was this that prevented Husky from being mounted until July. The final plan called for landings in south-east Sicily by the US Seventh Army commanded by Patton and Montgomery's Eighth Army. They would be preceded by an airborne assault. As a preliminary, the small island of Pantellaria, which lies midway between Tunisia and Sicily, was subjected to a prolonged air bombardment. Such was its intensity that, as the British assault forces reached its shore on 11 June, the Italian garrison surrendered without firing a shot. Pantellaria could thus be used as a forward air base.

At the conclusion of the Tunisian campaign the Allies held another strategic conference, this time in Washington, DC. This confirmed that Round Up was no longer possible in 1943, and that the invasion of Sicily should be the next step. This, however, was to be exploited in such a way as to knock Italy out of the war, which inevitably pointed to invasion of the Italian mainland.

The Axis, partially duped by Allied deception measures, believed that the next attacks would be against Sardinia, northern Italy, or Greece. Hitler also feared that his ally was about to collapse, and formed HQ Army Group B based at Munich. This was to be prepared to co-ordinate operations to secure northern Italy. Forces were also sent to Kesselring in southern Italy. To deal with the Balkan threat, he appointed Rommel C-in-C South-East. As for Sicily, the bulk of the defenders were lowgrade Italian troops – the best had been lost in North Africa or were on the Eastern Front. They were, however, stiffened by two German divisions.

The Sicily landings took place on 10 July. The airborne operation was not a success, largely because of high winds and poor navigation, and many of the paratroops were captured or drowned in the sea. The main landings were achieved without great difficulty. Once the beachheads had been secured, Montgomery began to push north towards Messina, while Patton advanced west and north-west to clear the remainder of the island. Eighth Army found itself up against the German divisions, which took maximum advantage of the mountainous terrain in the east of the island. Consequently, Montgomery, to his frustration, found it slow going. In contrast, Patton rapidly cleared western Sicily and then turned east, vowing to reach Messina before the British.

Hitler remained worried about the state of Italy, and on 19 July met Mussolini in northern Italy in an attempt to boost his flagging morale. It was too late. Six days later, the Fascist Grand Council, now totally disillusioned by the ever-worsening situation, arrested their leader. At the request of King Victor Emmanuel, Marshal Pietro Badoglio formed a new government, which was charged with exploring ways of making peace with the Allies. The fall of Mussolini, however, triggered the deployment of the German forces under Army Group B into northern Italy, with Rommel being brought back from Greece to command them.

The Axis forces began to evacuate Sicily on 3 August. Two weeks later Patton's troops entered Messina, but the German rearguard had already departed. Two days previously, Allied aircraft bombed Rome for the second time during the Sicilian campaign, and the Italian government now declared their capital an open city. They had already sent an emissary to neutral Portugal to open negotiations with the Allies, who insisted that Italy's surrender must be unconditional.

Simultaneously, another strategic conference was taking place in Quebec. Round Up, now renamed Overlord, was scheduled for 1 May 1944, and it was generally agreed that American Chief of Staff General George C. Marshall should command, leaving Eisenhower to look after the Mediterranean theatre. If for some reason Overlord did not prove feasible, Jupiter, the attack on Norway, would be considered in its place. Planning was also initiated for landings in the south of France to support Overlord. The Allies had already committed themselves to invading the Italian mainland, and the aim of this campaign, with Italy virtually out of the war, was to keep as many German forces tied down there as possible.

While Churchill wanted the Italian landings to take place as far north as possible, Eisenhower and his subordinates insisted that they should be in the south, within easy air range of Sicily. Montgomery's Eighth Army was to cross the Straits of Messina and land on the toe of Italy. Then the US Fifth Army, which contained both American and British troops and was commanded by Mark Clark, would land south of Naples, at Salerno – Montgomery, it was hoped, having successfully distracted the Axis forces. Much, however, depended on the secret armistice negotiations with the Italians. General Giuseppe Castellano, their emissary, had returned to Rome on 20 August armed with an Allied ultimatum that

American, British, and French soldiers bring in German and Italian prisoners at the end of the campaign in Tunisia.

the Italian government agree to the terms within ten days. Not until 1 September did the government accept them, and two days later Castellano signed the armistice in Sicily. It would come into effect on 8 September, the day of the Salerno landings, but would be kept secret until then.

The Germans knew what was in the wind and had made preparations to disarm the Italian forces as soon as the armistice came into being. They were also well aware that the Allies intended to land in southern Italy – the concentrations of amphibious shipping could not be disguised. There was, however, a debate on how the Germans should conduct the campaign in Italy. Kesselring believed that the terrain favoured a defence south of Rome and that this would help frustrate any Allied designs on the Balkans. Rommel, on the other hand, believed that this would lay the German forces open to being outflanked from the sea and that southern Italy should be evacuated. For the time being Hitler made no ruling, leaving Rommel with eight divisions in the north and Kesselring with ten in the south.

On 3 September, the day the Italian armistice was signed, the Eighth Army duly landed on the Italian toe and, in the face of minimal resistance, apart from demolitions, began to advance north. Two days later the Salerno force set sail from North Africa. On the 8th Eisenhower used Radio Algiers to announce the Italian surrender. The aim of knocking Hitler's ally out of the war had been achieved, but, at the operational level, Eisenhower's announcement was to create problems, since the landings at Salerno had not yet taken place.

Mussolini confers with one of his officers after the Allied invasion of Sicily. It was this that resulted in his removal from power by the Fascist Grand Council.

CHAPTER SIX

The Liberation of Russia (1943–4)

T-34 TANKS on the rampage. In the aftermath of Stalingrad the Red Army took to the offensive all along the Eastern Front. The contrast between its performance now and that of two years earlier, during the German invasion, was most marked. The Red Army took the lessons of the disasters of 1941 to heart. This, and its overwhelming numerical superiority over the Wehrmacht, meant that the end result could never be in doubt.

THE LIBERATION OF RUSSIA 1943–4

The Soviet tanks thrust into the German advanced formations at full speed and penetrated the tank screen. The T-34s were knocking out Tigers at extremely close range, since their powerful guns and massive armour no longer gave them an advantage in close combat. The tanks of both sides were in the closest possible contact. There was neither time nor room to disengage from the enemy and re-form in battle order, or operate in formation. The shells fired at extremely close range pierced not only the side armour but the frontal armour of the fighting vehicles. At such range there was no protection in armour, and the length of the gun barrels was no longer decisive. Frequently, when a tank was hit, its ammunition and fuel blew up, and torn off turrets were flung through the air over dozens of yards.

LT GEN. PAVEL A. ROTMISTROV ON THE TANK BATTLE AT PROKHOROVKA, KURSK, JULY 1943

THE DESTRUCTION of the German Sixth Army at Stalingrad meant that the Red Army could now set about the liberation of western Russia. It had learnt much from the previous twenty months' fighting and had been entirely re-formed, both in organization and tactics. The emphasis was now on maximum concentration of armour and artillery. Tank armies made up of tank and mechanized corps were now being formed, while the Stavka kept huge numbers of

Russian infantry prepare to move forward to the next bound. The Red Army soldier was renowned for his endurance. Compared to the soldiers of the western Allies, his wants were few.

Manhandling a Russian Model 42 45mm anti-tank gun into position. It was based on the PAK37, a number of which were purchased from Germany before the war. Capable of firing high explosive, as well as anti-armour shells, the Model 42 was a highly effective close support weapon for the infantry.

guns under its direct control to deploy for offensives. Furthermore, air armies of 200–300 aircraft were created and allocated to fronts, with the Stavka holding additional air corps to be used as reinforcements.

Everything was now directed towards breakthrough operations. The first phase was to consist of a concentrated artillery bombardment, during which time small probing attacks would be made, to identify weak points in the German defences. The break-in would be made by infantry, supported by tanks. If the defences were in depth, a second echelon would be used to complete the breakthrough. As this was achieved, the tank armies would be released. Operating in what were termed 'mobile groups', they would break out and penetrate as fast and deeply as they could before casualties and lack of fuel forced them to a halt. Where possible, the breakthroughs would be achieved in a number of places to keep the German reserves off balance. For the same reason, the Red Army also adopted a policy of rolling offensives. As one began to run out of momentum another would be launched elsewhere. The Russians also placed increasing emphasis on the use of deception (*maskirovka*) to further surprise. Likewise, they recognized the importance of co-ordinating the activities of their partisans behind the German lines with the main offensives.

The Red Army had begun to mount fresh offensives before the Stalingrad pocket

Georgi Zhukov was one of the outstanding Soviet commanders of the war. He epitomized the ruthlessness with which the senior Russian officers were imbued from 1942 onwards. There could be no excuse for failure and those who failed were often reduced to the ranks and sent to punishment battalions in which life expectancy was low.

had been reduced. In the Caucasus the now over-extended German Army Group A was attacked on New Year's Day 1943 and soon forced to give up many of its gains of the previous year. An operation to lift the siege of Leningrad was partially successful in that the Germans were cleared from the south shore of Lake Ladoga, enabling the resupply of the city's defenders to be improved. The pressure on Army Group B also continued, with the Voronezh Front attacking across the Don and encircling the Second Hungarian and Eighth Italian Armies. This triggered a general German withdrawal to west of the river, but the Russian pressure continued. They now had the recapture of Rostov-on-Don, Kursk and Kharkov in their sights.

While the remnants of Army Group A began to withdraw across the Straits of Kerch into the Crimea, the Soviet fronts west of Stalingrad maintained their attacks, regaining both Rostov and Kursk. There was also another offensive in the north, this time to remove the Demyansk salient north of Smolensk. All this forced a reluctant Hitler to sanction further withdrawals, but when von Manstein, now commanding the reconstituted Army Group South, voluntarily gave up Kharkov, Hitler was furious. He went straight to von Manstein's HQ, intending to sack him. Von Manstein, however, pointed out that by shortening his line he had been able to create additional Panzer reserves. Noting that Nikolai Vatutin's South-west Front was becoming over-extended, he proposed to counter-attack, to which Hitler eventually agreed.

Von Manstein launched his counter-stroke on 20 February. The Russians had believed that, coming on top of the victory at Stalingrad, the recent German withdrawals indicated that they were no longer capable of offensive effort and were taken by surprise. So over-extended was Vatutin that his mobile group was down to a mere twenty-five tanks when von Manstein struck. Even so, he was convinced that the Germans were merely trying to cover their withdrawal, and continued to advance westwards, thus making himself even more vulnerable.

The Russian situation was aggravated when Vatutin's northern neighbour, Filipp Golikov and his Voronezh Front, counter-attacked the Germans and was bloodily repulsed. Vatutin was now forced to withdraw and the Germans were able to recapture Kharkov, albeit after bloody street fighting. Von Manstein wanted to press on further east, but the spring thaw now arrived, bringing its usual temporary halt to active operations.

The operations around Kharkov had shown that the German army in Russia was still powerful and full of fight. Among the troops which played a major role in them was the SS Panzer Corps. The Waffen-SS, which was ultimately under the control of Heinrich Himmler and had a separate code of discipline, had been distrusted by the army during the early Blitzkrieg campaigns because of its inferior training. It was on the Eastern Front, however, that it began to come into its own. SS formations were generally better equipped than their army counterparts and their troops were more ruthless. Instilled with National Socialism to a degree that the army never was, the Waffen-SS fought the Russians with its own brand of fanaticism and ferocity. Army commanders might be suspicious of what the SS men stood for, but they admired their fighting spirit. Indeed, as the war on the Eastern Front dragged on, the Waffen-SS formations were increasingly used as 'fire brigades' which were deployed to critical spots to throw back Russian attacks.

The original German plan for the early summer of 1943 was to continue the offensive operations in the Kharkov area. Hitler, however, noted the huge salient further north, which jutted into the German lines and was based on Kursk. He

Coping with 'General Mud'. The spring thaw and the autumn rains placed a brake on mobile operations on the Eastern Front.

therefore decided that this must be eradicated. Not only would this considerably shorten the German line, but it would, he hoped, result in huge numbers of Russian casualties. This would delay the Red Army's build-up for further offensives. The salient was to be attacked by the Fourth Panzer Army from the north and Ninth Army from the south.

Preparations for Operation Citadel began towards the end of March, but the Russians soon became aware of them. This was partly through their very effective Lucy spy ring, which was based in Switzerland, and also from intelligence officers who had infiltrated the German lines. The Stavka was tempted to mount pre-emptive attacks, but Stalin ruled these out. Instead, the fronts within the salient

The PzKw VI Tiger. Its very thick frontal armour and 88mm gun made it a formidable adversary on both the Eastern and Western Fronts. It was, however, in defence that it was most effective.

The Ferdinand tank destroyer Jagdpanzer (tank hunter) was the German term for this type of armoured fighting vehicle. It was used to support conventional tanks in the attack and was placed in sniping positions in defence.

were to construct concentric defensive lines. Behind these armour would be concentrated for a counterstroke designed to cripple the attacking German forces. German air reconnaissance soon noted these preparations and Hitler's commanders urged him to allow them to attack sooner rather than later. Hitler, however, was more concerned in building up the largest possible assault force. Worse, in early May he decided to postpone Citadel still further to allow new weapons to be deployed.

Hitler had particularly in mind three new armoured fighting vehicles (AFVs). Two were tanks – the PzKw V Panther, and the larger PzKw VI Tiger, which had made its combat debut in Tunisia. These, especially the Tiger, were more heavily armoured and more powerfully armed than any other tank of the time. There was, too, the Ferdinand tank destroyer. This represented a new range of AFVs. By 1943 the loss of German tanks, especially in the Eastern Front, had risen at such a rate that production could not match it. The solution was AFVs with no turrets and a limited traverse gun mounted in the hull. These assault guns and tank destroyers were very much

PzKw VI

The anatomy of a Tiger tank's armour. The top priorities for protection were, in descending order, the front, sides, and underneath (to combat the mine threat). The top and rear were the least armoured since these were the least likely parts to be exposed to the enemy.

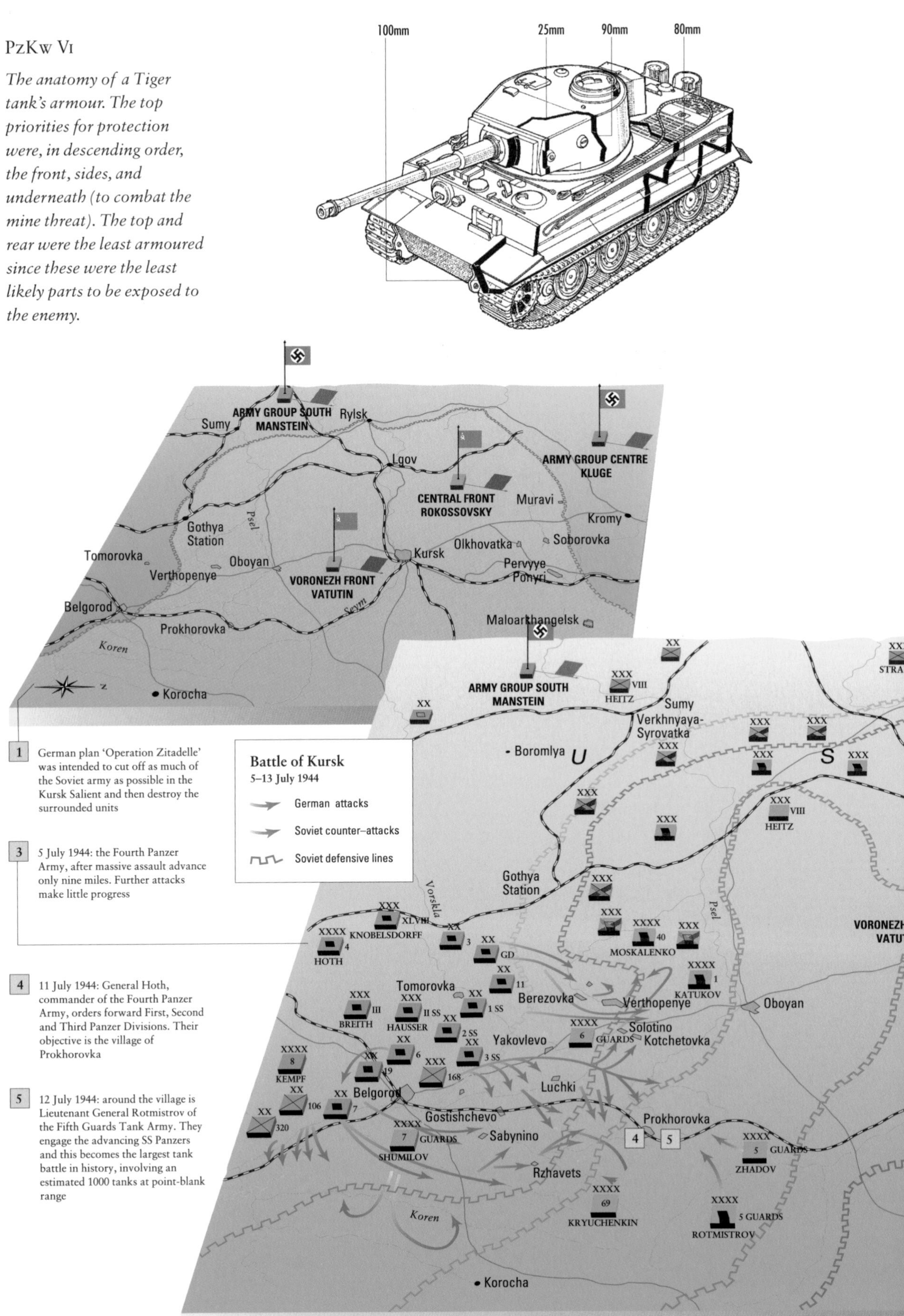

1 German plan 'Operation Zitadelle' was intended to cut off as much of the Soviet army as possible in the Kursk Salient and then destroy the surrounded units

3 5 July 1944: the Fourth Panzer Army, after massive assault advance only nine miles. Further attacks make little progress

4 11 July 1944: General Hoth, commander of the Fourth Panzer Army, orders forward First, Second and Third Panzer Divisions. Their objective is the village of Prokhorovka

5 12 July 1944: around the village is Lieutenant General Rotmistrov of the Fifth Guards Tank Army. They engage the advancing SS Panzers and this becomes the largest tank battle in history, involving an estimated 1000 tanks at point-blank range

Russian infantry and tanks counter-attack during the closing phases of the battle of Kursk.

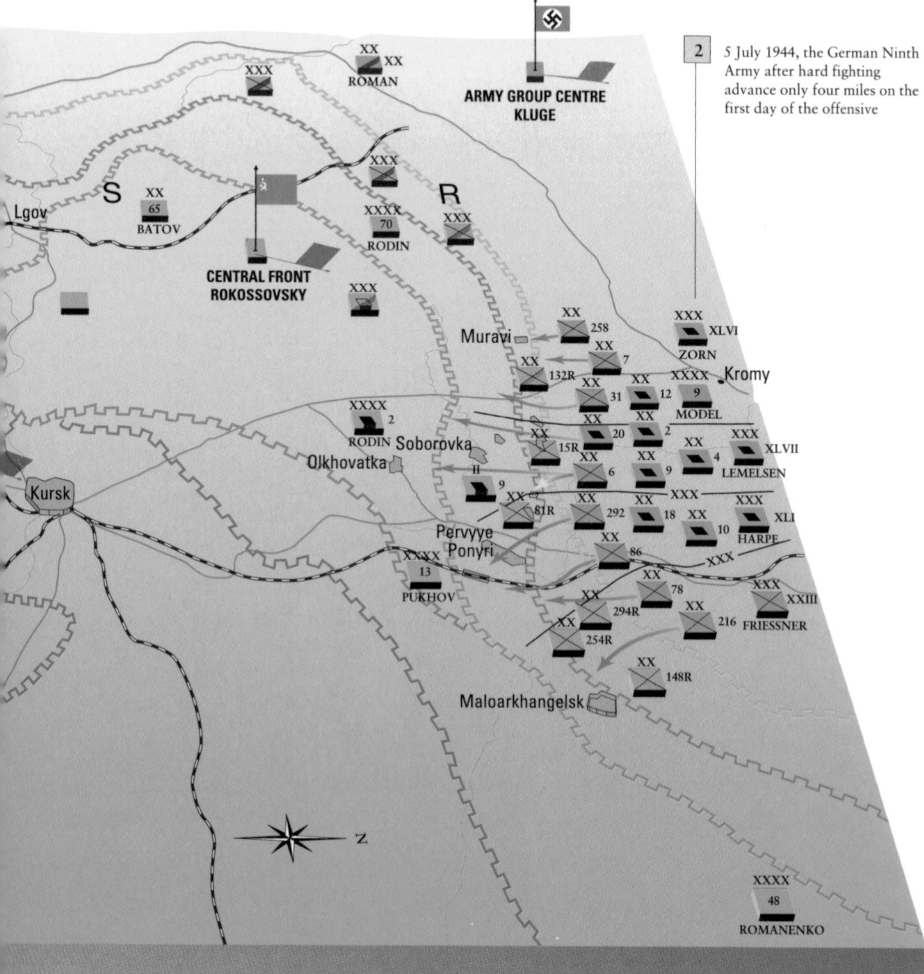

Kursk

Essentially it consisted of two separate battles, as Army Group Centre and Army Group South attempted to eradicate the salient through attacks from the north and south respectively. Apart from being well aware of Operation Citadel, the Russians also had the advantage of operating on interior lines.

simpler to produce than the conventional tank, and hence could be used in part to offset the increasing German numerical inferiority in AFVs.

The German offensive on the Kursk salient eventually began on the afternoon of 4 July with massive air and artillery bombardments. They had assembled a total of 900,000 men and 2,500 tanks and assault guns, but the Russian defenders outnumbered them with 1,300,000 men and 3,000 tanks. That night the German engineers cleared lanes through the Russian minefields. At dawn Fourth Panzer and Ninth Armies attacked. They initially made some progress, but the sheer depth of the Russian defences began to take its toll. By the end of 6 July Walther Model's Ninth Army was at a standstill. Hermann Hoth struggled on in the south for the next six days before the Russian armoured reserves mounted their counterstroke. The subsequent fighting was centred on the village of Prokhorovka north of Belgorod. No fewer than 1,300 tanks and assault guns, two thirds of them Russian, were involved, making it the largest tank battle of the war.

On that same day, 12 July, the West and Bryansk Fronts launched an attack against the rear of Ninth Army. The following day Hitler called off Citadel. Conscious of his mounting casualties and the fact that the western Allies were ashore on Sicily, he finally accepted that his armies in the east must go on to the defensive. As if to reinforce this, the Russians threatened Hoth, with an offensive directed on Kharkov. This was liberated for the second and final time on 23 August. By that time the Kursk salient had been eradicated, but by the Russians.

The Russian counter-offensives at Kursk were the start of a series of rolling attacks which were to take in the whole of the Eastern Front, apart from the extreme north. Stalin was determined to allow the German armies no respite and laid down that the next task was to be the liberation of eastern Ukraine and the destruction of Army Group South. To this end, once the operation around Kharkov had been completed, the Voronezh and Steppe Fronts were to advance to the Dnieper and secure bridgeheads across it. They were to be joined by other fronts armed with the missions of liberating Kiev and securing the lower Dnieper. Eventually, Army Group South was to find itself facing no less than nineteen thrusts by eight fronts. To distract neighbouring Army Group Centre, the Kalinin, West, and Bryansk Fronts were charged with assaulting the northern part of its sector. Here the line had been quiet for some months, enabling the Germans to construct formidable defences. These fronts were therefore unable to make much progress during August, but they did prevent von Kluge from passing reserves to von Manstein in the south. This was especially important since Hitler had warned him, after the arrest of Mussolini, that he must be prepared to send divisions to Italy.

Indeed, Hitler was facing a dilemma. He had, in early August, ordered the construction of new defences to the rear. The East Wall, otherwise known as the Panther Line, ran from the Estonian border almost due south to the Dnieper and then along the river before turning south to Melitopol on the Sea of Azov. But he decreed that there were to be no withdrawals to this as yet. Even so, von Manstein, under increasing pressure and short of reserves, gave Hitler a stark choice when the

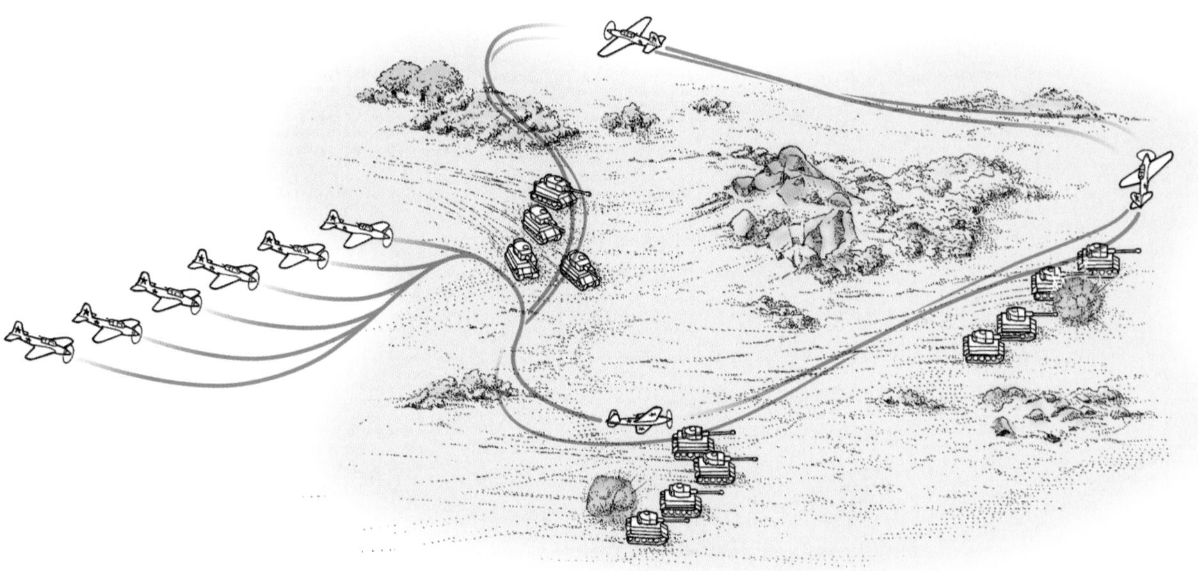

These diagrammatic representations show the ways in which Ilyushin Il-2 ground attack aircraft (Shturmovik) operated against German tanks. They were heavily armoured, which enabled them to carry out their attacks at very low level. One tactic (ABOVE) *was for a flight to attack the line astern and approach the target from the rear, flying in a roughly circular path. They would normally attack with anti-tank rockets. A second option* (BELOW) *took advantage of the fact that tanks were less heavily armoured at the sides than in the front and provided a larger target. The flight would jink one at a time backwards and forwards over the column. Tight turns meant that it was very difficult for flak guns to track and engage the aircraft.*

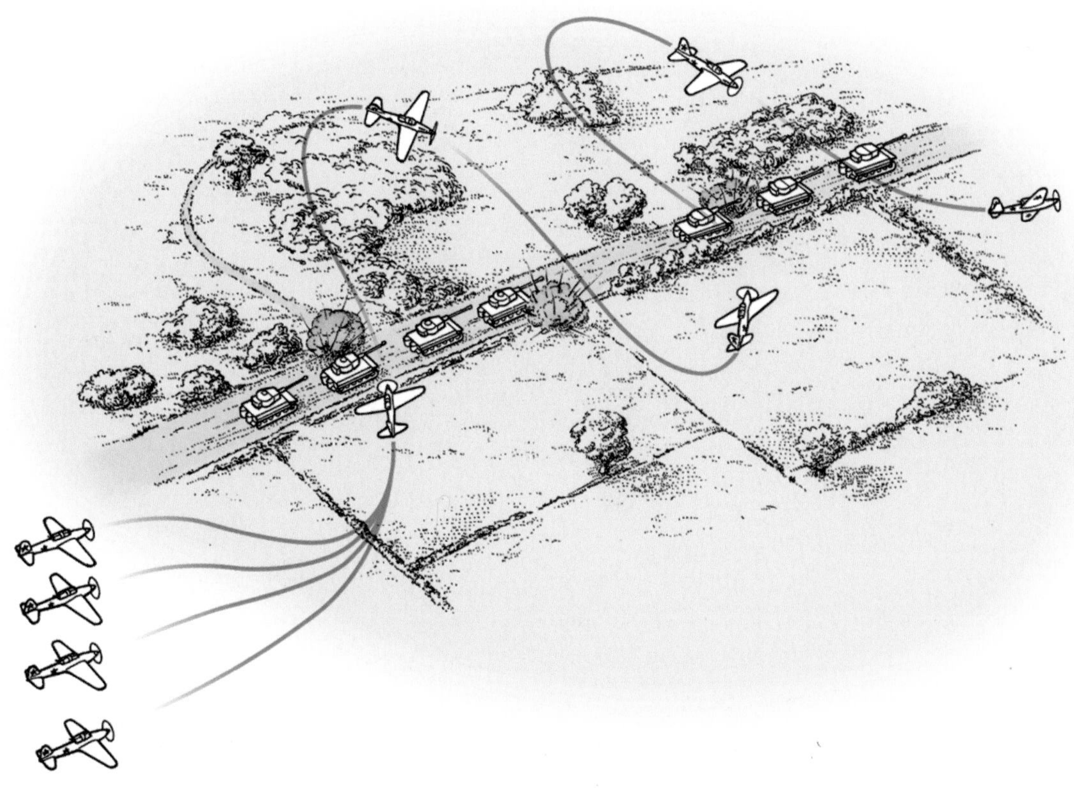

The beginning of a German counter-attack. On the left lies a knocked out T-34 tank, and on the right an assault gun, another means of providing infantry with intimate fire support.

Führer visited him at his headquarters. Unless Army Group South was quickly reinforced it would have to withdraw behind the Dnieper if it was not to be destroyed. Hitler, still preoccupied by events in the Mediterranean, would not make a decision. Two weeks later, on 8 September, von Manstein met Hitler again. This time Ewald von Kleist, whose Army Group A still had a toehold in the Caucasus, on the Taman peninsula, was also present. Hitler permitted Taman to be evacuated and allowed von Manstein a limited withdrawal back to the Dnieper.

The day after this meeting, Stalin stated that those soldiers involved in forcing the first crossings over the Dnieper would be awarded the Soviet Union's highest decoration, Hero of the Soviet Union. With von Manstein now trying to get his army group back across the river intact, a race developed. The result was a virtual dead heat. While von Manstein was successful, the Voronezh and then South-west Fronts also seized crossings over the river. This was even though their leading armies had left their bridging equipment far behind and had to rely on makeshift rafts.

This meant that in the south the East Wall had been compromised. Worse, the Russian sweep through the Donets basin cut off the remnants of Army Group A in the Crimea. The pressure on Army Group Centre increased, too, during September, with Smolensk being liberated on the 23rd.

On 12 October 1943, as Army Group Centre also fell back on the East Wall, Günther von Kluge, its commander, wrote a personal letter to Hitler. He stated that his army group was now 200,000 men under strength and what replacements he was receiving were poorly trained and of low calibre. Army Group South was in a similar parlous situation, with some divisions down to little more than a thousand men. Hitler, however, did not reply; von Kluge himself was badly injured in a traffic accident two weeks later and was replaced by Ernst Busch. But the Red Army, too, was suffering and was to lose 2.4 million men during the course of 1943. Indeed, the Germans could take some comfort from the fact that among the soldiers they were capturing were some who were little more than

Exhausted German troops withdraw with their wounded, autumn 1943. Every effort was made to evacuate wounded, since to leave them to the enemy was very bad for morale. This was a fact recognized by all armies.

children and others who were old men. None of these had been in the army for more than a few weeks.

The Soviet pressure continued throughout the autumn. In early October the attacks against Army Group Centre were expanded northwards across its boundary with Army Group North. The East Wall had now become meaningless as far as the other two army groups were concerned and they were driven west of it. Only furious counter-attacks, which knocked the Russians temporarily off balance, and the autumn rains prevented a total breakthough.

The one part of the Eastern Front which had remained quiet throughout the summer and autumn of 1943 was the extreme north; there Leningrad remained under siege from the Finnish South-east Army, which continued to be anchored on the 1939 Russo–Finnish border, and the German Eighteenth Army, which was

German supply convoy on a bleak Russian steppe, winter 1943–4. The Germans made much use of the panje, *a heavy Polish cart widely used in agriculture.*

investing the city from the south. Indeed, this was the only German formation still east of the Panther Line. It had, however, been forced to send most of its armour to help stem the Russian onslaughts in the south, and was now to be subjected to a fresh offensive designed finally to relieve Leningrad. Von Kuechler, commanding Army Group North, wanted to pull the Eighteenth Army back behind the Panther Line before the Russian attack took place, but Hitler forbade it, especially since the army commander had voiced his confidence at being able to hold on in his present positions. Furthermore, to withdraw from Leningrad would leave the Finns totally isolated.

The offensive opened on 14 January 1944 and Eighteenth Army was soon under unbearable pressure, which included 35,000 partisans harrying its lines of communication. The Moscow–Leningrad railway was cleared on the 26th and this

marked the final lifting of Leningrad's 900-day siege, the longest in modern times. The fighting continued, however, and when von Kuechler eventually allowed Eighteenth Army to withdraw to the River Luga, still over fifty miles east of the Panther Line, Hitler promptly sacked him, appointing Model, who had, in the aftermath of Citadel, established a reputation for himself as a general who would dispute every inch of ground. But even Model could not prevent the loss of further ground and in mid February was finally given permission to withdraw to the Panther Line. The Russians had also continued to attack elsewhere, giving the Germans no respite on any part of the front. Most serious was an offensive by Vatutin's 1st Ukrainian Front astride the boundary between Army Groups Centre and South. In the course of two days' fighting at the end of January they reached the pre-war Soviet–Polish border in the area of the River Styr.

The Russians now turned to liberating the remainder of the Ukraine. Once again this was achieved through a series of rolling offensives. Among the partisans operating here were groups dedicated to setting up an independent Ukraine. They had originally offered their services to the Germans, but Hitler was not interested in an autonomous Ukraine and so these partisans turned against the Germans while continuing to fight the Russian forces. At the end of February, they ambushed Nikolai Vatutin, who had by now established himself as one of the outstanding front commanders, and mortally wounded him. First Ukrainian Front was therefore taken over by Zhukov.

By the spring of 1944 the Russians were approaching the borders of Hungary and Romania and there were signs that Germany's allies were beginning to crack. German troops were therefore sent into Hungary to ensure her continued loyalty, as well as to secure the Balaton oilfields in the west of the country. Marshal Ion Antonescu of Romania flew to Berlin to ask that his troops now be allowed to concentrate on the defence of their own country. To this Hitler agreed, probably thinking that this would help to keep Romania on his side, especially since her oilfields were still supplying a significant proportion of Germany's needs. The Finns, now totally cut off from the main body of the German forces on the Eastern Front, sent a delegation to Moscow in April to seek an armistice. Stalin would only agree to this if their mutual border of March 1940 was restored, Finland expelled all German forces on her territory, and paid $600 million in reparations over five years. The parliament in Helsinki rejected this and the Finns fought on.

The Russian answer to the Tiger was the JS-2, named after Stalin himself. This weighed 46 tons, 10 tons less than the Tiger, and was armed with an 85mm gun. It entered service in 1944.

On 1 May 1944 Stalin announced his intentions for the coming summer. His main aim was to liberate Poland, Czechoslovakia and the 'fraternal' Slav nations. The cornerstone was to be Operation Bagration, whose object was nothing less than the destruction of the German Army Group Centre, which now occupied a vast salient, with its southern flank lying on the virtually impassable Pripet marshes. Not only would this enable Poland to be liberated, but it would also satisfy the request of the western Allies for an offensive to coincide with the long-awaited cross-Channel invasion of France. Two diversionary operations were to be mounted as part of Bagration. A feint in the north was designed to knock Finland finally out of the war and tie down

Contrasting reactions to liberation: Red soldiers welcomed with flowers by peasant women (OPPOSITE). *A Russian woman* (ABOVE) *searches for her loved ones, victims of another German atrocity. The Red Army would wreak terrible vengeance when it entered German territory.*

Army Group North, while, in the south, a thrust towards Lvov would similarly prevent Army Group South from sending reinforcements to its neighbour. *Maskirovka* also played a large part. Deception measures were put in place to make the Germans believe that the main operation would be towards the Balkans. A threat was also posed to northern Norway. This intentionally dovetailed with the western Allies' strategic deception plan Bodyguard (see Chapter 7), which also included an attack on Norway.

The final Bagration conference was held during 22–23 May and all the fronts involved were represented. They were told that the northern feint would be launched on 9 June and that the main offensive would follow twelve days later, on the third anniversary of the German invasion.

On the German side, Hitler had sacked more of his commanders on the grounds that they had withdrawn instead of standing and fighting. Two of his leading field marshals – Erich von Manstein and Ewald von Kleist – were removed from their posts for failing to hold up the Russian advance towards the Balkans. Neither would be re-employed. Increasingly, Hitler turned to men who were committed Nazis and who could be relied upon to obey his orders to the letter. Now, as May wore on,

Ernst Busch, commanding Army Group Centre, became increasingly convinced that the Russians were intending to attack him. Hitler, however, refused to allow him to shorten his line by withdrawing from much of the huge salient which Army Group Centre was holding. While he agreed that an offensive was likely, he was convinced that it would be directed towards Romania and the Balkans.

The Russian offensive against the Finns was launched on 10 June. The contrast with the performance of the Red Army three and a half years earlier during the first Russo–Finnish war was most marked. This time, attacking on both sides of Lake Ladoga, the Russians quickly placed the Finns under impossible pressure and the disputed port of Viipuri soon fell. German forces in the country did come to their aid, but only after the Finnish president had signed an agreement that his country would not make a separate peace with the Soviet Union.

The Warsaw uprising, August 1944. Members of the Polish Home Army bringing up supplies of mortar bombs. Some are wearing bits of captured German uniform, but their armbands distinguish them as Poles.

Bagration itself was launched on time. The Red Army had assembled no fewer than 1,254,000 men, 2,715 tanks, 1,355 assault guns, and over 24,000 guns, heavy mortars, and multiple-launch rocket systems. Army Group Centre had a mere 500,000 men and 630 tanks to defend nearly 700 miles of front. The Russians also enjoyed air superiority. The initial attack was made by 1st Baltic Front, after a short but intense pre-dawn artillery barrage, in the Vitebsk area. The Germans here were caught largely by surprise and, by the end of the day, the Russians had penetrated to a depth of 7.5 miles. The following day, after a series of probing attacks, five other breakthrough operations were mounted against the German salient. Within a week the heart of Army Group Centre had been torn open, as the Russians crossed the River Beresina and thrust towards the Polish border.

Hitler, whose attention up until now had been largely held by the fighting in Normandy, reacted by sacking Busch and replacing him with the ever dependable Model, who had been moved from Army Group North to Army Group North Ukraine and was now expected to command both. Georg Lindemann, commanding Army Group North, also lost his command after Hitler forbade him to withdraw so as to protect his ever more exposed southern flank. These measures, however, were not enough to halt the remorseless Russian advance. On 4 July they liberated Minsk, after trapping sizeable German forces to the east of the city. By the time this pocket was reduced a week later, with 57,000 German troops being made prisoner, the four Soviet fronts involved in Bagration had destroyed the equivalent of twenty-eight German divisions.

On 10 July the 2nd Baltic Front attacked Army Group North and, later joined by 3rd Baltic and the Leningrad Front, began to press the Germans back into Estonia and Latvia. Three days later, Ivan Koniev's 1st Ukrainian Front attacked towards Lvov. All this meant that Army Group Centre could expect no help from its neighbours and on 20 July 1st Belorussian Front reached the pre-war Polish border west of Kovel.

It was now that Poland's future became a matter of debate. After Germany had invaded Russia in June 1941, Stalin agreed to release the Poles he held as prisoners of war. Under the leadership of General Wladislaw Anders, these Poles, who were in camps in Siberia, made their own way to the Middle East, where they formed an army corps which became part of the British Eighth Army in Italy. This left several Polish officers unaccounted for, but Moscow denied all knowledge of them. Then, in April 1943, the Germans announced the discovery of a mass grave, containing the bodies of 4,500 Polish officers, at Katyn, near Smolensk, and claimed that the Soviet secret police, the NKVD, had been responsible. The Russians immediately accused Berlin of this atrocity, and the British government, unwilling to create friction with its ally, supported this. However, the Germans then arranged for a committee to investigate under the auspices of the International Red Cross. This noted that none of the corpses had documents on them dated later than April 1940 and that all had been shot in the back of the head with Russian ammunition. While the British tried to play down the matter, the Polish government-in-exile continued to press the Russians for an explanation.

Once the region had been liberated, the Russians organized their own inquiry and again claimed that the Germans were responsible. The London Poles refused to accept this and the result was a complete break between them and Moscow. Stalin now established an alternative government-in-exile, formed from Polish communists. His grounds for this was that it would enable Poland to govern itself

THE LIBERATION OF BELORUSSIA

The Soviet summer 1944 offensive, codenamed Bagration, broke the back of Army Group Centre. By extending the attack south of the Pripet Marshes, the Russians were able to prevent the German army group being reinforced by its southern neighbour.

BELOW: *Russian troops enter the Romanian capital Bucharest, 31 August 1944. For the Romanians, who had been allies of Germany, relief that the fighting was at an end overwhelmed any feelings that they might have had about being forced to surrender.*

after liberation. The London Poles were aghast and, on Churchill's advice, sent a deputation to Moscow at the end of July 1944.

Within Poland itself there was a secret army, the Polish Home Army, commanded by General Tadeusz Bor-Komorowski and controlled by the London Poles. Now, with the Red Army rapidly approaching the River Vistula, Bor-Komorowski ordered his forces to prepare for an uprising against the German occupier and asked London for permission to attack, requesting the support of the Polish Parachute Brigade and Polish RAF squadrons based in Britain. The Polish C-in-C in Britain, General Kazimierz Sosnkowski, was against the uprising because the British government refused to sanction the use of this external support, but he was in Italy at the time and there was a delay in transmitting his views. The London Poles therefore left the decision to Bor-Komorowski.

By 29 July the Warsaw Poles could hear the sounds of fighting on the other side of the Vistula as Konstantin Rokossovsky's 1st Belorussian Front warded off counter-attacks by three Panzer divisions. On that same day, a Russian-sponsored Polish radio station called for the uprising to begin. It did so three days later, but by then German reinforcements had moved into Warsaw. Furthermore, on the previous evening the Stavka had decided to halt Rokossovsky's offensive on the grounds that it had run out of momentum.

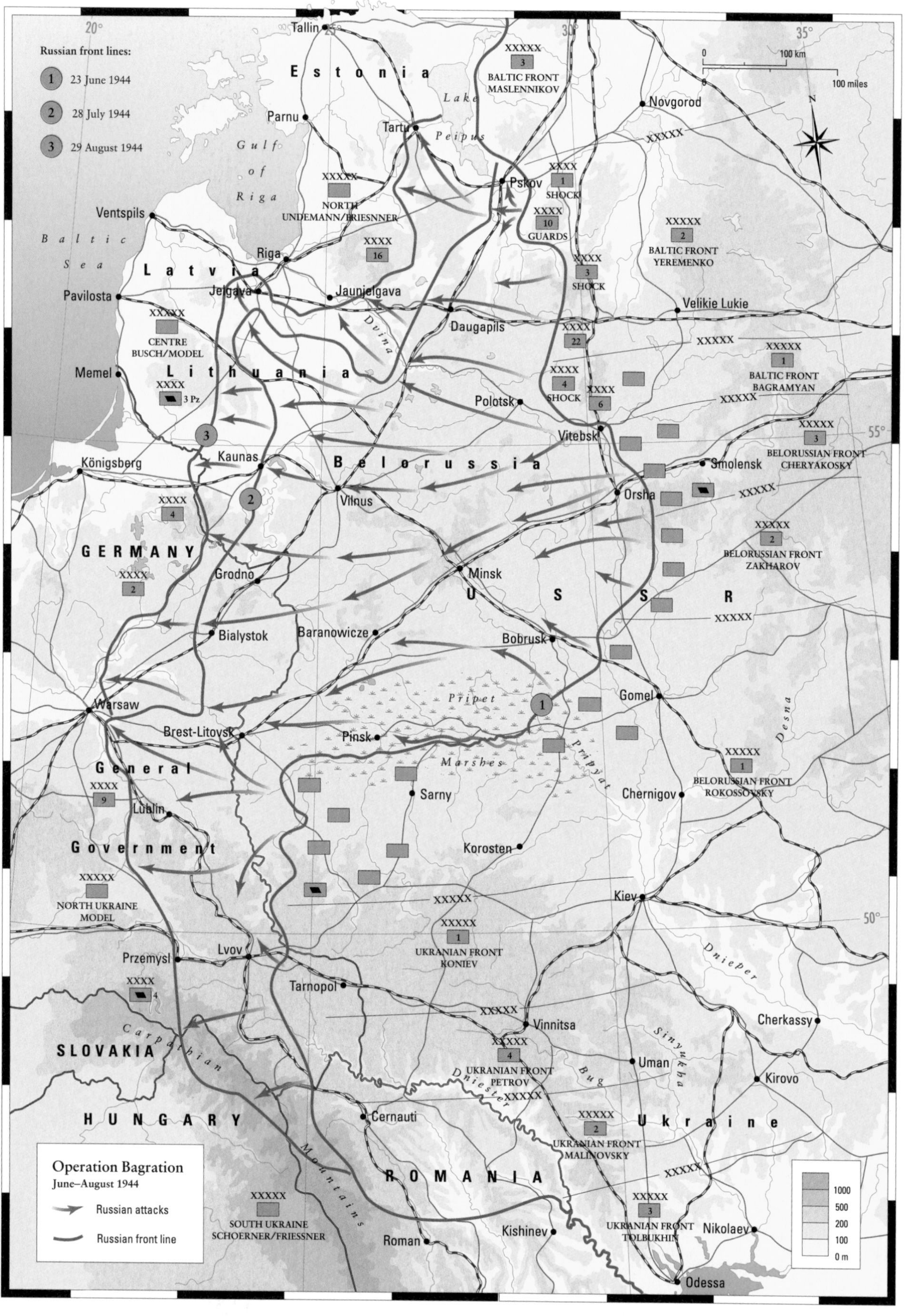
Russian front lines:
1 23 June 1944
2 28 July 1944
3 29 August 1944
Operation Bagration
June–August 1944
Russian attacks
Russian front line
Estonia
Latvia
Lithuania
Belorussia
GERMANY
General Government
SLOVAKIA
HUNGARY
ROMANIA
Ukraine
U S S R
Gulf of Riga
Baltic Sea
Lake Peipus
Pripet Marshes
Carpathian Mountains
Dvina
Dnieper
Desna
Pripyat
Sinyukha
Bug
Dniester
Tallin
Parnu
Tartu
Pskov
Novgorod
Ventspils
Riga
Pavilosta
Jelgava
Jaunjelgava
Daugapils
Velikie Lukie
Memel
Polotsk
Vitebsk
Smolensk
Orsha
Königsberg
Kaunas
Vilnus
Minsk
Grodno
Bialystok
Baranowicze
Bobrusk
Warsaw
Brest-Litovsk
Pinsk
Gomel
Sarny
Chernigov
Lublin
Korosten
Kiev
Przemysl
Lvov
Tarnopol
Vinnitsa
Cherkassy
Uman
Kirovo
Cernauti
Kishinev
Roman
Nikolaev
Odessa
XXXXX 3 BALTIC FRONT MASLENNIKOV
XXXXX NORTH UNDEMANN/FRIESNNER
XXXX 1 SHOCK
XXXX 10 GUARDS
XXXX 16
XXXXX 2 BALTIC FRONT YEREMENKO
XXXX 3 SHOCK
XXXXX CENTRE BUSCH/MODEL
XXXX 22
XXXXX 1 BALTIC FRONT BAGRAMYAN
XXXX 3 Pz
XXXX 4 SHOCK
XXXX 6
XXXXX 3 BELORUSSIAN FRONT CHERYAKOSKY
XXXX 4
XXXXX 2 BELORUSSIAN FRONT ZAKHAROV
XXXX 2
XXXXX 1 BELORUSSIAN FRONT ROKOSSOVSKY
XXXX 9
XXXXX NORTH UKRAINE MODEL
XXXXX 1 UKRANIAN FRONT KONIEV
XXXX 4
XXXXX 4 UKRANIAN FRONT PETROV
XXXXX 2 UKRANIAN FRONT MALINOVSKY
XXXXX SOUTH UKRAINE SCHOERNER/FRIESSNER
XXXXX 3 UKRANIAN FRONT TOLBUKHIN
0 100 km
0 100 miles
N
20°
25°
30°
35°
55°
50°
1000
500
200
100
0 m

On 4 August Stalin, having kept it waiting for some days, finally met the London Poles delegation. He told them that there could not be two governments-in-exile and expressed his annoyance at not having had prior warning of the uprising in Warsaw, whose chances of success he considered low. That same day he rejected a British request to air-drop supplies to the Home Army, and would continue to do so for the rest of the month. Unsupported, the Poles continued to fight on in Warsaw. In mid September the Russians relented over air drops and even began to parachute in supplies themselves, although the area of the city controlled by the Poles was now so small that most fell into the hands of the Germans. There was, too, a Polish army fighting under the Russians and this tried to establish a bridgehead on the west bank of the Vistula, but was beaten back. Eventually, the Home Army survivors were reduced to the city's cellars and sewers and on 1 October Bor-Komorowski decided that further resistance was pointless and surrendered. A quarter of Warsaw's population had been killed during the fighting and in the aftermath the city itself, which had already suffered from the September 1939 bombing and a rising by the Jews in its ghetto in spring 1943, was almost razed to the ground by the Germans.

The Russian failure to give timely help to the Polish Home Army must, in spite of the protestations of Soviet historians, be laid at Stalin's door. It is reasonable to assume that Rokossovsky could have forced the Vistula and Stalin forbade it because he saw the presence of an organized underground force answerable to the London Poles in the country as an obstacle to establishing a Communist state. As it was, many Poles felt bitter resentment towards their countrymen in Britain for their failure to give material support to the uprising and they began to accept the inevitability of their country coming under the domination of the hated Russians.

Yet, while Bagration had finally come to a halt, other offensives continued and fresh ones were opened. The Red Army maintained its pressure against the Finns, who again asked for an armistice. President Ryti had resigned and his successor, Marshal Carl von Mannerheim, considered that he was no longer bound by the pact made with Berlin earlier in the year. Consequently, under the terms of the armistice, which was signed on 19 September, Finland was allowed to retain her independence, but within her March 1940 borders with the Soviet Union. She also had to pay reparations to Moscow, which now set about clearing the German forces from northern Finland.

The offensive into the Baltic states was resumed in mid September. Within a month these had been liberated and the remnants of Army Group North trapped in Latvia's Courland peninsula. Chernyakovsky's 3rd Belorussian Front also entered East Prussia. In the extreme south the 2nd and 3rd Ukrainian Fronts had thrust into Romania on 20 August. Most Romanian formations quickly surrendered and three days later King Carol of Romania declared the hostilities over, leaving the German forces in the country to escape as best they could. On 30 August the Red Army occupied the Ploesti oilfields, now reduced to a complete shambles by an Anglo–US bombing campaign mounted from Italy. Thereafter Romania changed sides.

OPPOSITE: *Soviet partisans. They played an increasingly valuable role in the liberation of Russia, with their attacks against the German lines of communication being closely co-ordinated with the Red Army's main offensives.*

Simultaneous Soviet advances now threatened Bulgaria, Yugoslavia, and Hungary. The Bulgarians laid down their arms on 9 September, almost as soon as the Red Army crossed the borders. The thrust into Yugoslavia threatened the German forces in the Balkans. These consisted of Army Group E in Greece and Army Group F in Yugoslavia and they now began to withdraw northwards, harried by Resistance groups and partisans.

The word 'partisan' comes from the Russian *partizan*, meaning 'irregular soldier'. In Yugoslavia those commanded by Tito caught the imagination of the western Allies. Tito's proper name was Josip Broz, but he adopted a *nom de guerre* and was forever afterwards known as Tito. A convinced Moscow-trained communist, Tito was secretary of the Yugoslav Communist Party at the time of the April 1941 Axis invasion. He waited, however, until the Soviet Union had been invaded to issue his call to arms, which was not just directed against the occupiers of his country, but also had a revolutionary aim. At the time resistance was in the hands of Colonel Drava Mihailovic and his royalist Cetniks, who were supported by the British. The partisans had not only the Italians and Germans to contend with, but also Ante Pavelic's Croatian-based Ustase movement. This was ultra-nationalist and succeeded in persuading the Axis to create the 'independent' state of Croatia, which included not only Croatia *per se*, but also Bosnia and Herzegovina. Once in power, the Ustase set about cleansing their territory of all Serbs. This helped to swell the ranks of the two resistance movements. They themselves enjoyed an uneasy alliance, but, by the end of 1941 they began to split. Mihailovic was increasingly content to court the Italians to protect his Cetniks from the Ustase. The Axis pressure was therefore mainly on Tito. Throughout the period September 1941 until the spring of 1944 his partisans were subjected to a series of offensives, sometimes involving up to 200,000 troops, which kept them pinned down in the mountains.

British agents soon came to admire the fortitude and discipline of Tito's partisans and the fact that they were tying down so many Axis troops. Consequently support was switched from Mihailovic, but the Russians, too, were providing aid and Tito initially regarded the British with suspicion. At the end of May 1944 Tito was driven from the mainland and withdrew to the Adriatic island of Vis, which was occupied by the British. Both Churchill and Stalin now wooed him and Tito, concerned to maintain his country's integrity after the war, had to walk a delicate tightrope. Nevertheless, it was the Russians who entered Belgrade in October 1944, although Tito's partisans were there to meet them.

As the German Army Groups E and F withdrew northwards from the Balkans, the Russians swept into Hungary. At the beginning of November they were held up by determined German resistance in front of Budapest. Hitler ordered the Hungarian capital to be defended to the last and, although surrounded, it was still holding out at the end of the year.

Meanwhile in the far north the Russians began the clearance of the German forces out of the now-vanquished Finland. By the end of 1944 this operation had been largely achieved and the Germans had been driven back into northern Norway, where they began to operate a scorched-earth policy as they withdrew. Thus, everywhere in the east the Soviet forces were pressing in for the final kill. And in the west the same situation prevailed.

Marshal Tito outside his headquarters near Drvar in the mountains of Bosnia. It was a surprise German airborne assault here on 25 May 1944 which forced Tito temporarily to flee Yugoslavia.

CHAPTER SEVEN

North-west Europe and Italy (1944)

An American infantryman during the bitter fighting in the Huertgen Forest towards the end of 1944. German resistance in both North-west Europe and Italy remained tough until almost the very end of the war, as the British and Americans often found to their cost. Indeed, both after the entry into Rome in June 1944 and the liberation of France that August, the German defence congealed once more, forcing the Western Allies to pay dearly for further advances.

NORTH-WEST EUROPE AND ITALY 1944

The most effective method of attack proved to be by the combined action of infantry, artillery and tanks with some of the tanks equipped with dozer blades or large steel teeth to punch holes through the hedgerows. It was found necessary to assign frontages according to specific fields and hedgerows instead of by yardage and to reduce the distances and intervals between tactical formations. Normal rifle company formation was a box formation with two assault platoons in the lead followed by the support platoon and weapons platoon.

US FIRST ARMY REPORT ON FIGHTING IN THE NORMANDY *BOCAGE*

ON 1 APRIL 1943 the British General Frederick Morgan was formally appointed Chief of Staff to the Supreme Allied Commander (COSSAC). As such he was charged with drawing up the plan for the cross-Channel invasion of France and was given a joint Anglo-American staff to assist him. The date of the assault was confirmed as 1 May 1944. As yet no overall commander for the invasion had been appointed, and so Morgan found himself answering directly to the Combined Chiefs of Staff.

Morgan was able to make use of the numerous British staff studies of the problem which had been undertaken during the previous two and a half years. There

Photograph taken by an Allied reconnaissance aircraft of the beach defences along the Atlantic Wall. These were designed to cripple landing craft at high water. Note the German soldiers working on them diving for cover.

was also the experience being gained from amphibious operations, both small scale at home and major landings in the Mediterranean theatre. One crucial lesson had been learnt from the disastrous raid against Dieppe by the Canadians in August 1942: to base the landings around a port would be to court disaster since the defences were likely to be strong. Thus open beaches would have to be used, but many parts of the northern French coastline were not suitable. Another limiting factor was that the landing area had to be within range of fighter aircraft based in England.

Eventually Morgan and his staff were left with two options – the Pas de Calais and Normandy. While the former had the major advantage that the English Channel is at its narrowest here, it was, in German eyes, the most likely landing point. Consequently, Normandy was selected. Morgan realized, however, that the size of the landings depended on the amount of amphibious shipping available. From the production forecasts he calculated that the amphibious lift would provide for an initial landing force of three divisions. They would land north of Caen. The next task would be to secure Cherbourg for use as a port before advancing south into Brittany and east across the River Seine.

Morgan presented his plan in draft to the British chiefs of staff in mid July 1943 and it was approved in principle by the Combined Chiefs of Staff at the Quebec Conference that August. By now the cross-Channel invasion had received a new code name, Overlord. To safeguard it and to ensure that the Germans did not significantly reinforce Normandy, especially with mobile divisions, an elaborate deception plan, Bodyguard, was drawn up. This presented threats to Norway and the Balkans, and also tried to concentrate German attention on the Pas de Calais and the Belgian coast. Another plan aimed to deceive the Germans into believing that the cross-Channel attack would take place before the end of 1943. To this end a large amphibious exercise was carried out on the English south coast in early September, but the Germans were not fooled.

The need to tie down German troops gave added justification for the campaign in Italy. Eisenhower's precipitate announcement of the Italian surrender provoked a rapid German reaction. The landings at Salerno were fiercely opposed; the Germans also set about disarming the Italian armed forces. Thousands of Allied prisoners of war who had been held in Italy suddenly found themselves free. Many managed to reach the Allied lines, including Generals O'Connor and Neame, who had been captured during Rommel's spring 1941 offensive in Libya. Others were recaptured by the Germans. By virtue of a daring glider *coup de main*, the Germans also succeeded in rescuing Mussolini, who was being held in a ski resort in the Abruzzi mountains east of Rome. Before September was out, Mussolini had raised his banner once more in northern Italy, declaring it a socialist republic, but it was never to be more than a puppet state.

The virtual vacuum which existed in the days immediately succeeding the Italian surrender caused Churchill to look again at the Balkans. He wanted to seize the Dodecanese in the Aegean, hoping that this would both threaten the Balkans and finally bring Turkey into the war on the Allied side. The Americans, suspicious of his motives, would not go along with the plan, and so it had to be an entirely British effort. Troops were landed on some of the smaller islands, although they were foiled on Rhodes, the largest, where the Italian garrison surrendered to the Germans. Only very limited air and naval support was available. This meant that the British garrisons were virtually isolated and by the end of October the Germans had captured the islands.

At Salerno the Allies had to beat off heavy German counter-attacks before the beachhead could be secured. On 16 September, however, Montgomery's Eighth Army, advancing from the south, linked up with Fifth Army and the Germans began to withdraw northwards. The debate between Rommel and Kesselring over whether to defend north or south of Rome had not yet been resolved, with Kesselring commanding Army Group C south of Rome and Rommel remaining with Army Group B in northern Italy. Kesselring, however, had begun to construct defences, using the mountains south of Rome. These became known as the Gustav Line. After a Hitler conference at the end of September, Rommel was ordered to pass two divisions across to Kesselring, who was instructed to hold the Allies as long as possible on the Bernhard Line, subsidiary defences in front of the Gustav Line. Thus it would seem that Kesselring was winning the argument, but not for

British troops come ashore from a landing craft tank (LCT) at Salerno, September 1943. The initial landings were achieved at little cost, but the Germans reacted fiercely when the Allies were consolidating their beachhead prior to advancing inland.

The British Eighth Army's advance northwards towards the Gustav Line. Track links were often fitted to the glacis plates of both Allied and German tanks to increase frontal protection.

another month did Hitler appoint him commander-in-chief in Italy and move Rommel to other duties.

The Allies advanced with Mark Clark's predominantly American Fifth Army in the west and the British Eighth Army in the east. But southern Italy is blessed with numerous lateral river lines, especially on the Adriatic side. These bought Kesselring valuable time as he was able to force the Allies to halt and conduct set-piece river crossings. Not until mid November did Mark Clark penetrate the Bernhard Line. With winter now upon them, the Allies were unable to break through the Gustav Line, although Montgomery did penetrate it, before being forced to halt because of heavy casualties.

Fearing stalemate, Eisenhower, still Supreme Allied Commander in the Mediterranean, decided that the only way to capture Rome was by outflanking the Gustav Line through an amphibious operation, with Anzio, fifty miles south of Rome, being selected as the target. However, the bulk of the amphibious shipping in the Mediterranean had to be returned to Britain in preparation for Overlord. Furthermore, the Big Three – Churchill, Roosevelt and Stalin – meeting at Tehran at the end of November 1943, had confirmed that Overlord must take priority over Italy, from where veteran British and US divisions, earmarked for the Normandy landings, were already being withdrawn. In addition, it had also been agreed that there would be landings in the south of France, using troops currently fighting in Italy. The Anzio landings therefore appeared to be the one chance of striking a decisive blow in Italy. Thus they were allowed to go ahead, with the date 22 January 1944 being selected. The amphibious shipping used would have to be returned to Britain two weeks later.

OVERLEAF (TOP): *German paratroops occupy the ruins of the monastery on top of Monte Cassino after its bombing by Allied aircraft on 15 February 1944.*

The end of 1943 saw much reorganization in the the western Allies' Mediterranean camp. Wladyslaw Anders' II Polish Corps replaced the British divisions sent home for Overlord. Fifth Army, which was providing the Anzio force, received Alphonse Juin's French Expeditionary Force, composed largely of indigenous troops from north-west Africa. Italy was becoming a very cosmopolitan theatre, with Canadian, South African and Indian divisions, as well as Italians, now fighting on the Allied side.

Personalities at the top also changed, largely because of Normandy. Morgan had recommended that the supreme commander for Overlord be an American, with British single-service commanders-in-chief under him. Admiral Sir Bertram Ramsay, who had overseen the evacuation from Dunkirk, was made naval commander and Sir Trafford Leigh-Mallory, who had played an important part in the

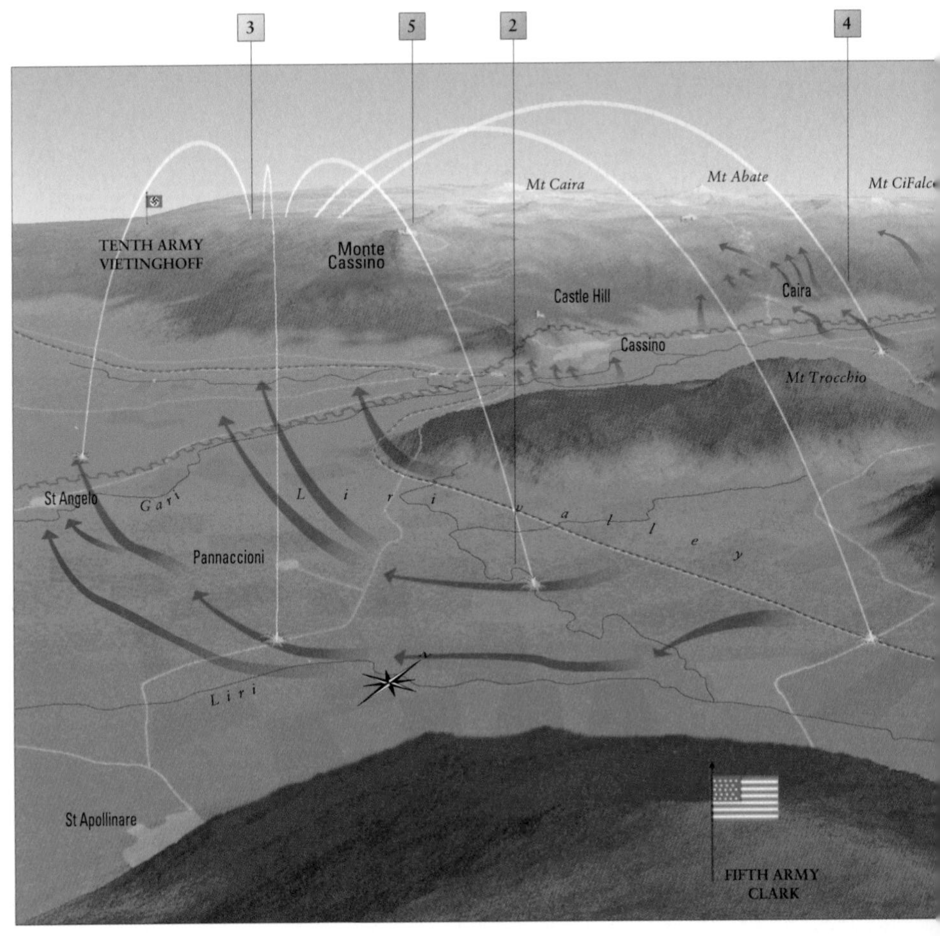

ITALY 1944–5

Kesselring took maximum advantage of Italy's mountainous spine, forcing the Allies into costly attacks, notably against Cassino, key to the Gustav Line, and against the Gothic Line later in 1944.

1 17 January: General Clark orders a frontal attack to seize river crossings and break the Gustav Line. By 11 February the attacks are called off with little progress

2 Allied troops advance over the floor of the Liri Valley overlooked by a well concealed enemy in the hills

3 German artillery fires on the Allied advance accurately guided by observation posts on surrounding hills

4 15 February: a second assault is ordered and as a precaution it is decided to destroy the Monastery of Monte Cassino. By 20 February the attack had failed

5 16th February: the ruins are occupied by German paratroops, and is turned into an almost impregnable stronghold

Italy 1944-5
Allied attacks
German retreat
Allied front line
German front line
German fortified defensive line
4000
3000
2000
1000
500
200
0 m
A U S T R I A
LICHTENSTEIN
SWITZ
Innsbruck
Brenner Pass
Predlidz
Villach
Bolzano
Belluno
Udine
Ljubljana
Trento
Rovereto
Alpine Line
Italian Partisans
Varese
Como
Biella
Busto Asizo
Bergamo
Ivrea
Milan
Brescia
Vercelli
Turin
Casale
Treviso
Vicenza
Venitian Line
Verona
Padova
Venice
Chioggia
Trieste
Koper
Novigrad
Fiume
Pola
Cremona
Mantova
Piacenza
Alessandria
Parma
Modena
Ferrara
Codigoro
Bologna
Argenta
Ravenna
Genova
Savona
Imola
Forlì
Florence
La Spezia
Cerrara
Viareggio
Lucca
Pistoia
Rimini
Pescara
Pisa
Gothic Line
Urbino
Livorno
Ancona
Iesi
Arezzo
Siena
Gubbio
Cortona
Fabriano
Macerata
Perugia
Fermo
Foligno
Piombino
Grosseto
Ascoli
Orvieto
Terni
Teramo
Viterbo
Rieti
Pescaro
L'Aquila
Civitavecchia
Sulmona
Tivoli
Gustav Line
Rome
Anzio
Cassino
Terracina
Naples
Salerno
I T A L Y
Ligurian Sea
Adriatic Sea
Po
Ticino
Mincio
Piave
XXXX 7
XXXX 14 LEMELSEN
XXXX 10 HERR
XXXX YUGOSLAV
XXXXX C VIGTINGHOFF
XXXX 1 LIGURIAN (Italian)
XXXX 10 VIETINGHOFF
XXX LXVI
XXXX 14 MACKENSEN
XXX LI (Mtn)
XXX XIV
XXXX 8 McCREERY
XXXX 5 TRUSCOTT
XXXXX 15 CLARK
XXX Fr Exp
XXXX 10 VIETINGHOFF
XXXX 14 MACKENSEN
XXX V
XXXX 8 LEESE
XXXXX 15 ALEXANDER
XXX XIII
XXXX 5 CLARK
XXX Fr Exp
XXXXX 15 ALEXANDER
XXX III
XXX VI
XXX X
XXXX 5 CLARK
Mt South Croce
StElia
EIGHT ARMY LEESE
Rocca
San Ambrogio
Garigliano
Allied front lines:
1 22 May 1944
2 end of May 1944
3 4 June 1944
4 17 June 1944
5 end of December 1944
6 23 April 1945
N
0 100 km
0 100 miles

Battle of Britain when in command of No. 12 Group, was air commander. Another British airman, Sir Arthur Tedder, who had been Eisenhower's air commander in the Mediterranean, was made Deputy Supreme Allied Commander. Not until the beginning of December was the decision made over the Supreme Allied Commander himself. Up until then the general belief had been that General George C. Marshall, chairman of the US Joint Chiefs of Staff, would take on the role. Certainly he had impressed everyone, including the British, and was desperately keen to do the job. But Roosevelt had come to rely on him too much and, in the end, would not release him. The mantle therefore fell on Eisenhower, who by now was well experienced in conducting coalition campaigns. The ground force commander for Overlord took a few days longer to select. Eisenhower wanted Alexander, who was commanding the ground forces in Italy and with whom he got on well. Churchill, however, had other ideas. He wanted the dynamic and thrusting Montgomery, and so it was to be.

Both Eisenhower and Montgomery made it their top priority to examine the COSSAC plan and both of them, especially Montgomery, disliked it. The three-division frontage was too narrow. They therefore insisted that the initial landings must be made by five divisions, with airborne divisions used to secure the flanks of the beachhead. The additional amphibious shipping, especially the Landing Ships Tank (LST), identified as the crucial item, would just have to be found.

Across the other side of the English Channel the Germans, too, were preparing for the inevitable. Up until autumn 1943 Hitler had given little priority to the defence of the west. France and the Low Countries were garrisoned by low-grade divisions. Others were sent there to recover after fighting on the Eastern Front, but no sooner had they been refitted and brought back up to strength than they were sent back to Russia. This was intensely frustrating for C-in-C West, Gerd von Rundstedt, but his complaints that he had too few troops to guard the 1,600 miles of coastline that was within his command fell on deaf ears. Hitler believed that the so-called Atlantic Wall, which had been under construction since 1941, was sufficient to repel the invader, even though work on it had progressed slowly and it was still very incomplete.

Not until the autumn of 1943 did Hitler begin to wake up to the threat. This was in part thanks to a lengthy report that von Rundstedt submitted to him. He pointed out that a rigid defence in the form of the Atlantic Wall could not be maintained for any length of time and that the outcome of the battle depended on mobile reserves. He had a mere three Panzergrenadier divisions, two of which were still forming to fulfil this role. Hitler's response was to issue a directive calling for reinforcement of the west. He also dispatched Rommel on a tour of inspection.

Rommel was regarded by von Rundstedt and many other senior German commanders as a 'young cub', who had not experienced the 'real war' on the Eastern Front and had distinguished himself merely in minor theatres. Rommel, on the other hand, believed that those who had spent their time fighting the Russians had little comprehension of the vast amounts of weaponry that the western Allies had at their disposal. There was, thus, mutual antipathy between von Rundstedt and Rommel, although relations did improve as time went by. Rommel presented his report to von Rundstedt at Christmas time. He believed that if the Allies were allowed to establish a lodgement the battle would be lost. Consequently, they had to be defeated on the beaches. This meant that the mobile reserves had to be deployed well forward, especially in the Boulogne–Somme sector, which Rommel reckoned was the most likely invasion target. Von Rundstedt was not so sure, believing that it was essential to confirm that the landings were the main Allied attack before the armour was totally committed.

Rommel's view provoked an argument with Geyr von Schweppenburg, commanding Panzer Group West, which contained all the mobile reserves. He believed even more strongly than von Rundstedt in a central reserve which could react once the main Allied attack had been identified. Eventually, von Rundstedt compromised, allotting one third to Rommel's Army Group B, which was now responsible for the defence of northern France and the Low Countries, a third to Army Group G, covering southern France, with the remainder held centrally. Hitler, however, now intervened. The Allied deception measures served to maintain his doubts as to where the invasion might come. While he accepted that the Pas de Calais was the most likely objective, and that Normandy was also a possibility, invasion might come anywhere. Thus, so as to maintain personal control over events, he insisted that the central mobile reserves must be under his direct control. As for Rommel, he worked tirelessly during the early months of 1944 to strengthen the beach defences of northern France.

While the Overlord staffs in Britain wrestled with the myriad pieces of jigsaw that made up one of the most comprehensive operational plans in military history, in Italy eyes were turned on Anzio. The landings duly took place, but there was a failure to exploit the initial surprise gained, partly because Mark Clark's orders did not make it clear whether this should be done before the beachhead had been properly secured. One of the noticeable features of the German army during 1939–45, as it had been during 1914–18, was its ability to mount immediate counter-attacks after losing ground in an attack. It did so now and successfully kept the Allies pinned on the beachhead for the next four months. This meant that some of the amphibious shipping had to be retained here instead of returning to Britain for Overlord. Indeed, the last LSTs required for the Normandy landings did not arrive back until just a bare few weeks before they took place.

Failure at Anzio also meant that the doors to the Gustav Line remained locked and there was no other option but to attack it frontally. The fighting itself centred on Monte Cassino; amid appalling weather and in rocky and bleak terrain a series of attacks were launched against it. The defenders, German paratroops and Panzergrenadiers, resisted fiercely, as French, New Zealanders, and then Indians flung themselves against it, but with little success. It was the same for the Americans attacking to the south. Such were the casualties that British and Dominion formations were beginning to run short of infantry. This was a problem that the British would also face in north-west Europe and Montgomery would be eventually

By the last year of the war both sides recognized multiple-launch rocket systems as highly effective in producing short concentrated bombardments.

forced to go as far as disbanding infantry divisions. As it was, in Italy the problem provoked Mark Clark to accuse his British subordinates in Fifth Army of lacking drive, not appreciating that the US manpower barrel was still relatively full and that he could afford to be more profligate.

While the assaults on Monte Cassino continued, Alexander drew up a new plan, Diadem. The objective was Rome and it meant switching the bulk of the Eighth Army to the western side of the Apennines for a more concentrated punch through the Gustav Line. In conjunction with this, there would be a break-out from Anzio to cut the German lines of communication running northwards to the Italian capital. There was to be a concerted air campaign too, also aimed at communications, under the apt code name of Strangle. Alexander could not mount this attack until May, and was unable to do so without using the troops earmarked for Anvil – the landings in the south of France. The Americans, especially, wanted these to coincide with Overlord. The Combined Chiefs of Staff agreed on Diadem, however, which meant postponing Anvil until after Overlord had taken place.

GERMAN SD KFX ROCKET VERSION

US ROCKET-FIRING SHERMAN

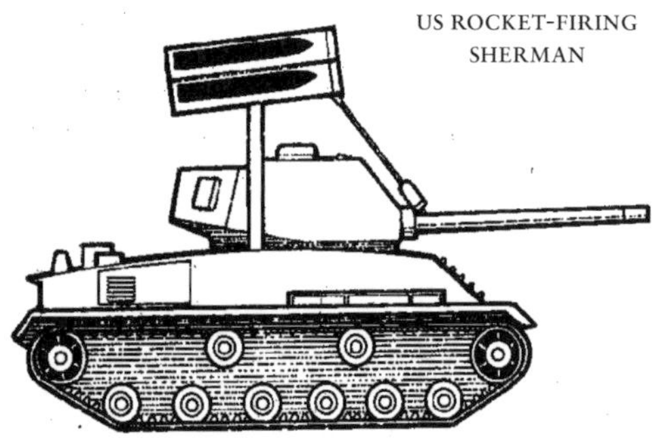

SOVIET KAYUSHA SYSTEM

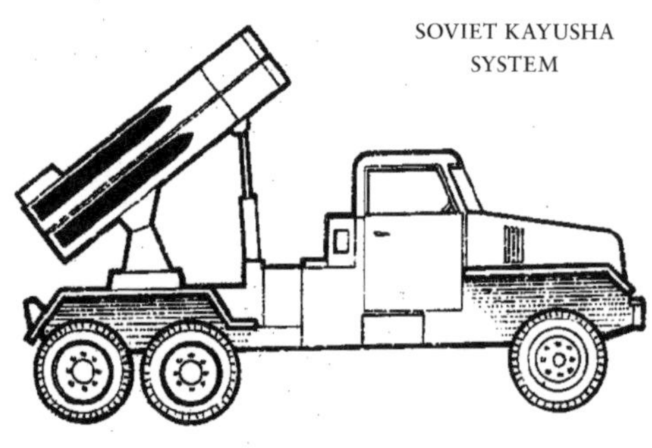

GERMAN NEBELWERFER

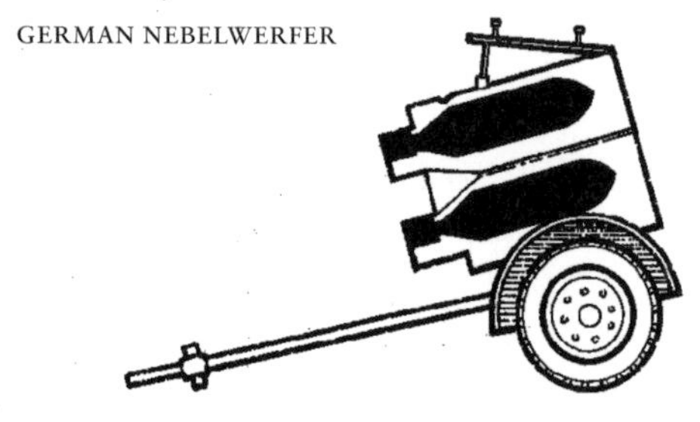

Alexander launched his offensive on the night of 11/12 May. The Poles attacked Monte Cassino, but they made little headway. Likewise, although British troops got across the Rapido river, they could not exploit their bridgeheads. In the Fifth Army sector the progress was better, with the French breaking through the Aurunci Mountains, believed by the Germans to be impassable. This provided the key to the Gustav Line and Kesselring ordered a withdrawal to a subsidiary defence line, but not before the Poles had again attacked Monte Cassino, which the Allies finally secured after four months of some of the grimmest fighting in western Europe during the war. Increasing Allied pressure now forced further German withdrawals and on 23 May the US VI Corps finally broke out of Anzio, linking up with Fifth Army two days later. The plan now was for Fifth Army to thrust eastwards in order to cut off the withdrawing German Tenth Army, but Mark Clark became mesmerized by Rome and instead advanced northwards. Kesselring managed to hold him for a few days in the Alban Hills, but he then received permission from Hitler to evacuate the capital, entered by the Allies on 5 June. This triumph was quickly overshadowed, however, by the Normandy landings, which took place on the following day.

As the preparations for Overlord became ever more advanced it was increasingly difficult to conceal them from the Germans. Consequently, the emphasis on deception became more pronounced. A mythical British Fourth Army was created in Scotland to maintain the threat against Norway, while in south-east England the 1st US Army Group (FUSAG), which had a real commander in George S. Patton, was designed to make the Germans believe that the Pas de Calais was the main objective, with Normandy being merely a subsidiary attack. Besides wearing down the Luftwaffe, the Allied air forces, including the strategic bombers, diverted from their pounding of Germany, engaged in a lengthy campaign against communications in northern France. The purpose of this was to hinder the deployment of German reinforcements to Normandy. The French Resistance was also primed to assist in this.

In spite of concerns over the weather, which forced Eisenhower to make a last minute postponement of the landings by twenty-four hours, the Allied forces stormed ashore on the morning of 6 June. The weather had, in fact, helped the deception plan, since the Germans did not believe that the landings would take place that day and many key commanders were absent from their posts. This and the overwhelming Allied air supremacy and massive weight of supporting naval gunfire enabled all five beachheads to be secured by the end of the day, with no fewer than 155,000 men landed. The only real problem was that congestion within the

Poster emphasizing the role played by the British Empire in the war. It was in Italy especially that Commonwealth troops made up a significant part of the British Eighth Army. The noticeable exception was Australia, whose troops were withdrawn to fight against the Japanese after the battle of El Alamein had been won.

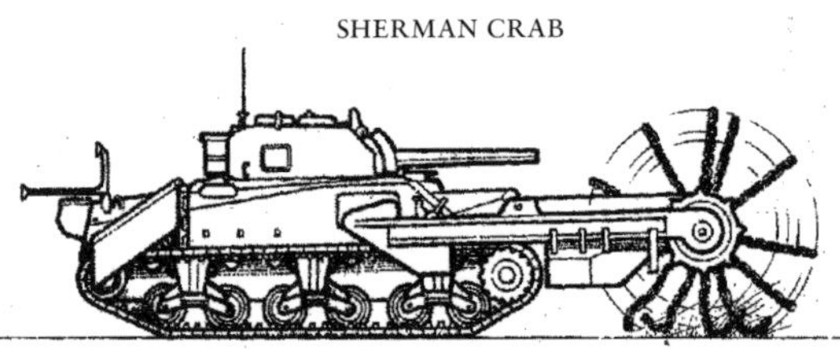

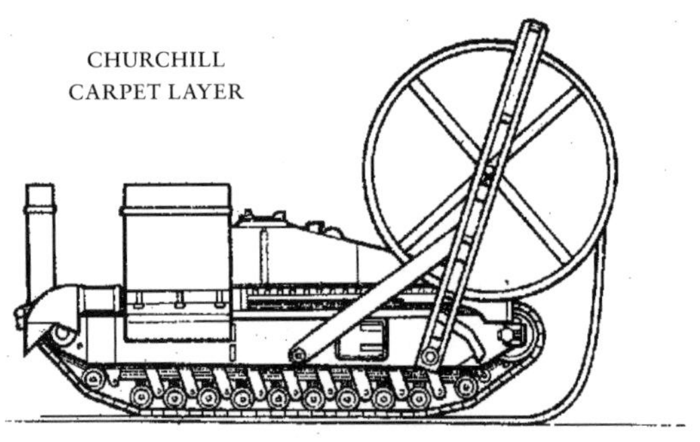

THE FUNNIES

Some of the specialized armour used by the Allies for the Normandy invasion. The DD Sherman was used in the initial landings. The tank was driven through the water by a propellor attachment fitted to its rear. The Sherman Crab was fitted with a flail attachment for clearing lanes through minefields, while the Churchill carpet layer laid a track over boggy ground. Other types included flamethrower tanks, armoured recovery vehicles, various types of bridgelayer tank, tanks with explosive hoses (another method of creating lanes in minefields), and special assault engine tanks with fascines for dropping into ditches and a 165mm gun for engaging concrete strongpoints.

OPPOSITE: *An artist's impression of the landings on Omaha beach, where, because their landing craft were launched too far from the coast, the troops had most difficulty in getting ashore.*

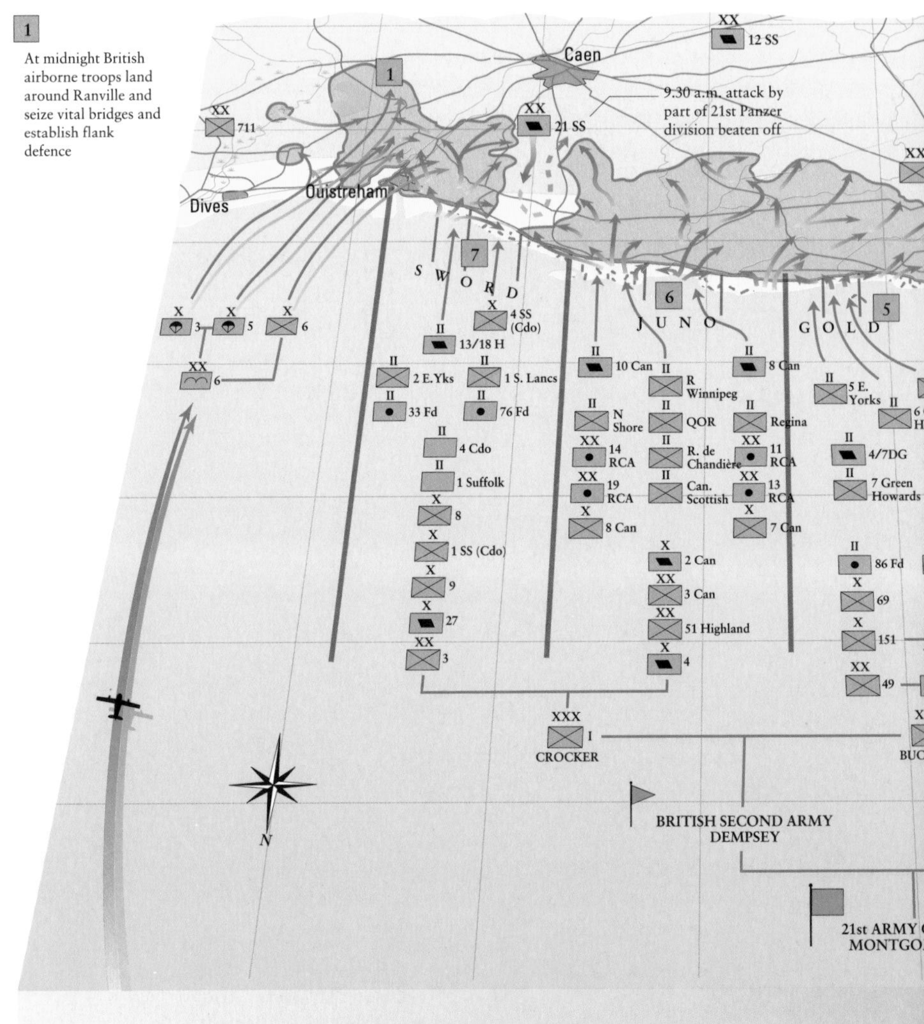

THE NORMANDY LANDINGS

The map shows the airborne drops and the order in which units landed on each beach.

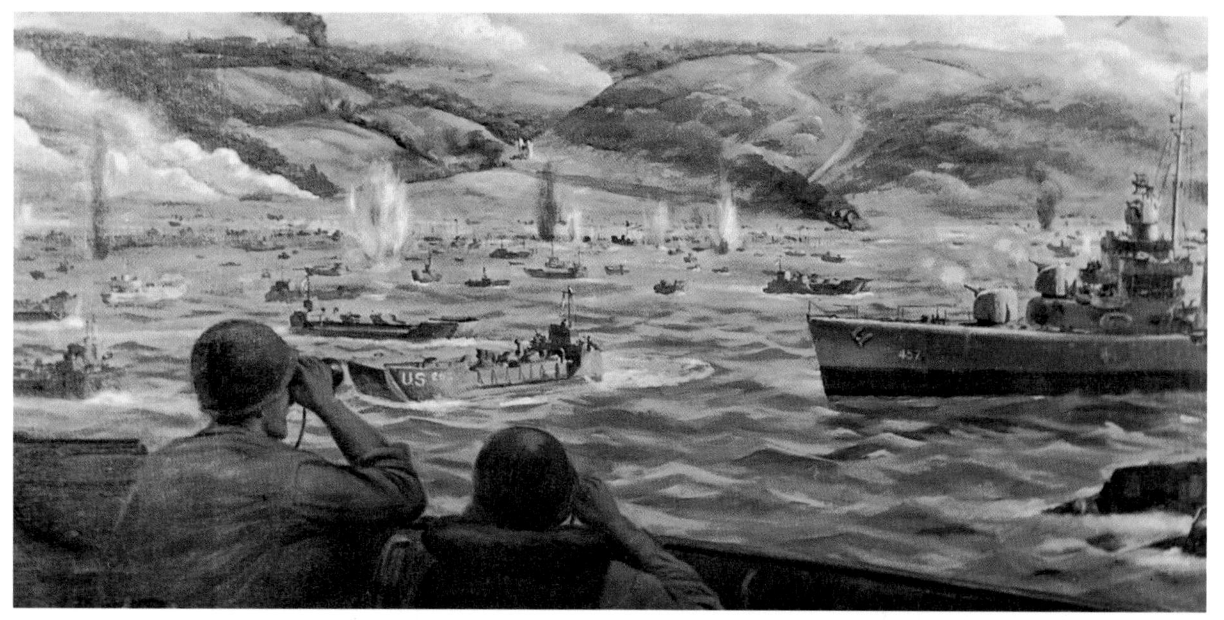

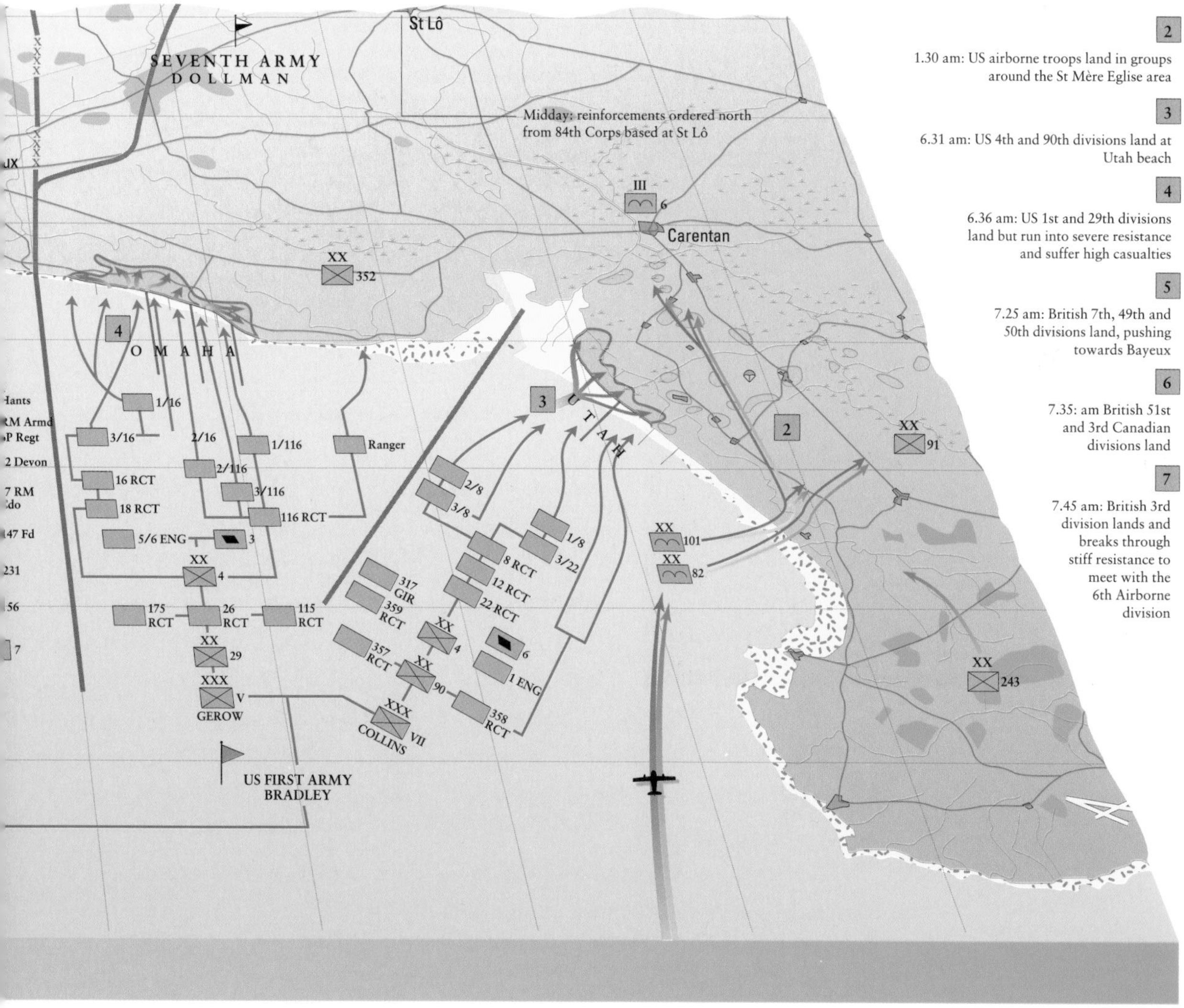
St Lô
SEVENTH ARMY
DOLLMAN
Midday: reinforcements ordered north from 84th Corps based at St Lô
Carentan
OMAHA
UTAH
XX 352
XX 91
XX 243
III 6
1/16
3/16
2/16
1/116
2/116
3/116
Ranger
16 RCT
18 RCT
116 RCT
5/6 ENG
XX 4
175 RCT
26 RCT
115 RCT
XX 29
XXX V GEROW
2/8
3/8
1/8
3/22
8 RCT
12 RCT
22 RCT
317 GIR
359 RCT
357 RCT
XX 4
XX 90
6
1 ENG
358 RCT
XXX VII COLLINS
XX 101
XX 82
US FIRST ARMY
BRADLEY
Hants
RM Armd
P Regt
2 Devon
7 RM
Cdo
47 Fd
231
56
7
2
1.30 am: US airborne troops land in groups around the St Mère Eglise area
3
6.31 am: US 4th and 90th divisions land at Utah beach
4
6.36 am: US 1st and 29th divisions land but run into severe resistance and suffer high casualties
5
7.25 am: British 7th, 49th and 50th divisions land, pushing towards Bayeux
6
7.35: am British 51st and 3rd Canadian divisions land
7
7.45 am: British 3rd division lands and breaks through stiff resistance to meet with the 6th Airborne division

beachheads slowed the advance out of them. This meant that the final D-Day objectives, notably the city of Caen, had not been reached by the end of the day. It also enabled the one mobile formation in the area, 21st Panzer division, to deploy, although it was not in a position to counter-attack before the day ended.

The German dilemma was uncertainty whether Normandy represented the only Allied landings or whether the main blow would be against the Pas de Calais. Certainly, Hitler believed the latter and refused to release the mobile reserves from Panzer Group West until late in the afternoon. Likewise, von Rundstedt would not allow the two Panzer divisions located north of the Seine to be switched to Normandy. When the mobile reserves did begin to deploy, the effects of the Allied air interdiction campaign and Resistance attacks on key bridges, combined with the continual presence of Allied aircraft overhead, meant that their moves took considerably longer than anticipated and they were committed piecemeal. This meant that no really co-ordinated and effective counter-attack against the beachheads could be launched and the Panzer formations found themselves committed to helping the infantry hold the ring.

General Dwight D. Eisenhower. As supreme Allied commander for Overlord he faced a tough test. Not only did he have to weld the British and Americans into one, but also their ground, naval and air elements.

But not all went the Allied way. Much of the Normandy terrain is made up of *bocage* – small fields enclosed by hedge-topped banks. While the Allied forces had been highly trained for actually getting ashore, not enough account had been taken of the claustrophobic nature of the *bocage*, which favoured defensive operations. The Allied armour, especially, was nonplussed by this. Outgunned by the German Panther and Tiger tanks, and highly vulnerable to sniping anti-tank guns, it suffered severely. The fighting also revealed that, compared to the Germans, Allied combat organization and tactics were still overly rigid. Normandy thus saw the Allies learn the hard way as they slowly inched forwards. Indeed, it became a matter of simply wearing down the defenders.

Montgomery now concentrated on drawing the bulk of the German armour eastwards to the British Second Army front so as to enable the Americans to break out in the west. He did this by a series of attacks around Caen. The Germans, notably the fanatical youngsters of the 12th SS Panzergrenadier Divison (*Hitlerjugend*), offered fierce resistance and Caen itself did not fall until five weeks after D-Day.

Even so, the unrelenting pressure on the Germans was slowly beginning to tell. Pleas to Hitler by von Rundstedt and Rommel for infantry reinforcements so that the Panzer formations could be withdrawn from the line to mount a concerted counter-attack fell on largely deaf ears. They then proposed evacuating Normandy altogether in favour of a new defence line on the River Seine, but Hitler rejected this out of hand. Indeed he sacked von Rundstedt, replacing him by von Kluge, recently recovered from his motor accident in Russia.

Then, on 17 July, Rommel was gravely wounded by a marauding Allied fighter. Three days later came the attempt on Hitler's life at his headquarters at Rastenburg in East Prussia. In Paris the military governor, Karl von Stuelpnagel, arrested Gestapo and SS men, but his action was premature. In Berlin Josef Goebbels, ascertaining that Hitler had survived the bomb blast, organized the Wachbattallion Grossdeutschland, an army guard unit stationed on the outskirts, to surround the Reserve Army HQ. The key plotters, who occupied senior positions in this, were arrested and summarily executed.

Most of the senior German commanders engaged in active theatres had been approached, but largely took the attitude of von Manstein, who declared: 'Prussian field marshals do not mutiny!' They were too bound by their oath of loyalty to Hitler, whatever they personally thought of him. In any event, they were engaged in what was now a desperate struggle against the Allies on all fronts and this took priority. Some, however, were implicated through their knowledge of the plot. Thus, von Kluge was recalled at the beginning of August, but committed suicide on his way back to Germany. Rommel, too, was eventually forced to take his own life after his family was threatened.

Gerd von Rundstedt, Commander-in-Chief West, discusses plans for countering the Allied invasion with Hitler. In spite of von Rundstedt's pleas for reinforcements, it was not until it was almost too late that the Führer released them, faced as he was with continuous and mounting Soviet pressure in the East and the need to keep the Western Allies tied down in Italy.

On 25 July, five days after the attempt on Hitler's life, the Americans began their break-out from Normandy. The assault was preceded by an attack on the German positions by Allied heavy bombers, a tactic that had been previously employed in the fighting around Caen. While it certainly numbed the defenders for a time, 'carpet bombing' was a two-edged weapon. It tore up the ground to such an extent that it restricted the attacker's mobility and, as happened on 25 July, caused casualties to his own troops. Even so, after six days the break-out had been achieved and the time had come to release the newly landed Third US Army under Patton through the gap.

The Allied forces were now reorganized into two army groups – Bradley's 12th and Montgomery's 21st. While Montgomery had been the Allied land commander for Overlord, Eisenhower had always intended to take charge once the break-out from Normandy had been achieved, and this is what he now began to do.

Patton's forces quickly advanced west into Brittany, as well as south and east, with Montgomery's forces also pressing out of Normandy in an attempt to trap the German Seventh Army. Much of this was destroyed from the air around Falaise, but

The airborne assault during the Dragoon landings in the south of France, 15 August 1944. The 1st Airborne Task Force was an Anglo-US formation, whose role was to drop inland from the beaches in order to provide immediate depth to the beachhead.

elements did manage to evade encirclement. Nevertheless, the German forces had lost cohesion and they withdrew rapidly eastwards. The liberation of France was now really under way.

On 19 August the Allies secured their first lodgement over the River Seine, west of Paris, and on the same day the French Forces of the Interior (FFI), an amalgam of all the Resistance groupings, rose against the Germans in the capital. Six days later the Allies entered Paris, with Charles de Gaulle arriving that evening to forestall a plan by French Communists to seize control. But while liberation provoked intense joy among people who had been under Nazi rule for four years, there was a dark side to it. The desire to punish those who had collaborated with the Germans was strong – many young women suffered public humiliation by having their heads shaved. There is no doubt, too, that some used this as cover to settle private scores. Indeed, the scars of the Occupation are still carried by France to this day.

By the time Paris had been liberated the Germans were facing a new threat in France. The Allied landings in the south of the country had taken place on 15 August and the US Seventh and French First Armies began to advance rapidly northwards.

In the north, however, as the Allied onrush eastwards continued, a new problem was rapidly emerging. The Allied supplies were still coming through Cherbourg. The reason for this was that Hitler had declared all the Channel and French Atlantic ports *Festungen* (fortresses to be defended to the last). Siege operations had to be mounted to reduce them and when they were finally captured the port installations had been wrecked. To overcome the problem of ever-stretching supply lines, the Americans organized the Red Ball Express, an endless conveyor belt of trucks operating between Normandy and the front. But as the distance between the two increased, these trucks consumed more and more of the fuel they were carrying and shortages began to appear.

For the moment, though, the advance continued, with the British liberating Brussels on 3 September and, far to the south, French troops entering Lyons on the same day. By now Eisenhower was firmly in control and issued a directive the following day. While Montgomery was to pursue the German armies into the Ruhr, Bradley was to advance to the Saarland. Montgomery, conscious of the growing logistics problem, protested that a broad front advance could not be maintained.

ALLIED TANK BUSTER

How rocket-firing Typhoons operated against German armour. They aimed their eight 60lb anti-tank rockets from a shallow dive. They were not especially accurate against tanks, but they did affect the morale of the German tank crews, who would sometimes abandon the vehicles in the face of an attack by Typhoons.

This marked the beginning of a controversy which was to dog the Allies throughout the remainder of the campaign in north-west Europe. While Montgomery's argument was militarily sound, Eisenhower also had to consider the political implications. A narrow-front advance would involve just one army group, leaving the others, which included the newly formed US 6th advancing from the south, out of the limelight. This would undoubtedly cause a major rift in Anglo-US relations and Eisenhower was determined to avoid this at all costs. His broad-front strategy therefore prevailed.

On 11 September American patrols crossed the German border near Luxembourg, but such were the Allied fuel shortages that everywhere the advance was grinding to a halt. This at last gave the near-shattered Germans a chance to draw breath. Allied hopes of a quick victory in the West began to fade, but there was still just a chance of striking a decisive blow.

Early in the year the First Allied Airborne Army had been formed in Britain. Three of its divisions – one British and two American – had taken part in the D-Day landings. Some twenty plans for its employment during the subsequent fighting in Normandy and beyond had been considered, but none had come to anything. Montgomery now proposed to Eisenhower that elements of this be used in an

US troops advance through a heavy mortar barrage during Operation Cobra, the break-out from Normandy.

The Red Ball Express in operation. On 29 August 1944 alone 5,958 trucks delivered 12,342 tons of supplies to the forward troops. However, the trucks themselves consumed on average 300,000 gallons of fuel per day.

operation designed to turn the German flank by thrusting across the Lower Rhine in Holland. No fewer than three airborne drops would be made to secure bridges over canals in the Eindhoven area, the River Maas at Grave and River Waal at Nijmegen, and, finally, that over the Rhine at Arnhem. At the same time XXX British Corps would advance into Holland, linking up with the airborne forces in turn.

Operation Market-Garden was launched on 17 September. At first all went well, with the US 82nd and 101st Airborne Divisions seizing the Eindhoven, Grave and Nijmegen bridges, and quickly linking up with XXX Corps at Eindhoven. At Arnhem, however, the dropping zone was a good six miles from the bridge. There were also two SS Panzer divisions refitting in the area after fighting in Normandy. Allied intelligence had not appreciated the significance of this, but they soon made their presence felt on the British 1st Airborne Division and the Polish Parachute Brigade which reinforced it. These did manage to seize the Arnhem bridge, but came under increasing pressure from the more heavily armed Waffen-SS men. Worse, north of Eindhoven XXX Corps found its advance restricted to what was virtually a single road, with wet, low-lying country on either side. German attacks into its flanks slowed its progress, as the paratroops at Arnhem found themselves engaged in an ever more desperate battle.

Eventually XXX Corps reached the Rhine and managed to link up with the Polish paratroops, but it was unable to reach 1st Airborne Division, only a fifth of which was able to escape across the river. Market-Garden has often been criticized as being overly ambitious, but its failure was narrow. Even so, it represented the last opportunity for the western Allies to end the war in Europe in 1944. Against a congealing defence, skilfully conducted by von Rundstedt, whom Hitler had recalled, the Allied advance towards the upper Rhine became increasingly hard. The Americans, in particular, fought a fierce battle to capture the first significant German town, Aachen, and then another in the Huertgen Forest to its east.

By the late autumn most of the French Atlantic and Channel ports had been liberated, although Dunkirk would hold out until the very end of the war. But these were still a long way from the front. True, the city of Antwerp had been captured in early September, but its port, one of the largest in western Europe, could not be used because the Germans still held both banks of the River Scheldt on which it lies. An operation was mounted to clear them from the Breskens pocket on the south bank. This was followed, on 1 November, by landings on the island of Walcheren at the mouth of the river. It was secured after a week's fighting in appalling weather. The Scheldt then had to be cleared of mines. Even so, the port of Antwerp was open for

A truck bogged down in the mud during an American withdrawal in the opening days of the Ardennes counter-offensive.

business and receiving supply ships before November was out. It was, however, too late to affect Allied fortunes in 1944.

In Italy, too, the Allies found themselves deadlocked once more by the end of the year. The euphoria resulting from the liberation of Rome soon evaporated. The advance continued north of the capital but had to be halted when it reached the River Arno. This was because the forces earmarked for Anvil had now to be withdrawn, together with a significant proportion of 15th Army Group's artillery. An army corps from Brazil, which had entered the war in August 1942, and an American black division, the first such combat formation to be created in the US Army, replaced the Anvil contingent, but neither had any previous combat experience. Even so, Alexander still believed that he could break through Kesselring's next major belt of defences, the Gothic Line, which took maximum advantage of the Apennines.

Alexander mounted his assault against the Gothic Line on 12 September. Over six weeks' bitter fighting, often in heavy rain, saw the US Fifth Army make one penetration into the mountains before casualties and the impossible conditions forced it to a halt. In the east, the British Eighth Army found itself once more faced by an endless succession of river lines. It crossed these, one after another, amid worsening weather. Pushing through the Gothic Line, its advance was increasingly separated from its neighbour by the Apennines. By late December it was exhausted and could do no more. Alexander, now promoted Mediterranean theatre commander, therefore halted all offensive operations until the spring.

As he did so, his attention was diverted to newly liberated Greece, where a tussle for power between Communist and non-Communist Resistance groups had erupted into all-out civil war. British forces had to be sent from Italy to bring the fighting to an end and oversee the establishment of an effective government.

Back in north-west Europe, 1944 did not, as in Italy, go out with a whimper. Since the early autumn Hitler had been planning an ambitious counter-offensive. Its object was to split the British from the Americans by thrusting towards Antwerp. In this way he hoped to be able to buy time in the west so as to be able to concentrate on stemming the now inevitable Russian offensive across the River Vistula and towards Berlin. Both von Rundstedt and Model, his subordinate now in charge of Army Group B, blanched when Hitler told them what he had in mind and proposed a more modest attack to trap the Americans around Aachen. Hitler, however, would have none of it. He did, however, agree to postponing the offensive from 25 November until mid December.

The Ardennes, where the attack was to be launched, was considered by the Americans as a quiet sector and was manned by divisions fresh from the United States and others recovering from the bitter combat in the Huertgen Forest. During the early part of December the Allied intelligence agencies, including Ultra, identified a growing number of indicators pointing to an attack, even though the German security was tight, with all deployments being done under the cover of darkness. But while the indicators were there, the commanders, convinced that the

Members of the US 1st Infantry Division during the German withdrawal from the Ardennes. Known as the Big Red One, from its divisional symbol, this formation was a veteran of the Torch landings and the Tunisian and Sicilian campaigns. It landed on Omaha Beach on D-Day and thereafter fought its way across France and into Germany. During the Ardennes fighting it operated on the northern shoulder of the German 'bulge'.

Waffen-SS troops of Sixth Panzer Army, distinguishable by their camouflaged uniforms, after ambushing an American column during the opening days of the Ardennes counter-offensive. Sepp Dietrich's men found that the hill and wooded terrain in their sector operated against them, especially after snow fell. Shortage of fuel was another problem. To their south Hasso von Manteuffel did better, but his failure to capture Bastogne told against him since it stood astride vital supply routes. The Allied fallback position was the River Meuse and Montgomery's forces were deployed to secure and defend the bridges over it. As it was, the German offensive stopped short of the river. By this time its long open flanks made it vulnerable to a counter-stroke.

Battle of the Bulge
16–24 December 1944
German attacks 16–20 December
German paratroop drop
US front lines

The Battle of the Bulge

It was the rapidly mounted thrust into the German southern flank by Patton's Third US Army and its relief of Bastogne which forced the Germans to withdraw.

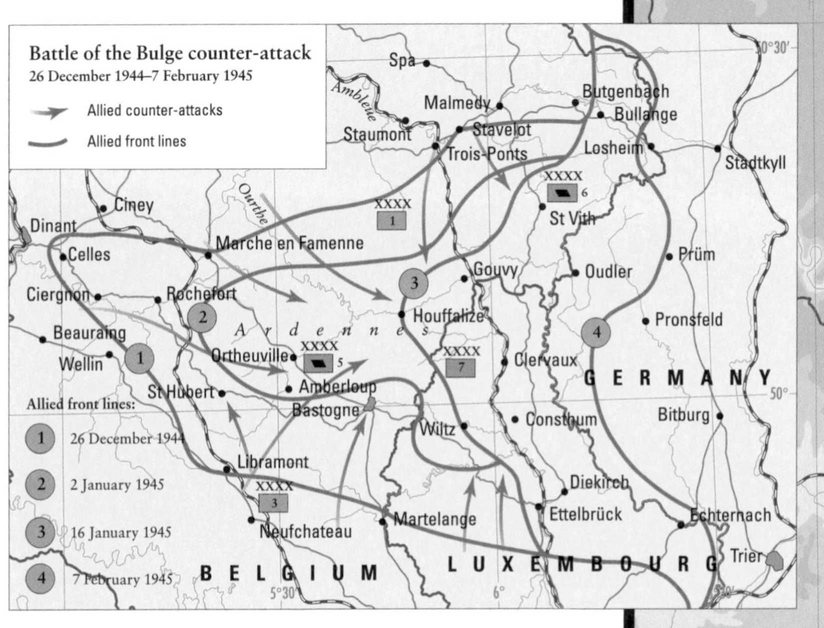

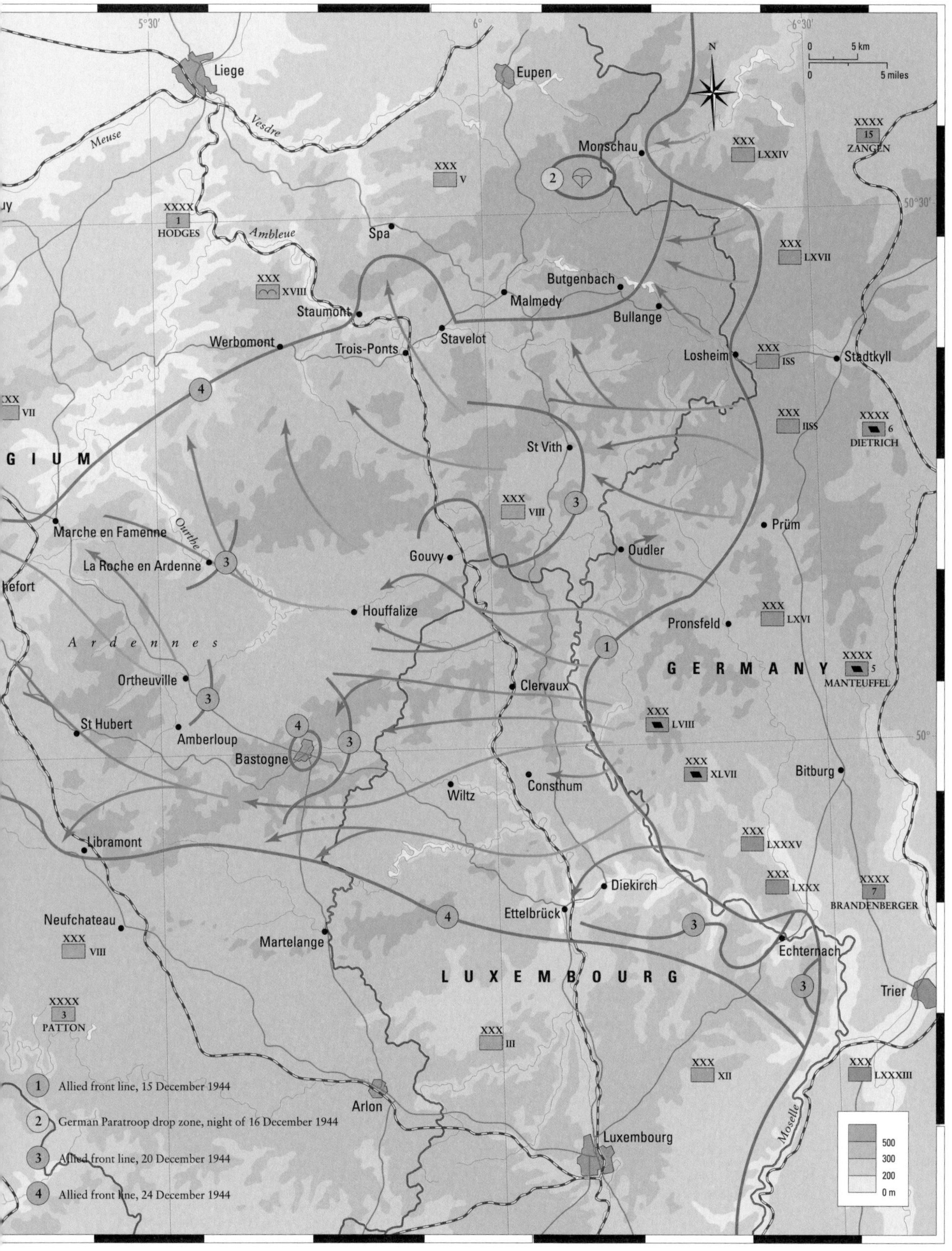

Liege
Eupen
Meuse
Vesdre
Monschau
XXX V
XXXX 1 HODGES
Ambleue
Spa
XXX LXXIV
XXXX 15 ZANGEN
XXX LXVII
XXX XVIII
Butgenbach
Malmedy
Bullange
Staumont
Stavelot
Werbomont
Trois-Ponts
Losheim
XXX ISS
Stadtkyll
XXX VII
XXX IISS
XXXX 6 DIETRICH
St Vith
XXX VIII
Prüm
Marche en Famenne
Ourthe
La Roche en Ardenne
Gouvy
Oudler
Houffalize
Ardennes
Pronsfeld
XXX LXVI
Ortheuville
Clervaux
GERMANY
XXXX 5 MANTEUFFEL
XXX LVIII
St Hubert
Amberloup
Bastogne
XXX XLVII
Bitburg
Consthum
Wiltz
XXX LXXXV
Libramont
Diekirch
XXX LXXX
XXXX 7 BRANDENBERGER
Ettelbrück
Neufchateau
XXX VIII
Martelange
Echternach
LUXEMBOURG
Trier
XXXX 3 PATTON
XXX III
XXX XII
XXX LXXXIII
Arlon
Moselle
Luxembourg
0 5 km
0 5 miles
500
300
200
0 m
1 Allied front line, 15 December 1944
2 German Paratroop drop zone, night of 16 December 1944
3 Allied front line, 20 December 1944
4 Allied front line, 24 December 1944

Christmas 1944 in the Ardennes. Conveniently camouflaged by the snow, these Shermans prepare to advance during Patton's counter-stroke into the German southern flank.

days of major German offensives were long gone, refused to take them seriously.

As the tanks and guns of Hasso von Manteuffel's Fifth and Sepp Dietrich's Sixth Panzer Armies moved into position, Hitler arrived at one of his now many field HQs to supervise the attack personally. Indeed, in the course of two days he lectured all commanders down to and including corps level and insisted on dealing directly with Model's staff, bypassing von Rundstedt entirely.

On 16 December, after an early brief artillery barrage, the offensive opened. Fog, so often an attacker's ally, was present. The American defenders were taken totally by surprise and chaos began to reign, helped by infiltrators in American uniforms and jeeps, who altered signposts and cut telephone cables. For the next two days the attack made good progress, but then a number of factors started to take effect. Snow began to fall, making it difficult for the heavy German tanks to manoeuvre in the

narrow and twisting Belgian lanes. An astute US engineer battalion also slowed their progress by blowing bridges in Sixth Army's attack sector, forcing the Panzers to make time-consuming detours. They also failed to secure a vital US fuel dump. In von Manteuffel's sector the key communications centre of Bastogne, reinforced by paratroops of the veteran 101st Airborne, refused to fall. Finally, the weather cleared, enabling Allied air power to resume its dominance of the skies.

Montgomery stepped in and took control of the northern half of the newly created German salient. In the south, Patton, anticipating that his Third Army would be required, switched its axis through ninety degrees and was ready when the order came to relieve Bastogne. By the 23rd Sixth Panzer Army had been halted and three days later Bastogne was relieved. But Hitler had already departed, realizing that he had shot his last bolt in the West.

CHAPTER EIGHT

The Final Campaign (1945)

A surprisingly cheerful Canadian infantry section take a ride on a Sherman Firefly during the bitter fighting in the Reichswald in February 1945. The Firefly was armed with a long-barrelled 17pdr (76.2mm), considerably more powerful than the 75mm on the conventional Sherman. The Firefly was introduced to combat the Tiger and PzKw V Panther. The infantry are wearing bandoliers containing additional rifle ammunition – an indication that they are on their way to the front line.

THE FINAL CAMPAIGN 1945

He was wearing a filthy bandage on his head and he was riding on the back of an ox, which was pulling a small ammunition truck, which had run out of gas. He maintained, with the sense of romance common to all soldiers of experience, that he had been riding the ox and pulling the truck all the way from Stalingrad, and if he hadn't been, the Allies might still be in fairly serious trouble. I asked him what he intended to do with the ox now that the war was nearly over. 'Eat it,' he said and there can't be the slightest doubt that he did.

COLONEL NICHOLAS IGNATIEFF, RUSSIAN-BORN CANADIAN SERVING WITH BRITISH MILITARY INTELLIGENCE, TORGAU, RIVER ELBE, 25 APRIL 1945

GERMANY AT THE BEGINNING of 1945 was in a desperate situation. Her future on the ground rested on the River Rhine in the west and the River Vistula in the east. Although its capital Budapest still held out, most of Hungary had been overrun and Austria was under threat. In Italy, too, it was inevitable that the Allies would resume their offensive. Germany was being pounded from the air by day and night. Fuel supplies ran almost dry, and road and rail communications were disrupted. Defeat stared her in the face. Yet the German people continued to fight.

A Churchill AVRE (Armoured Vehicle Royal Engineers) during the fighting in the Reichswald. The Churchill started life as an infantry support tank, but took on many specialized armour roles. The AVRE had a 165mm Petard mortar in its turret. This fired a 25lb explosive charge contained in a 'dustbin'. It was used against concrete strongpoints and other reinforced structures.

Much of the reason for this lay in the innate discipline of the Germans combined with the fact that the country had been under a rigid dictatorship for twelve years. The Nazi propaganda machine made great play of the Allied demand for unconditional surrender, asserting that it meant that the country would lose everything and be reduced to a wasteland. There was therefore nothing to be gained from seeking terms with the Allies. Hitler, who had now taken up residence in the *Führerbunker* in Berlin, promised a new generation of 'miracle weapons', which would surely turn the tide. At the same time he, and many of his people, nourished the hope that the western Allies would finally wake up to the true threat to western Europe – *Bolschewismus* from the East.

Yet not until after the July 1944 bomb plot had Hitler finally ordered mobilization for 'total war'. During the next six months a new type of division, *Volksgrenadier*, was created, with a smaller organization than the standard infantry

A Maxim 1910 machine-gun covers Soviet infantry during the Vistula-Oder offensive of January 1945. Like the British Vickers machine-gun, the Soviet Maxim had a long life, being continuously in production from 1910 until the end of the war in 1945. Its last appearance in combat was during the Korean War.

OPPOSITE: *Equipped with lifejackets, British infantry move up to cross the Rhine during Operation Plunder, March 1945.*

division and geared to defence. The *Volksturm* was also formed. This was a home guard, drawn largely from the over six million males in reserved occupations, and those above and below military age. Many were armed with just the *Panzerfaust*, one of the new generation of hand-held recoilless anti-tank weapons which had come into service on both sides during the second half of the war.

If Nazi propaganda had become ever more strident as Germany prepared for the last battles, so had that of the Russians. Ilya Ehrenburg, who had become the equivalent to Goebbels, preached a simple message to the Red Army as it prepared to enter the Third Reich proper. 'Bread for Bread, Blood for Blood' meant that the atrocities that the Germans had committed in Russia must be revenged in kind. The result was to be rape and pillage on a scale not known in Europe for centuries.

The long-awaited Russian offensive across the Vistula opened on 12 January 1945. The first to attack was Koniev's 1st Ukrainian Front in the extreme south and this achieved an immediate breakthrough, penetrating up to twelve miles on the first day alone. Next day, in the north, the 3rd Belorussian Front struck into East Prussia. Rokossovsky's and Zhukov's fronts then crossed the Vistula north and south of Warsaw and finally liberated the Polish capital. Preceded by columns of terrified refugees, bringing with them horrific tales of atrocities, the Russians swept westwards. By the end of the month Zhukov had closed to the River Oder and Koniev to the Neisse. The German hold on East Prussia had been reduced to a small pocket around Koenigsberg.

The other active front in the east was Hungary. The capital Budapest was still holding out at the beginning of 1945 and throughout January Woehler's Army Group South struggled to relieve it, reaching as close as twelve miles to its outskirts. It was to no avail, and after bitter street fighting, Budapest finally fell to Malinovsky's 2nd Ukrainian Front on 13 February. Hitler, however, had not finished his offensive operations in Hungary. He was determined to regain the oilfields around Lake Balaton and to this end, in the aftermath of the Ardennes counter-offensive, he ordered the transfer of Sepp Dietrich's Sixth SS Panzer Army from the west.

Under the code name Spring Awakening, Dietrich attacked alongside Hermann Balck's Sixth Army in the early hours of 6 March. The weather was against them, though. The spring thaw had made the ground very wet and the advance was a struggle from the outset. After a week's fighting, which ended with the 3rd Ukrainian Front mounting a counterstroke which threatened Balck's and Dietrich's communications, the offensive was halted and the Germans were forced to withdraw. So furious was Hitler that he ordered the Waffen-SS formations involved to remove their prized divisional cuff bands.

In the north the Germans had also been on the offensive when, on 15 February, Walther Wenck's Third Panzer Army began to strike from Pomerania into the now long and exposed northern flank of the 1st Belorussian Front. The attack initially made good progress, but faltered after Wenck himself was injured in a car crash. Even so, Zhukov realized that Pomerania would have to be dealt with before the final assault towards Berlin could be mounted. Consequently, both he and Rokossovsky

attacked northwards, quickly clearing the region, although a now totally isolated Koenigsberg still held out. Simultaneously, Koniev cleared the area between the Oder and the Neisse.

To the south, the remainder of Hungary was quickly overrun and the Russians crossed the border into Austria. By 6 April they were at the gates of Vienna, which fell after a week's fighting. Koenigsberg finally surrendered on 10 April and all Soviet attention could now be concentrated on Berlin.

In the west the German failure in the Ardennes did not mean that their defences had cracked. On the contrary, the Allies faced stiff opposition as they closed up to the Rhine. In the far south de Lattre de Tassigny's First French Army spent a tough week at the beginning of February reducing the Colmar pocket on the east bank of the river. Patton's Third and Hodges' First US Armies had a somewhat easier task, although it included recapturing the ground lost during the Ardennes counter-

The Allied airborne operation during Operation Plunder, 24 March 1945. Both British and US airborne troops took part, their objective to secure high ground beyond the east bank of the Rhine. Unfortunately, their dropping zones were in and around the German gun lines. This resulted in casualties to transport aircraft and gliders. Even so, they had achieved their aim by the end of the day.

offensive, and the distances involved meant that it took them considerably longer to reach the Rhine. Montgomery's 21st Army Group had some very tough fighting in wintry conditions as they pressed Eugen Mendl's First Parachute Army back to the Lower Rhine. In particular, the British and Canadians experienced conditions reminiscent of France and Flanders in 1914–18 as they struggled to clear the heavily wooded Reichswald.

By early March von Rundstedt finally received permission from Hitler to withdraw his forces east of the river and to demolish the remaining Rhine bridges. On the 7th, however, elements of the First US Army succeeded in seizing a bridge at

Remagen, south of Bonn, before it could be totally demolished. This coup cost von Rundstedt his command for the third and final time during the war. Throughout the next two weeks the Germans made desperate attempts to destroy the bridge, including air attacks and frogmen. Eventually it collapsed, but, in any event, the terrain on the east bank was such that the Allies could not exploit this unexpected success and had to await crossings elsewhere.

Troops from Patton's Third Army land from their assault boats on the east bank of the Rhine during one of his opportunity crossings of the Rhine.

Hitler, whose reason was beginning to leave him, now declared a scorched earth policy. Nothing of value must be left to the Allies and the whole of the German people was to be moved to the centre of the country. This was clearly impossible to achieve and no effort was made to carry it out. As for laying waste Germany, it was Albert Speer, Hitler's munitions minister, who managed to prevent this from being carried out in the western part of the country, believing that the government had a duty to maintain a minimum standard of living for its people.

The first main Allied Rhine crossing took place on the night of 22/23 March at Oppenheim, above the junction of the Rhine and the Main. Patton's Third Army achieved a bounce crossing over the river straight off the line of march. Such was the degree of surprise that many Germans were caught asleep. In contrast, the crossing by the British Second Army in the Wesel area had been under preparation for some three weeks. In the last airborne operation in Europe, British and American paratroops and gliders were used to secure high ground beyond the far bank as the assault troops crossed the river. Thereafter several more crossings were achieved along the middle Rhine.

Once bridgeheads across the Rhine had been secured, pontoon bridges were quickly built to carry the armour and supplies necessary for the break-out phase.

Once across the river, the broad-front versus narrow-front debate erupted once more. On 28 March, without consulting the US or British governments, Eisenhower sent a message to Stalin stating that he had no intention of advancing on Berlin and was leaving this to the Russians. Instead, the western Allies would make their main thrust towards Dresden. In truth, Eisenhower was concerned not to risk any clash with the Russians which might sour the final victory. He was also worried about intelligence reports that the Nazis were intending to set a last-ditch *Festung* in the Alps, the so-called National Redoubt. While it is true that Hitler did order two HQs – OKW North and OKW South – to be established in Schleswig-Holstein and the Alps, this was to prepare for the country being split into two by the Allied offensives; the National Redoubt *per se* was a myth.

Be that as it may, Stalin, with his eye now firmly on the German capital, was delighted with Eisenhower's pledge and assured him that he would make it his top priority to link up with the western Allies so as to split Germany in two. He stated

that Berlin was no longer of significant interest to him and that he would begin his next offensive in the second half of May, once the ground had dried out. This, of course, was not what Stalin had in mind, but he wanted to lull British and American suspicions. Churchill, however, was aghast when he heard what had been done, declaring that Berlin was a strategic objective and that it was vital to meet the Russians as far east as possible. Montgomery, too, was horrified, having been led to believe that the 21st Army Group would conduct the main Allied thrust and that it would be directed at the German capital. As it was, Eisenhower laid down that once the Ruhr had been reduced, Montgomery would hand back Simpson's Ninth US Army, which had been under his command since the Ardennes, and concentrate on liberating northern Holland and clearing the north German coast.

The truth was that Britain was now the junior partner in the alliance. This had become very clear at the Allied strategic conference held at Yalta in the Crimea in early February 1945. A now very sick Roosevelt was prepared to make concessions

US soldiers bring in German prisoners during operations on the east bank of the Rhine. Many of those captured were little more than boys. The German manpower barrel was finally being drained dry.

to Stalin to encourage him to join in the war against Japan immediately after Germany had been defeated, and Churchill had found that there was little that he could do about it.

The Ruhr was encircled in a pincer operation by the US First and Ninth Armies. This tore a huge gap in the German defences, and Bradley's 12th Army Group was quick to take advantage of this, sending divisions racing eastwards as fast as they could go. Within the Ruhr pocket itself lay the remains of Walther Model's Army Group B, which had fought the western Allies from the Normandy beaches eastwards. It took eighteen days to reduce and yielded 325,000 prisoners, the largest surrender that the western Allies achieved in a single battle. Model himself committed suicide.

Meanwhile, the rapid advance eastwards continued, often with only small groups of still fanatical SS men standing in its way. As early as 11 April elements of Simpson's Ninth US Army reached the Ruhr at Magdeburg, just seventy-five miles from Berlin. Simpson pleaded to be allowed to go on to the German capital, but Eisenhower was adamant: none of his troops would advance east of the Elbe, even though the Russian assault on Berlin had not yet opened.

Events were moving just as rapidly in northern Italy. While there was little that the German troops in Italy could do to influence the worsening situation at home, the western Allies were conscious that if they were allowed to withdraw to the Alps it would be very difficult to winkle them out. Consequently, another offensive had to be mounted. The plan was literally to trap Army Group C, now commanded by von Vietinghoff, since Kesselring had been ordered to replace von Rundstedt as C-in-C West. The British Eighth Army was to seize the vital Argenta Gap between Lake Commacchio and the River Reno, while the US Fifth Army advanced north and west of Bologna. But as preparations for the attack were under way, the first signs that the Third Reich might be cracking became apparent. In early March the SS adjutant to the German military governor in northern Italy made overtures to the OSS (Office of Strategic Services – US equivalent to SOE) in Switzerland, proposing a separate armistice for the German forces in the country. However, Himmler, who had proposed to the western Allies earlier in the year that they join Germany against Russia, became aware of what was going on and put an end to the negotiations.

The final Allied offensive in Italy opened on 9 April. The German forces, short of fuel and with their lines of communication badly damaged from the air, could do little and the Allies were soon sweeping northwards. Von Vietinghoff, realizing that defeat was inevitable, decided to reopen negotiations with the Allies without informing Berlin. Not, however, until 27 April did Alexander sanction these. The following day saw the death of Mussolini, who had been captured by partisans. His body and that of his mistress were strung up in one of the main squares of Milan. Finally, on 29 April, the German forces in Italy signed an unconditional surrender. By then the war in Europe as a whole was almost at an end.

Eisenhower's Elbe halt order did not mean that the 6th and 12th Army Groups totally ceased their advance, merely that they had switched direction to the south-east towards Czechoslovakia and Bavaria, while Montgomery's forces continued to clear the north German coast, aiming especially for Bremen and Hamburg. But attention all the time was focused on Berlin.

Contrary to what he had told Eisenhower, Stalin had given orders that Berlin was be secured by 1 May. The plan had been personally approved by him on 1 April. While Zhukov was to capture the city itself and then advance to the Elbe, Ivan Koniev was to cross the Oder to the south, destroy all German forces in his path, and press on to Dresden. To the north, Rokossovsky was also to advance to the Elbe and make for the Baltic coast.The assault was to begin on 16 April.

The three fronts totalled nearly two million men. Marshalling them and the 6,250 tanks, 41,600 guns and mortars, and the 7,500 aircraft which were to support the attacks was an enormous challenge, especially given the short period of time in which it had to be done. To the east of the Oder every patch of woodland was crammed with vehicles and troops. Where natural cover was not available, acre upon acre of camouflage netting was used. That the preparations were completed on time is a measure of the high degree of efficiency attained by the Red Army after four years of war.

On the west bank of the Oder three German armies, with a total of a mere thirty-three under-strength divisions, stood awaiting the inevitable. West of Berlin was another motley army, Wenck's Twelfth, whose twelve divisions were defending the line of the Elbe. The Germans had had, however, plenty of time to prepare the Oder defences.

It was Zhukov who struck first. After a short concentrated air and artillery bombardment, and using artificial moonlight (searchlight beams reflected off the clouds), his troops crossed the river in the early hours of 16 April, but could make little impression on the Seelow heights which dominated this stretch of the Oder. In contrast, Koniev, who also attacked on this day, was poised to break through by the end of it. On the following day he was through the German defences, while Zhukov was still struggling to establish a bridgehead. Stalin, without telling Zhukov, told Koniev that he could now drive on to Berlin. In the north, Rokossovsky launched his attack on the 18th, but found the marshy ground an obstacle and made little progress during the first two days. Even so, he was able to prevent the Third Panzer Army from going to the defence of Berlin.

On 20 April Hitler celebrated his fifty-sixth birthday. He declared that he would remain in his capital, but gave permission for various government organs to leave. He ordered Grand Admiral Karl Doenitz to take command of all forces in northern Germany and Kesselring those in the south. On the following day Koniev's forces crossed the autobahn ring which marked the boundary of Berlin proper and his guns began to shell the centre of the city. Hitler, realizing that the western Allies did not intend to advance east of the Elbe, now rested his hopes on Wenck coming to the rescue. His belief that Wenck's twelve weak divisions could make any difference to the inevitable outcome merely reflected the total sense of unreality that now existed in the *Führerbunker*.

On 25 April Zhukov's forces, which had been ordered to thrust north of Berlin, linked up with those of Koniev, thus encircling the German capital. Simultaneously, Koniev's men also joined hands with Hodges' First US Army at Torgau, north-east of Leipzig, on the River Elbe. Germany was physically split into two.

Now began the final battle, as the Russians advanced ever closer to the centre of Berlin. Like all battles in urban areas, it was a slow and costly business, but on 29 April they reached the area of the Reichstag and Chancellery. Hitler made his last will and testament, declaring Doenitz his successor, and marrying his long-time mistress, Eva Braun. The following day he committed suicide. Others of his

THE SOVIET ASSAULT ON BERLIN

Once they had broken through the German defences west of the River Oder the Russians moved quickly to seal off Berlin and link up with the Western Allies.

entourage, including Goebbels and his family, took their lives on the following day. Finally, on 2 May, one day after Stalin's deadline, General Helmuth Weidling, the military governor of Berlin, surrendered the city.

Elsewhere the fighting continued. Montgomery's 21st Army Group had fought a bitter battle to take Bremen, but had then raced on to the Elbe. Hamburg fell without a fight on 3 May, and the British forces simultaneously advanced north into Schleswig-Holstein and east to secure Lübeck before the Russians arrived. Far to the south, Patton's Third US Army had crossed the Czech border and was pressing on eastwards against the remnants of the German Army Group Centre. This was also being forced back on the Czech capital, Prague, by no fewer than four Russian fronts. The First French and Seventh US Armies were closing on the Swiss border, while the Allied armies in Italy were advancing through the Alps and into Austria.

The first formal German surrender approach was made to Montgomery on 3 May. The German delegation wanted to surrender all their forces in northern Germany, including those withdrawing in front of Rokossovsky, but Montgomery would accept only that of the forces in north-west Germany, Holland and Denmark. The Germans then proposed a separate surrender to the western Allies, but Eisenhower turned this down. Meanwhile, the fighting in Czechoslovakia continued, with patriots in Prague rising against the German garrison.

Eventually the Germans accepted that they had no option but to surrender

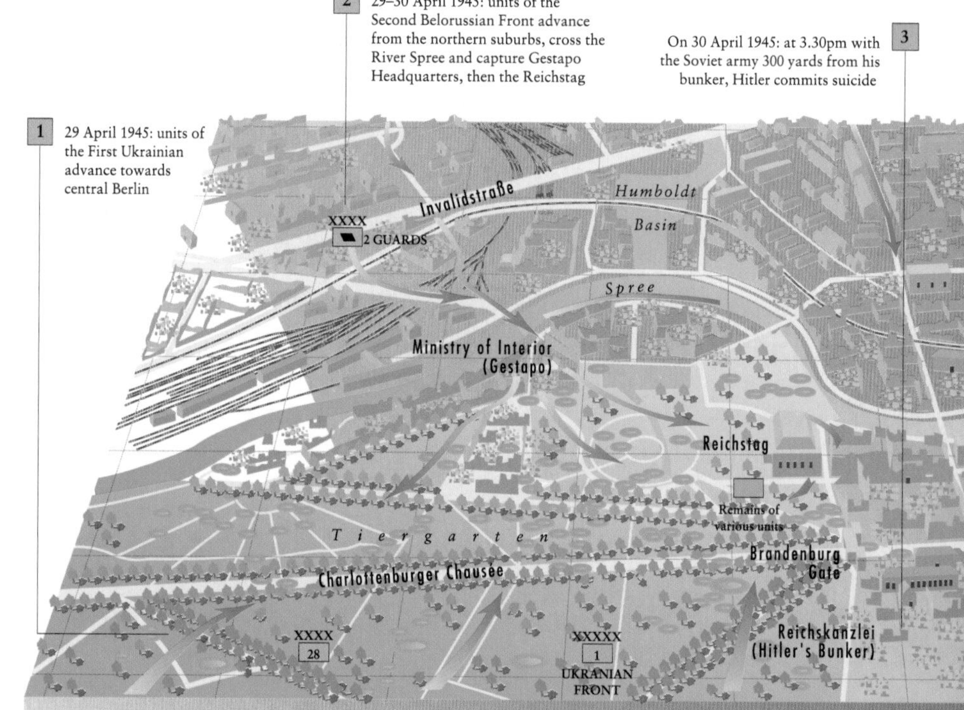

THE FINAL PHASES OF THE BATTLE OF BERLIN

The casualties were very high on both sides during the protracted street fighting. During the whole offensive, from 16 April, the three Soviet fronts suffered a total of over 350,000 casualties. No precise figures exist for the German side, but, including civilians, they were of much the same order.

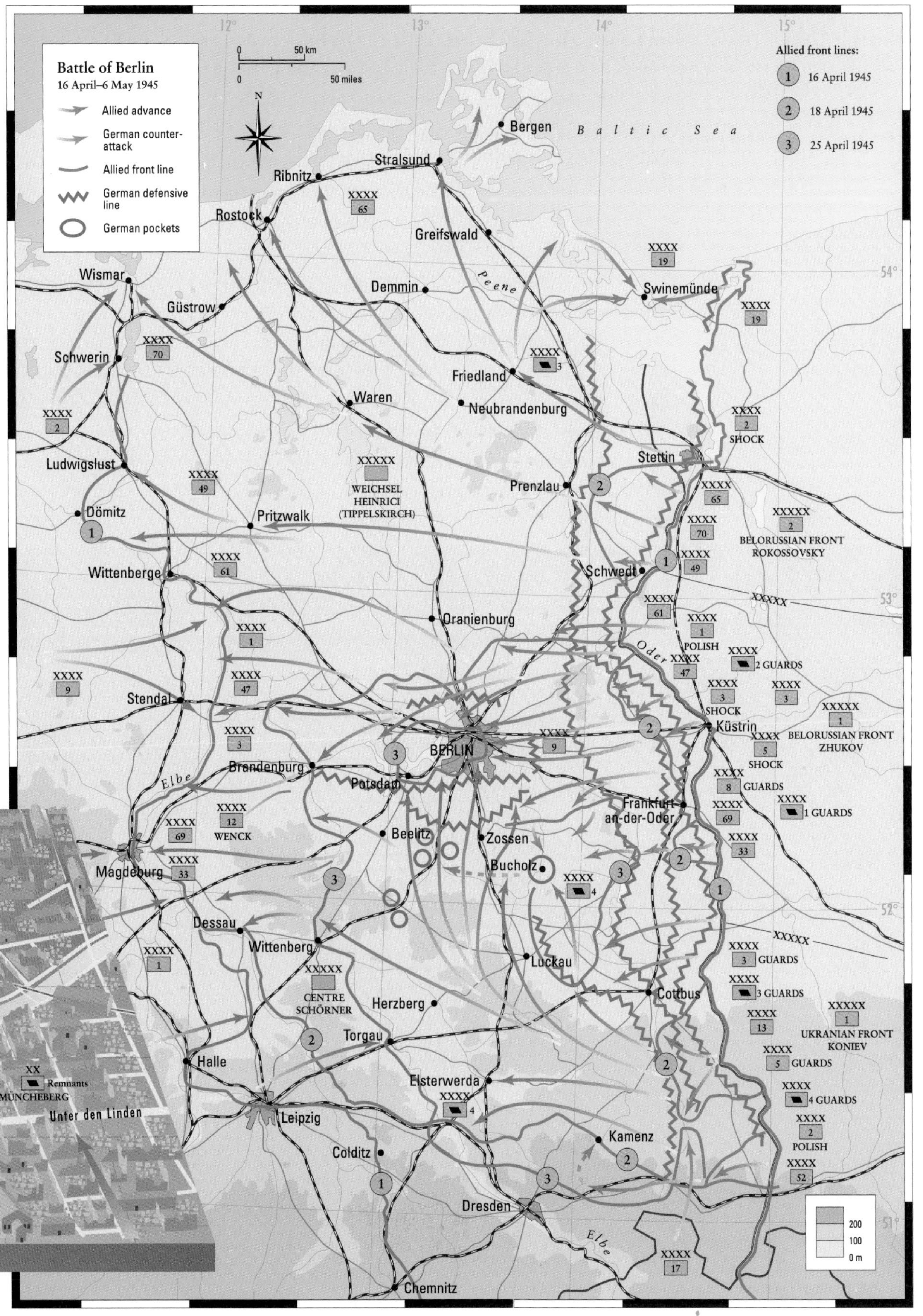
Battle of Berlin
16 April–6 May 1945
Allied advance
German counter-attack
Allied front line
German defensive line
German pockets
Allied front lines:
1 16 April 1945
2 18 April 1945
3 25 April 1945
Baltic Sea
Bergen
Stralsund
Ribnitz
Rostock
Greifswald
Wismar
Güstrow
Demmin
Peene
Swinemünde
Schwerin
Friedland
Waren
Neubrandenburg
Ludwigslust
Dömitz
Pritzwalk
Stettin
Prenzlau
WEICHSEL HEINRICI (TIPPELSKIRCH)
SHOCK
BELORUSSIAN FRONT ROKOSSOVSKY
Wittenberge
Schwedt
Oranienburg
POLISH
Oder
2 GUARDS
Stendal
Küstrin
BERLIN
BELORUSSIAN FRONT ZHUKOV
Brandenburg
Potsdam
Elbe
WENCK
Frankfurt an-der-Oder
8 GUARDS
1 GUARDS
Magdeburg
Beelitz
Zossen
Bucholz
Dessau
Wittenberg
Luckau
CENTRE SCHÖRNER
Herzberg
Cottbus
3 GUARDS
Torgau
UKRANIAN FRONT KONIEV
Halle
5 GUARDS
Elsterwerda
4 GUARDS
Remnants MÜNCHEBERG
Unter den Linden
Leipzig
Kamenz
Colditz
Dresden
Chemnitz
12°
13°
14°
15°
54°
53°
52°
51°
50 km
50 miles
200
100
0 m

OPPOSITE: *The end of a long road – Soviet troops on the roof of the badly damaged Reichstag in the centre of Berlin.*

unconditionally to all the Allies. The formal ceremony took place at Eisenhower's headquarters at Reims on 7 May, with hostilities coming to an end at 2301 hours Central European Time on the 8th. The British and Americans prepared to broadcast this to their peoples and to make the 8th Victory in Europe Day, but the Russians now demanded another surrender ceremony in Berlin on 8 May. The broadcasts were therefore cancelled, but the news was already out and so, as the second surrender took place, in western Europe, America, and elsewhere in the world millions of people celebrated.

Yet fighting continued in Czechoslovakia and not until 11 May did the German Army Group Centre finally lay down its arms. Three days later came the final German surrender, that of the remnants of Army Group E to Tito's forces in northern Yugoslavia. Even so, the Third Reich was not quite dead. The Allies had allowed Doenitz to keep his government in being at Flensburg in Schleswig-Holstein so that he could organize the surrender of the U-boats still on the high seas. On 23 May, once this had been done, Doenitz was arrested. The Second World War in Europe was finally over.

GI Joe meets Ivan at Torgau on the River Elbe, 25 April 1945.

CHAPTER NINE

In Retrospect

Tanks of the US Seventh Army enter Nuremberg, 20 April 1945. The destruction, which was largely the result of the sustained Anglo-American strategic bombing offensive against Germany, was typical of almost every large German town and city. Indeed, so much of the country's infrastructure had been destroyed that sustaining the German people in the immediate aftermath of their defeat was to prove a hard task for the Allies.

IN RETROSPECT

THE SECOND WORLD WAR in Europe was very much more total than its predecessor. The territory over which the fighting on the ground took place encompassed an area many times that of 1914–18. In Europe alone, it extended from the extreme north of Norway to the Italian toe and from the English Channel to the River Volga. In Africa the combat reached the extreme south of Abyssinia and stretched the length of the northern coastline. It was significantly more ferocious in nature, not just because weapons were more destructive than they had been during the Great War, but because this was a war between ideologies as opposed to empires.

Civilians were very much more in the firing-line, not just because they were subjected to prolonged air-bombing campaigns, but also because often the onrush of battle reached them before they had time to flee their homes to safety. There was, too, the Holocaust, which caused the deaths of some six million of Europe's Jews. As for military casualties, those in the West were proportionately less than they had been twenty-five years earlier, mainly because the prolonged and costly trench offensives of the Western Front 1914–18 did not take place. In the East, it was very different. The Soviet armed forces suffered over eight million fatalities and lost nearly four million others as prisoners of war. That the German armed forces lost 3.5 million killed on all fronts is, as much as anything, an indication of the relative value attached to human life. But the fact that the bulk of German deaths was on the Eastern Front was also an indicator of the ruthlessness with which the war there was conducted by both sides.

Knocked out Soviet tanks and rubble-strewn streets provide some impression of the severity of the final battle for Berlin.

Given the degree of emancipation of women that 1914–18 had triggered, it would be natural to suppose that the female cause would be further advanced during the Second World War. This, however, is true only to a degree. The increased technology made greater demands on industry, which led to a greater need for women factory workers in some countries, notably America, Britain and the USSR. By the same token, more women joined the armed forces. In the West, however, the anathema against women actually engaging in direct combat persisted, although, especially on anti-aircraft gun sites, they did everything except actually fire the gun. The Red Army had no such sensitivities, and neither did the partisans. It is, however, a curious fact that even when Germany had its back to the wall, Hitler still largely believed that a woman's place was at home.

Land warfare between 1939 and 1945 saw the pendulum swing back in favour of the offence. Ever more efficient internal combustion engines and the development of effective radio communications saw to this. Between them they restored fluidity to the battlefield. True, there were periods of static warfare, particularly in Italy, but these were caused by the terrain and the weather and not usually by bankruptcy of means or ideas to break through. But the increased pace of operations meant that commanders at all levels had to be very much more quick thinking than they had been twenty-five years before. They also realized, especially the Germans, that one of the keys to victory lay in the closest co-operation among all arms – infantry, armour, artillery and engineers.

An American White halftrack passes the body of an unknown German soldier. More than five and a half years of war cost the German nation the lives of three and a half million of its soldiers, sailors, and airmen, and two million of its civilians.

The last vestiges of the traditional one-dimensional appearance of the land battlefield also quickly disappeared. The advent of aircraft in the first decade of the twentieth century had begun this process, but by 1939 ground-force commanders were fully appreciating that, without enjoying a measure of air superiority at least

over the battlefield at the outset, the prospects of victory were much diminished. Thereafter, close air support and aerial interdiction, two air-power roles which had been developed during 1914–18, helped to ensure success on the ground, with improved air–ground communications making air forces that much more responsive. This multi-dimensional approach was further enhanced by the employment of airborne forces, although, apart from on Crete, they were never decisive when employed on their own. Properly used, with the guarantee of an early link-up by ground forces, they were a valuable member of the all-arms orchestra.

Navies, especially on the Allied side, also played their part. Indeed, between 1942 and 1944 amphibious operations dominated western Allied strategy in the European

Without doubt, the most horrific aspect of the Second World War in the West was the concentration camps. These inmates are seen shortly after liberation. For some of them this came too late; they were already dying and nothing could save them.

theatre, as they did in the Pacific. The landing of troops on hostile shores was developed into a fine art, entailing the development of special weapons, in particular armoured fighting vehicle variants to assist them to get off the beaches. Naval fire support also helped the ground forces, especially during the early days in Normandy.

The new mobile warfare of 1939–45 placed an ever-increasing strain on logistics, with fuel becoming the most vital commodity. The greater multiplicity of weapons, especially rapid-fire types, meant added problems for ammunition resupply. Where road and rail networks were sparse, as in Russia the supply difficulties were immense, especially during the winter months, at least for the Germans. It was for this reason that their armies were without winter clothing when they were halted before Moscow in December 1941. The Russians did not have quite the same problem. Indeed, the German General Hasso von Manteuffel noted: 'Behind the tank spearhead rolls on a vaste horde partly mounted on horseback. Soldiers carry sacks on their backs filled with dry crusts of bread and raw vegetables collected on the march from the fields and villages. The horses feed on the straw from the roofs of houses – they get very little else. The Russians are accustomed to carry on for as long as three weeks in this primitive way when advancing.'

In contrast, the soldiers of the western democracies, with their industrialized societies and relatively high standard of living, had greater expectations in the field. Hot food, suitable clothing, an efficient mail service, and rest and recreation centres were all considered to be important for the maintenance of morale. This and greater weapons and equipment sophistication meant that, while it took just two men on the lines of communication to support a Russian in the front line, the American combat soldier required eight. This was one reason why the Allies, especially the British, suffered from a shortage of infantry towards the end of the war.

The higher expectations of the American and British soldier have caused some to declare that their fathers who fought in the trenches during 1914–18 had much greater sticking power and could endure a much higher loss rate before becoming combat ineffective. Those who fought at Tobruk, Monte Cassino, and Bastogne would be the first to dispute this. The truth of the matter was that their generals had personally experienced the slaughter of the Western Front in the Great War, and they were determined not to subject the new generation of young men to the same horrors. Consequently, whenever possible they relieved units in combat sooner rather than later. When they were forced to remain longer in the front line than was desirable, there is no evidence to suggest that units showed any less endurance than they did during the Great War on the Western Front.

Another significant aspect of the Second World War in Europe was the treatment of casualties. Such were the improvements in medicine (notably the availability of penicillin) and casualty evacuation, which now included rescue by air, that a British soldier wounded in action had a twenty-five times better chance of survival than his predecessor of 1914–18. The same did not apply to the Red Army, with its primitive medical facilities, although the situation did improve as the war went on. The experience of the Great War also led to greater understanding of battle fatigue, with sympathetic treatment enabling a large proportion of British and American sufferers to return to combat fully restored in health. In the dictatorships of Germany and Russia, the problem was regarded as a military rather than medical one. Consequently, battle fatigue cases often continued to suffer harsh treatment.

Overall, it was the influence of national leaders on the war that so often dictated its shape. The dictators – Hitler and Stalin, and also Mussolini for a time – exerted an iron grip on its conduct. Stalin dominated entirely through fear: the firing-squad, penal battalions, and the labour camps of Siberia constantly hung like a noose over his military commanders. Hitler could always play the trump card that his generals had been duped into swearing personal loyalty to him. His early blitzkrieg successes also gave him the confidence to overrule his military commanders, who, during the early part of the war, had often expressed doubts over his strategy. Increasingly, he sacked those who objected to his diktats. But Churchill, too, loved to meddle in military affairs and it took a strong military chief of staff, Alan Brooke, to keep him within the bounds of what was feasible. Even so, as the British forays into the Balkans showed, Brooke was not always successful. The leader who was most amenable to military advice was undoubtedly Roosevelt, who became heavily dependent on his Joint Chiefs of Staff, notably their chairman, George C. Marshall. Sadly, Roosevelt was to die just weeks before the final victory over Nazi Germany.

But for the victorious Allied forces, in both East and West, who stood over the ruins of the Third Reich in May 1945, these reflections were for the future. They were conscious that the war with Japan continued and that some of their number, even now, were being redeployed to the Pacific. Amid a numbed and sullen population, and long columns of ex-concentration camp victims, former German conscripted foreign workers, refugees and newly liberated prisoners of war, there was much to do to resolve the chaos brought about by over five and a half years' destructive war. There were, too, differences in the agenda for postwar Europe between the Soviet Union and that of her western allies, and these were already becoming apparent.

Some leading commanders

American

Omar N. Bradley (1893–1981)
1915 Commissioned into Infantry; 1917–18 company commander Stateside; 1924–5 student Infantry School, Fort Benning; 1925–8 battalion commander, Hawaii; 1928–9 Command and General Staff School, Fort Leavenworth; 1929–33 instructor Infantry School; 1933–4 Army War College; 1934–8 tactics instructor West Point; 1938–9 G-1 (personnel) Division, War Dept; 1939–41 Assistant Secretary of General Staff; 1941 Commandant Infantry School; 1941–2 commanded and trained 82nd and 28th Divisions; 1943 deputy commander and commander II Corps in Tunisia and Sicily; 1943–4 Commanded US 1st Army in Britain and Normandy; 1944–5 commanded 12th US Army Group NW Europe; 1945–8 Head of Veterans' Association; 1948–9 US Army Chief of Staff; 1949–53 Chairman Joint Chiefs of Staff.

Mark Clark (1896–1984)
1917 Commissioned into Infantry; 1917–18 company and briefly battalion commander until wounded, then Supply Section HQ 1st US Army, France; 1928 infantry brigade executive officer; 1929–33 National Guard Division instructor; 1933–5 Command and General Staff College, Fort Leavenworth; 1935–6 Assistant Chief of Staff G-2 (Intelligence) and G-3 (Operations) at division and corps; 1936 Army War College; 1937–40 Assistant Chief of Staff G-2/G-3 at divisional HQ; 1941–2 served GHQ rising to Chief of Staff Army Ground Forces; 1942 commanded II Corps then made Deputy Supreme Allied Commander for Torch landings; 1943–4 Commanded US 5th Army North Africa and Italy; 1944–5 commanded 15th Army Group, Italy; 1945–7 Commander US Troops Austria; 1947–9 commanded US 6th Army; 1949–52 Chief, Army Ground Forces; 1952–3 C-in-C United Nations Command and Far East.

Dwight D. Eisenhower (1890–1969)
1915 Commissioned into Infantry; 1917–18 trained young officers and commanded tank training school; 1919–21 Infantry Tank School; 1922–4 Executive Officer infantry brigade, Panama; 1925–6 attended Command and General Staff School, Fort Leavenworth; 1927–8 Army War College; 1929–33 military assistant to Assistant Secretary of War; 1933–9 Personal Assistant to Gen MacArthur, when Army Chief of Staff and Military Adviser to Filipino govt; 1940–41 regimental executive officer and battalion commander; 1941 corps then army chief of staff; 1941–2 Deputy Chief of War Plans Division, War Dept; 1942 Chief of Operations Division, War Dept, then Commanding General US Army European Theatre of Operations; 1942–3 Allied commander Torch landings and Commanding General Allied Forces HQ North Africa, Supreme Allied Commander Mediterranean; 1944–5, and Europe; 1945–8 US Army Chief of Staff; 1950–52 Supreme Allied Commander Europe; 1953–61 President of USA.

George C. Marshall (1880–1959)
1902 Commissioned into Infantry; 1907–10 attended Command and General Staff School, Fort Leavenworth, then instructor; 1912–16 company commander USA and Philippines; 1917–18 divisional staff officer and Chief of Operations First US Army, France; 1919–24 chief aide to Gen Pershing; 1924–7 Exec. Officer 15th Infantry, Tientsin, China; 1927–32 Assistant Commandant Infantry School, Fort Benning; 1932–3 battalion and regimental commander; 1933–6 Chief Instructor Illinois National Guard; 1936–8 brigade commander; 1938–9 Chief of War Plans Division then Deputy Army Chief of Staff; 1939–45 Army Chief of Staff; 1945–6 President Truman's personal representative in China; 1947–9 Secretary of State for Foreign Affairs; 1950–51 Secretary of State for Defense.

George S. Patton (1885–1945)
1909 Commissioned into Cavalry; 1916 took part in Mexican Expedition; 1917–18 Post Adjutant HQ American Expeditionary Force then commanded light tank brigade before being wounded; 1919–20 Infantry Tank School; 1923–4 Command and General Staff College, Fort Leavenworth; 1924–8 corps and divisional staff USA and Hawaii; 1928–31 Office of Chief of Cavalry; 1931–2 Army War College;

1932–4 cavalry regiment executive officer; 1935–7 Head of G-2 (Intelligence) Hawaiian Dept; 1938–40 executive officer, then commanded cavalry regiment; 1940–2 armoured brigade and divisional commander; 1942 commanded I Armored Corps and Desert Training Center, then commanded Torch landings Morocco; 1943 commanded II Corps in Tunisia and 7th Army in Sicily – removed from command after slapping shell-shocked soldier in hospital; 1944–5 commanded 3rd Army in NW Europe; 1945 appointed to command 15th Army but killed in car accident in Germany.

British

Harold Alexander (1891–1969)
1911 Commissioned into Irish Guards; 1914–18 regimental service Western Front; 1919 Allied Relief Commission Poland and commanded Baltic Landswehr; 1922–6 battalion commander, including Chanak Incident; 1926 Staff College; 1930–32 Imperial Defence College; 1934–8 brigade commander, India, including Frontier campaigns; 1938–40 commanded 1st Division and I Corps; 1940–42 C-in-C Southern Command, Britain; 1942 Commanded British Forces Burma, then First Army in Britain; 1942–3 C-in-C Middle East; 1943–4 commanded 15th Army Group in Tunisia, Sicily, Italy; 1944–5 Supreme Allied Commander Mediterranean; 1946–52 Governor-General of Canada; 1952–4 Minister of Defence.

Claude Auchinleck (1884–1981)
1902 Commissioned, later joining 62nd Punjabis, Indian Army, including service in Tibet; 1914–18 served at regimental duty, Egypt and Mesopotamia; 1919 divisional staff, Kurdistan; 1920 Indian Staff College; 1927 Imperial Defence College; 1928–30 battalion commander, India; 1930–32 instructor Indian Staff College; 1932–6 brigade commander India, including Frontier campaigns; 1936–8 Deputy Chief C-in-C of General Staff India; 1938–40 district commander India; 1940 commanded IV Corps in England, northern Norway, V Corps, England, then Southern Command; 1941–2 C-in-C Middle East; 1943–7 C-in-C India.

Alan Brooke (1883–1963)
1902 Commissioned into Royal Artillery; 1914–18 served mainly on artillery staff at division, corps, and army level on Western Front; 1919 Staff College; 1920–27 staff; 1927 Student Imperial Defence College; 1920–32 commandant of School of Artillery; 1932 instructor Imperial Defence College; 1934–5 infantry brigade commander; 1935 Inspector of Artillery; 1936 Director Military Training; 1937 commanded Mobile Division; 1938 Anti-Aircraft Corps commander; 1939–40 commanded II Corps, France and Flanders; 1940–41 C-in-C Home Forces; 1941–6 Chief of Imperial General Staff.

Bernard Montgomery (1887–1976)
1908 Commissioned into Royal Warwickshire Regiment; 1914 badly wounded, France; 1915–18 served on brigade, divisional and corps staffs, Western Front; 1920 Staff College; 1921–6 brigade and divisional staff then company commander; 1926–8 instructor Staff College; 1929–34 regimental duty including battalion command in Egypt; 1934–7 instructor Indian Staff College; 1937–8 infantry brigade commander; 1938–9 divisional commander Palestine during Arab Rebellion; 1939–40 commanded 3rd Infantry Division, France and Flanders; 1940–42 corps commander and commanded South-Eastern Army, England; 1942–4 commanded Eighth Army North Africa, Sicily, Italy; 1944–6 commanded 21st Army Group; 1946–8 Chief of Imperial General Staff; 1948–51 Chairman Western European Union Chiefs of Staff Committee; 1951–8 Deputy Supreme Allied Commander Europe.

Archibald Wavell (1883–1950)
1901 Commissioned into Black Watch and served South African War and India; 1909–10 Staff College; 1912–14 Directorate of Military Operations; 1914–16 served on brigade staff (wounded) and GHQ France and Flanders; 1916–17 British military representative to HQ of Grand Duke Nicholas in Caucasus; 1917–20 liaison officer, staff of Allied Supreme War Council, corps chief of staff Palestine; 1921–30 War Office and divisional staff; 1930–34 infantry brigade commander; 1935–7 commanded division; 1937–8 commanded British forces Palestine during Arab Revolt; 1938–9 C-in-C Southern Command, Britain; 1939–41 C-in-C Middle East; 1941–3 C-in-C India and briefly Supreme Allied Commander South-West Pacific; 1943–7 Viceroy of India.

German

Walter Von Brauchitsch (1881–1948)
1900 Commissioned into 3rd Guards Regiment of Foot, but then transferred to Guards Field Artillery; 1910–12 War Academy; 1914–18 Served on divisional and corps staffs; 1919–32 battery and artillery battalion commander, and staff, rising to Maj Gen; 1932 Inspector of Artillery; 1933–7 divisional and corps commander; 1937 Commander 4th Army Group; 1938 Army C-in-C; 1941 Retired. Died in British captivity.

Wilhelm Keitel (1883–1946)
1901 Commissioned into Prussian Field Artillery; 1914 wounded; 1915–18 served on divisional and corps staffs; 1919–26 battery and artillery battalion commander; 1926–33 head of organization branch in Truppenamt; 1933 district infantry commander; 1934 divisional commander; 1935 Chief of Armed Forces office in War Ministry; 1938–45 Chief of OKW; 1945 found guilty of war crimes at Nuremberg and executed.

Albert Kesselring (1883–1960)
1904 in Bavarian Artillery; 1914 Western Front; 1915–17 Artillery staff France; 1917–18 divisional, corps, and army staffs, Eastern Front; 1922–31 Truppenamt; 1932 commanded artillery regiment; 1933 transferred to Air Ministry; 1936 chief of staff Luftwaffe; 1937 Commander 3rd Air Region; 1938 commander 1st Air Fleet including Polish campaign; 1940 commander 2nd Air Fleet in West and for invasion of Russia; 1941 C-in-C Mediterranean; 1944 C-in-C Italy and Army Group C; 1945 C-in-C West; 1947 tried by British for war crimes and sentenced to death, later commuted to life imprisonment; 1952 released.

Günther Hans Von Kluge (1882–1944)
1901 Commissioned into Lower Saxony Artillery Regiment; 1908–14 War Academy, and General Staff; 1914–18 staff officer Western Front; 1919–34 regimental and staff duty; 1934–7 divisional commander; 1937–8 corps commander; 1938–41 commanded Sixth (later Fourth) Army, Polish and French campaigns, and invasion of Russia; 1941–3 commanded Army Group Centre on Eastern Front until badly injured in car crash; 1944 C-in-C West Jul–Aug, but then dismissed. Committed suicide.

Erich Von Manstein (1885–1973)
1906 Commissioned into 3rd Foot Guards; 1914 severely wounded on Eastern Front; 1915–18 army group, army and divisional staffs; 1919 involved in planning post-Versailles army; 1920–34 regimental duty and staff; 1934 district chief of staff; 1935 head of army general staff operations branch; 1936 deputy army chief of staff; 1938 divisional commander; 1939 Chief of Staff Army Group South, Poland; 1940 corps commander during campaign in West; 1941 Panzer corps commander for invasion of Russia then commanded Eleventh Army; 1942 command of Army Group Don (later South); 1944 dismissed; 1949 tried by British for war crimes and sentenced to 18 years' imprisonment, later reduced; 1953 released.

Walther Model (1891–1945)
1910 Commissioned into 52nd Infantry Regiment; 1914–18 regimental and staff duty on Western Front; 1919–35 staff and regimental duty; 1935–8 general staff, Berlin; 1938 chief of staff IV Corps, and in Polish campaign; 1939–40 chief of staff 16th Army, campaign in West; 1940–41 Panzer division and corps commander, including invasion of Russia; 1942–4 commanded 9th Army Eastern Front; 1944 commanded Army Group North, Army Group N. Ukraine, Army Group Centre; 1944–5 briefly C-in-C West then of Army Group B. Committed suicide in Ruhr Pocket.

Erwin Rommel (1891–1944)
1912 Commissioned into 124th Infantry Regiment; 1914–16 served on Western Front and twice wounded; 1917–18 served with mountain troops in Romania and Italy; 1919–35 regimental duty and infantry instructor; 1935–7 instructor at War College; 1939 commanded Hitler's bodyguard during Polish campaign; 1940 Panzer division commander French campaign; 1941 commander Deutsches Afrika Korps then Panzergruppe Afrika, Libya; 1942 commander Panzerarmee Afrika; 1943 commander Army Group Africa, Tunisia then Army Group B, North Italy and France; 1944 severely wounded and later forced to commit suicide.

Gerd Von Rundstedt (1875–1953)
1893 Commissioned into Prussian Infantry; 1903–12 War Academy followed by staff appointments; 1914–18 divisional and corps staffs on Western and Eastern Fronts; 1919–27 infantry regiment commander and

staff appointments; 1928 cavalry division commander; 1932–8 district and group commander based in Berlin; 1938 Retired; 1939 recalled to plan invasion of Poland during which commanded Army Group South; 1939–40 commanded Army Group A during campaign in West and thereafter C-in-C West; 1941 Commanded Army Group South on Eastern Front, but retired at end of year; 1942–5 C-in-C West, but sacked in July 1944 and again finally in March 1945; 1949 charged by British with war crimes but found medically unfit to plead and released.

Russian

Ivan Stepanovich Koniev (1897–1971) 1916–17 served as a junior artillery NCO; 1918–25 military commissar; 1926 attended Frunze Military Academy; 1927–32 commanded a rifle regiment then a division; 1932–4 senior officers' course at Frunze Military Academy; 1934–7 commanded Belorussian Military District; 1937–41 corps commander Mongolia then commanded in succession 2nd Separate Red Banner Army in Far East, Transbaikal and Northern Caucasus Military Districts; 1941–2 commanded 19th Army during German invasion then Kalinin Front; 1942–3 commanded West Front; 1943–4 commanded North-West then Steppe (later 2nd Ukrainian) Fronts; 1944–5 commanded 1st Ukrainian Front; 1945–6 C-in-C Soviet Central Group of Forces in Austria and Hungary; 1946–56 C-in-C Soviet Land Forces and Deputy Defence Minister; 1956–60 C-in-C Warsaw Pact Forces and Deputy Defence Minister; 1960–61 Chief Inspector Ministry of Defence; 1961–3 C-in-C Soviet Forces Germany; 1963 reappointed Chief Inspector Ministry of Defence

Konstantin Konstantinovich Rokossovsky (1896–1990) 1914–17 served in a Dragoon regiment as junior officer; 1917–21 fought in Civil War rising to cavalry regiment commander; 1922–4 Far East, eventually commanding cavalry brigade. 1925–8 military mission to Mongolia; 1928 senior officers' course at Frunze Military Academy; 1929–30 commanded cavalry brigade on Sino-Russian border; 1930–37 commanded cavalry division and corps; 1937–1940 imprisoned as a result of the Purges; 1940–41 commanded cavalry then mechanized corps; 1941–2 commanded Sixteenth Army in defences of Moscow; 1942–3 commanded Bryansk then the Don (later Central) Fronts; 1943–4 commanded 1st Belorussian Front; 1944–5 commanded 2nd Belorussian Front; 1945–9 C-in-C of Russian troops in Poland; 1949–56 Polish Defence Minister; 1956–7 Deputy Soviet Defence Minister; 1957–8 Chief Inspector Soviet Ministry of Defence, then commanded Transcaucasus Military District; 1958–62 resumed as Chief Inspector Soviet Ministry of Defence.

Semyon Konstantinovich Timoshenko (1895–1970) 1914–18 Served as machine-gunner; 1918–20 joined Red Army and fought in Civil War, rising to command a cavalry division before being seriously wounded; 1921–33 commanded a cavalry corps and attended senior officers' courses; 1933–9 Deputy Commander, then commander various military districts; 1939 commanded Ukrainian Front for invasion of Poland; 1940 commanded North-West Front in war against Finland then Defence Commissar; 1941–2 on German invasion took command of West Front then South-West Theatre; 1942–3 commanded North-West Front; 1943–5 acted as Stalin's personal representative to various fronts; 1946–60 commanded various military districts; 1960 Inspector General Soviet Defence Ministry.

Georgi Konstantinovich Zhukov (1896–1974) 1914–16 Served in a reconnaissance unit and badly wounded; 1918 joined Red Army as a volunteer, rising to squadron commander and again wounded; 1923–33 cavalry regiment and brigade commander, attended Higher Cavalry School and other senior officers' courses; 1933–8 cavalry division and corps commander; 1938–9 deputy commander Bialystok Military District; 1939–40 commanded 1st Army Group on Mongolian border, including action against Japanese; 1940–41 commanded Kiev Military District; 1941 Chief of General Staff then commanded Reserve and Leningrad Fronts before command of defence of Moscow; 1942–4 Deputy Supreme C-in-C and First Deputy Defence Commissar; 1944–5 commanded 1st Ukrainian then 1st Belorussian Fronts; 1945–6 C-in-C Soviet zone of occupation in Germany; 1946–7 C-in-C Land Forces and Deputy Defence Minister then commanded Odessa Military District; 1948–53 commanded Urals Military C-in-C District; 1953–5 Deputy Defence Minister; 1955–7 Defence Minister.

FURTHER READING

Addison, Paul and Calder, Angus (ed.), *Time to Kill: The Soldier's Experience of War in the West 1939–1945* (Pimlico, London, 1997)

Ambrose, Stephen, *The Supreme Commander: The War Years of General Dwight D. Eisenhower* (Doubleday, NY, 1969)

Barnett, Correlli (ed.), *Hitler's Generals* (Weidenfeld & Nicolson, London, 1989)

Beevor, Antony, *Stalingrad* (Viking, London, 1998)

Creveld, Martin van, *Fighting Power: German and US Army Combat Performance, 1939–1945* (Arms & Armour, London, 1983)

Dear, I. C. B., and Foot, M. R. D. (ed.), *The Oxford Companion to the Second World War* (OUP, 1995)

Erickson, John, *The Road to Stalingrad* (Weidenfeld & Nicolson, London, 1975)

Erickson, John, *The Road to Berlin* (Weidenfeld & Nicolson, London, 1983)

Graham, Dominick, and Bidwell, Shelford, *Tug of War: The Battle for Italy 1943–45* (Hodder & Stoughton, London, 1986)

Greenfield, Kent Roberts (ed.), *Command Decisions* (Methuen, London, 1960)

Harris, J. P., and Toase, F. N. (ed.), *Armoured Warfare* (Batsford, London, 1990)

Hastings, Max, *Overlord and the Battle of Normandy, 1944* (Michael Joseph, London , 1984)

Horne, Alistair, *To Lose a Battle: France 1940* (Macmillan, London, 1969)

Keegan, John (ed.), *Churchill's Generals* (Weidenfeld & Nicolson, London, 1991)

Lewin, Ronald, *Ultra goes to War: The Secret Story* (Hutchinson, London, 1978)

Macksey, Kenneth, *Crucible of Power: The Fight for Tunisia 1942–43* (Hutchinson, London, 1969)

Messenger, Charles, *World War Two Chronological Atlas* (Bloomsbury, London, 1989

Niepold, Gerd, *Battle for White Russia: The Destruction of Army Group Centre June 1944* (Brassey's, London, 1987)

Shukman, Harold (ed.), *Stalin's Generals* (Weidenfeld & Nicolson, London, 1993)

Strawson, John, *The Battle for North Africa* (Scribner, NY, 1969)

Weigley, Russell, *Eisenhower's Lieutenants: the Campaigns in France and Germany 1944–45* (Sidgwick & Jackson, London, 1981)

INDEX

PICTURE CREDITS

Every effort has been made to contact the copyright holders for images reproduced in this book. The publishers would welcome any errors or omissions being brought to their attention.

pp. 8, 16, 19, 31, 32, 34, 36, 37, 40, 42, 46, 50, 52, 59, 62, 66, 668, 69, 73, 74, 78, 84, 88, 93, 97, 98, 103, 104, 106, 107, 108, 133, 140, 141, 143, 152–3, 154, 156, 157, 158, 160, 162, 184, 198, 206, 212, endpaper Hulton Getty; 22, 25, 28, 48, 60, 79, 86, 120, 138, 144, 145, 210 The Tank Museum, Dorset; 27, 30, 43, 61, 64, 70, 80, 82, 85, 92, 95, 99, 115, 116, 118, 123, 125, 126, 142, 149, 150, 151, 165, 170, 171, 172, 178, 179, 181, 182, 186, 188, 189, 192, 194, 195, 197, 199, 200, 201, 208, 211 Corbis UK Ltd; 38, 56, 57, 65, 90, 94, 96, 100, 101, 102, 109, 112, 114, 137, 166, 177, 190–91, 207 Peter Newark Military Pictures; 76, 168, Imperial War Museum.

The pictures on pp. 119, 130, 136–7 are reproduced by kind permission of the author.

The illustrations on the title page and on pp 23, 45, 67, 85, 146, 149, 176, 178, 183 are by Peter A. B. Smith and Malcolm Swanston.

ENDPAPER: *D-Day 6 June 1944: American troops in landing craft head for Omaha Beach.*